REWIND

REWIND

LESSONS FROM FIFTY
YEARS OF ACTIVISM

T WILLIAMS WITH DAVID LAWRENCE GRANT

MINNESOTA
HISTORICAL
SOCIETY PRESS

CLEAN
WATER
LAND &
LEGACY
AMENDMENT

mnhspress.org   @mnhspress

The Minnesota Historical Society Press is a member of the Association
of University Presses.

Manufactured in the United States of America.

10 9 8 7 6 5 4 3 2 1

♾ The paper used in this publication meets the minimum requirements
of the American National Standard for Information Sciences—
Permanence for Printed Library Materials, ANSI Z39.48–1984.

International Standard Book Number
ISBN: 978-1-68134-292-4 (paperback)
ISBN: 978-1-68134-293-1 (e-book)

Library of Congress Control Number: 2024949111

CONTENTS

INTRODUCTION

Through a long career, I have seen how one person can instigate significant change by helping energize and focus the work of our communities' own homegrown institutions. Over and over, I have seen how these institutions have played an underappreciated role as mediating forces throughout the history of the Black struggle for justice and equity. I wanted to tell this story. Several grants from the Minnesota Historical Society, starting in 2012, made possible the oral history project that has resulted in this book.

After George Floyd was murdered on May 25, 2020, my purpose expanded. The atmosphere of crisis that quickly escalated, sending intense aftershocks across the entire world, made me realize that some of my experiences as a community activist over the past fifty years and more might also provide valuable insight to young leaders about how to help a community navigate a crisis like this one—beginning with a clear-eyed view of its historical context. All of us, young and old, understood that just as surely as this was not the first such killing, it would not be the last. We vowed to use this moment of collective anguish to move our communities toward a future where such incidents become less and less common, bringing us to a place where, in the not-too-distant future, they are relegated to the dustbin of history.

I begin with relevant stories from my youth because I can now see clearly that the values and commitment to community I learned from my family provided me with a solid foundation for the challenges that lay ahead. My early childhood in Mississippi showed me a deep and pernicious American racism. But it also filled me with pride, purpose, and a strong sense of identity. I learned how the community that raised and nurtured me was able to manage the insults, the hurts, and the dangers of Jim Crow with courage, resilience, and grace.

Once my family moved north to Chicago, I quickly learned that these coping and survival skills were still very much needed for life in the northern states, even though the ways in which racism manifested itself north of the Mason–Dixon line were different, and often more subtle. My experiences in Chicago and beyond—high school, college, and my time in the military—helped prepare me to navigate the leadership opportunities that would come my way after I married and my young family and I settled in Minneapolis. These included a sojourn as executive director at the Phyllis Wheatley Community Center; helping found and direct the Urban Coalition of Minneapolis; serving as the first Minnesota ombudsman for corrections; and carrying out duties for subsequent positions at Minneapolis Public Housing, at the Hubert H. Humphrey School of Public Affairs at the University of Minnesota (Humphrey Institute), at Rainbow Research, Inc., and on the Minneapolis Board of Education.

As my family settled into life in Minneapolis in the mid-sixties, America was in crisis because a question asked fully a century before, during another national crisis, had still not found a comprehensive answer: Is the Negro to be embraced as a full-fledged citizen?

Our national mythology has always insisted that the Civil War, followed by the ratification of the Thirteenth, Fourteenth, and Fifteenth Amendments to the Constitution, had settled this question once and for all. But the largely unacknowledged truth is that in the decades following Reconstruction, the South was allowed to win back in the political and cultural arena much of what it had lost on the battlefield.

The Thirteenth Amendment abolished slavery. The Fourteenth Amendment guaranteed full citizenship to the formerly enslaved and their descendants. But state by state, a host of Jim Crow laws made a mockery of the amendments' intents, effectively allowing at best only a kind of second-class citizenship to Black Americans. Even where not reinforced by racist laws, anti-Black sentiment throughout most of the nation long created and sustained a culture in which rampant discrimination against Black people was, and continues to be, widely unacknowledged and widely tolerated.

The Fifteenth Amendment guaranteed Black citizens the right to vote, but across most of the post-Reconstruction South, state and municipal laws created so many impediments to Black voting that, in effect, the intent of the Fifteenth Amendment was almost entirely neutralized. Throughout most of the old slaveholding South and beyond, what was given with one hand was taken away with the other, and Black citizens lost the primary symbol and tool of their citizenship: their right to vote.

During the tumultuous days of the mid-sixties, there was a Southerner in the White House—Lyndon Baines Johnson—who decided that answering the old, lingering question about Black citizenship, resoundingly and without ambivalence, would be the cornerstone of his legacy. He concluded that only a politician from the old Confederacy could construct the bipartisan coalition that would be required in order to help deliver "the new birth of freedom," of which President Abraham Lincoln spoke so eloquently and soulfully at Gettysburg. Johnson's belief was probably correct, but it certainly didn't hurt that he was arguably one of the most skillful politicians who has ever served as president.

At the sociopolitical moment when he took office in 1964, there was a mighty grassroots movement in Black communities across the nation for civil rights, augmented by the activism of significant numbers of culturally diverse allies. Johnson recognized the power and visibility of this movement. It was being closely watched around the entire world and would help create the social conditions necessary for him to advance his ambitious agenda. He and his allies in Congress seized the moment and delivered the Civil Rights Act of 1964, the Voting Rights Act of 1965, the Fair Housing Act of 1966, and many of the hard-fought, hard-won initiatives of the War on Poverty.

But during this period there were also loud, discordant voices on the white supremacist extreme right whose "solution" was essentially the same as the one promoted by bitter, unreconstructed Confederates in the aftermath of the Civil War—a deeper, permanent codification of second-class citizenship for Black Americans, separate and unequal in every sense of the word—that, or an all-out race war.

Despite the powerful example of nonviolent protest for civil rights, the race war scenario about which the racist far right opined was made to feel quite credible to many—and close at hand—through the bloody police response to civil rights demonstrations, the bombing and burning of Black churches, the murder of civil rights leaders and organizers, and the images of urban burning, violence, and looting that often dominated the evening news as the decade marched on. Long-repressed Black rage was boiling over and finding expression in this way too—rage fueled by generations of unchecked police brutality, the effects of deep-seated institutional racism, and anxieties over the escalating war in Vietnam.

All of this was going on just when it appeared that we might be on the verge of meaningful progress. But history shows that it is precisely during times of rising expectations and hope that people whose aspirations for a better future have been profoundly repressed often rise up in open revolt. Dr. Martin Luther King was quoted during this period as saying, "The riot is the language of the unheard."[1]

I was there in North Minneapolis—1966 and 1967—when the phenomenon of the "long, hot summer" (roughly, 1964 through 1969) swept through my new hometown, mostly along Plymouth Avenue. I was part of the solution cobbled together to develop and begin to implement a few Minneapolis-centered answers to some of that national discontent.

We were fortunate at that critical moment to have cadres of creative community leadership at the grassroots level, people like Gleason Glover, executive director of the Minneapolis Urban League; Sam Richardson at the Minneapolis NAACP; Syl Jones and Gwen Jones Davis of The Way; Ernestine Belton at Pillsbury Neighborhood Services; Bill English at Sabathani Community Center; Dennis Banks, Russell Means, Clyde Bellecourt, and Emily Peake of the American Indian Movement. They found allies during this period in leaders from the local government sector like Minneapolis Mayor Art Naftalin and his highly respected special assistant, Josie Johnson, and Lillian Anthony of the Minneapolis Civil Rights Department. Their efforts were supported and augmented by corporate leaders who were willing to listen, learn, and act—leaders like John Cowles Jr., a vice president of the Minneapolis Star and Tribune Company, which was owned by his family; Donald Dayton and his brothers, the founders and owners of Dayton's, the department store that would later also spawn Target; Wheelock Whitney, investment banker; Steve Keating, president of Honeywell, Inc.; Earl Ewald, president of Northern States Power (later Xcel Energy); Paul Parker, a vice president at General Mills; and Dean McNeal, executive vice president at the Pillsbury Company—all of them people who believed that it was time to step up and partner in meaningful ways with the communities where their businesses were based.[2]

Suddenly, our Black community was beginning to be seen not just as a marginalized group of people rife with problems but as a group of resilient, capable citizens, ready for an opportunity to work with people who had the resources and the will to help solve problems and right old wrongs. As these corporate leaders dove into the work before them, they were surprised to learn that, in a state whose reputation is politically and socially progressive, racial disparities were (and still remain) among the worst in the nation, including persistent disparities in education, poverty, housing, employment, and access to equal justice. To their eternal credit, this situation felt personal to some of them, and their desire to address these disparities in meaningful and lasting ways was deeply felt. Our challenge as members of the grassroots Black leadership was to seize the day and channel as much of that energy, goodwill, and intention as possible into making lasting political, social, and cultural change.

Black people have been finding their way to Minnesota and settling here since before the Civil War—since before statehood was declared. However, to my knowledge, this communal crisis marked the first time that white civic leaders had ever made an organized attempt to identify and reach out to Minnesota Black grassroots leadership for the express purpose of accurately assessing Black community wants and needs and partnering with them to strategize about effectively beginning to meet those wants and needs.

I would argue that many in the Black community showed up willing to "speak truth to power" because this time it was corporate leaders and not just politicians who were listening. These Twin Cities business leaders, men with high national and international profiles, were an element of the local power structure. Even though all their corporate headquarters were just a few miles away, most of the community had had very limited exposure to them. With their presence and active participation at the table, there was a real chance to break the all-too-familiar cycle of *talk, talk, and more talk, but no action.*

Shortly after the assassination of Dr. King in 1968, the Urban Coalition was tasked with presenting community demands to the civic leaders who had signed on to listen, set goals, and fashion action plans. Because so many business leaders were at the table, one of the first demands laid before them was for aggressive hiring and promotion initiatives at their companies and throughout the wider business community for Black people and other people of color. There was a call for significant aid to Black businesses, including a program to step up soliciting bids for everything from construction and cleaning services to catering, facilitating easier access to capital, and mentoring. The community also made a strong push for affordable housing and for both police and criminal justice reform.

For a number of reasons, meaningful police reform remains elusive, as across most of America. But during those Urban Coalition years, we did have an opportunity to spark a groundbreaking, grassroots effort at rethinking the role and nature of policing. What began as an emergency response to community violence driven by volunteers who walked the streets, calming frayed nerves and quashing dangerous rumors, the Soul Patrol soon evolved into an unarmed, volunteer resource that offered a unique, experimental glimpse into at least what one part of a community-centered rethinking of public safety might look like.

We all held our breath, and for a while it worked. We made progress. We avoided further communal violence. It worked because the things we managed to accomplish, or at least to begin, left everyday people with a genuine sense of momentum and hope that this ambitious agenda for change could, and would, make a real difference.

Can we look back on the experiences of a different era for clues about how best to respond to today's issues? I believe that the history through which I've lived over the past fifty years and more may offer some insight into how to think through solutions to our current crises.

I speak in these pages about the power of community-based institutions. During my time as a community leader, I had the honor of helping establish two new institutions that were to function as vehicles for both social progress and crisis intervention: the Minneapolis Urban Coalition in 1967–68 and Minnesota's Office of the Ombudsman for Corrections in 1972—the first such ombudsman in the country.[3]

Born in response to the violence along Plymouth Avenue in 1967, from that time until 1980 the Urban Coalition was one of Minneapolis's most consequential institutions for addressing social and economic justice issues in marginalized communities. Its history is virtually unknown in Minneapolis today. I am uniquely qualified to tell the story of its origin and early impact on the community.

The creation of Minnesota's Office of the Ombudsman for Corrections was consequential to the move toward the more equitable administration of justice in the Minnesota prison system for thirty years. The story of the first ombudsman in Minnesota is an important part of the history that I'm uniquely qualified to tell, since I was part of the process that created the position to which I was named in 1972.

From 1965 to 1972, I also served as executive director of one of our community's oldest institutions: Phyllis Wheatley Community Center (PWCC). Phyllis Wheatley was established as a settlement house in North Minneapolis in 1924 to help enhance the quality of life of Minneapolis's growing Black community.

All three of these institutions fit the description of what Peter Berger and John Neuhaus refer to as "mediating institutions": "those institutions standing between the individual in his private life and the large institutions of public life." They help bridge the gap between each one of us and the overarching society in which we live. They serve as a safety net, and they are often the places to which we turn in times of need.[4]

Through my deep involvement in these institutions, I had a chance to be part of solutions—cobbled together during times of crisis—to problems of racial injustice. As a result, I've learned to look within a crisis for the lessons we can apply to the next crisis and for guidance as to how best to respond. Because there will always be a next crisis.

Today, five years after the murder of George Floyd, the United States is in crisis yet again over precisely the same question: Do Black Americans, now and forever, have a fully equal place in this society? Only this time, the voices that seek to answer in the affirmative are somewhat quieter and harder to hear. Under the guise of seeking to counter alleged large-scale voter fraud, those who fear the browning of America and demographic changes long in motion have been able to spearhead the passage of a round of bills across many states, some of them draconian, that would suppress the Black and brown vote. And alarmingly, voices on the extreme white supremacist right—still calling for race war—are louder than ever. Sadly, their poisonous influence in the political arena has grown, edging the country closer to the racial violence they espouse.

In the aftermath of George Floyd's murder, we here in Minneapolis were witness to what that doomsday scenario might look like in its early stages. There was some evidence—and there were widespread rumors—of individual actors or small groups of white supremacists from other states setting fires or encouraging others to set fires and loot in tense neighborhoods wherever large numbers of people remained on the streets after peaceful demonstrations had wound down. For me, their outrages were profoundly disturbing to witness, because they felt personal. This is my Minneapolis—the place I've called home for over fifty years. The place where I raised my children. This is my backyard.[5]

We must fight against this racial violence and for the equality that our Constitution promises. My experience proves that a single person can intervene and put into motion significant change on behalf of their community. My hope is that this book will inspire many others to do the same in years to come.

1

LIFE IN MISSISSIPPI

The Deep South of my youth, in the thirties, was profoundly divided by race. Black people were only a couple of generations away from slavery, and white people made sure everyone remembered that fact. We were subservient—at least in public. If a white person was approaching on the sidewalk, we were expected to step aside and let him pass. All whites were addressed as "Mr." or "Miss," even young children. Imagine a grown Black man addressing a ten-year-old white child as "Mr. Gregory" while neither that child nor their parents were expected to show any such respect toward him. He lived his entire life in this community, knowing he would never be addressed as "Mr." To call him by such a proper title would imply equality, and this was something Mississippi law and custom were determined never to allow.

Even though I grew up in a world defined by racial inequality, my family made it clear that the way whites demeaned Blacks did not reflect on the kind of people *we* were. Their attitudes and behaviors were, instead, indicators of the kind of people *they* were. Regardless of reassurance from my parents and grandparents that none of this ugly behavior toward us was personal, it was infuriating because it always somehow *felt* personal. It felt like a constant weight on my shoulders—a feeling that troubled my sleep and filled every day with anxiety, a feeling that I must have done something wrong to make them treat me the way they did.

Momma and Daddy insisted times would change—they had seen times change. They knew and had taken to heart the old saying, "We ain't what we wanna be, and we ain't what we gonna be ... but thank God, we ain't what we was." Their stance was that positive change will happen: not today—but change *will* happen. Well, I was a child, and from my point of view, their perspective was hard to see. If change was coming, it wasn't coming fast enough for me. I was still at an age when, in the days and weeks after Thanksgiving, waiting for Christmas felt like an eternity. And *that* was a set point in time. Imagine at my tender age waiting for something as complex and ambiguous as social change to happen.

An impatient child, number seven of eight, can exhaust the best and most empathetic of parents. Fortunately, my parents had plenty of practice with my siblings. As I expressed my distaste for the injustices we were experiencing (mostly the injustice I was experiencing—because I was a child, and the world revolved around me at that time), Momma and Daddy and all my parental influencers countered with, "Get an education. They can't take that away from you."

The Influencers—and Moving North

Education was just about the only necessary thing in life that was free for us. My father was a sharecropper in Shaw, Mississippi, and there were many mouths to feed in our family. So we always made sure to take full advantage of any good thing offered to us for free. There was no charge for advice from Daddy either. Along with teaching us how to protect ourselves from the white man's wrath and handle ourselves when out of his sight, he told us, "Don't limit yourself to thinking you're as good as the white man. You have to prepare yourself to be *better*—so much better—even to be considered as good as him." Like most people of my generation, I always remembered that admonition, and I have passed it along to my children and grandchildren as well. It became second nature for me to constantly look for opportunities to demonstrate that I can and have achieved at the highest level.

I am third-generation free. My great-grandfather, Anthony Williams, was born enslaved in 1840 and died in 1944 at the age of 104. My grandfather, Mack Williams, was born free in 1876. My father, Fred Mack Williams Sr., was born free in 1899. And I was born on the family-owned farm in Sunflower County, Mississippi, in 1934, the seventh of eight children. In our community, elders vie for the opportunity to name the children born into a family line. By the time I came along, my maternal grandmother complained that she hadn't had her turn to name one of us yet. Although the tradition was generally to name children after one of their ancestors, she named me Theartrice after a man she had known in her hometown—a grocer widely loved and admired for his kindness.

Moving North

Shortly after my sixteenth birthday in 1950, I realized my desire to get out of Mississippi. My sister, Leola, provided me with my literal ticket out that summer when she booked passage for me and our brother Anthony—we called him Sporty—on a Greyhound bus to her hometown of Portland, Maine. The plan was for me to come and be caretaker for her two-year-old son and my sister Sylvia's one-year-old boy. Sporty, who was just a year older than me, would look for a job. It was a long bus ride from Shaw to Portland, and we were traveling from the Deep South to the far Northeast during a time of absolute segregation. This meant we had to ride in the back of the bus until we crossed the Mason–Dixon line. It was also our first trip ever out of Mississippi. Until then, Shelby, Mississippi, thirty-two miles away, was as far north as I had ever been. My mother knew we didn't have enough money to buy food at the rest stops—and that most rest stops wouldn't serve Black people anyway—so she prepared two shoeboxes filled with fried chicken and cake.

Riding the bus was fun, but it was long and tiring. Across the length of Mississippi, all we could see along US Highway 61 were cotton fields. As we entered Tennessee, the cotton fields disappeared, and we began to see city streets and lights. Soon, we arrived in Memphis, where we would change buses. I remember mentioning to my brother that we must be somewhere near the Peabody Hotel. We had grown up listening to a lot of radio broadcasts originating from the Peabody Hotel in Memphis, so as far as we were concerned, that had to be the most famous hotel in the world. Even though I don't think we ever caught a glimpse of it, our arrival in Memphis did serve to mark our entry into the great, wide world beyond the state of Mississippi. I had the sense that, even though I might return to visit family and friends, I had well and truly left my childhood home.

It was inevitable that my brother and I would run out of stuff to talk about on such a long trip. That gave me a lot of time to imagine what it might be like in Maine and reflect on the only world I had ever known during my childhood in Mississippi. Everyone in my school thought I was the smartest kid in my class. And truly, I might have been. But I began to obsess now over how I would measure up, compared to my classmates in a northern school.

In rural Mississippi, children of all grades attended the same small school. Although relatively uneducated themselves, my parents believed strongly in education for their children, so we attended religiously, and we studied hard.

But a major feature of the Jim Crow system was a conscious effort to systematically limit the horizons of Black citizens—to put it more starkly, to stifle any form of Black ambition. And our completely segregated educational system played a key role in this. The credo of "separate but equal" was a cruel, cynical lie.

Only pennies were spent on Black students for every dollar spent by the system on whites. The education of Black students didn't have to be equal to the education provided for white students, because the mostly unspoken expectation was that there was no need to prepare Black students for any future that was thought to be "above their station."

Any healthy society on earth will naturally seek to encourage, nurture, and reward both excellence and ambition as its young people receive an education and move toward careers. But my siblings and I grew up within a system that was not only unfriendly toward Black aspirations for a better future—it was downright hostile. Everything about the way the system operated was guided by the principle that education for Black students should prepare them for lives of labor and servitude and nothing more.

This driving principle expressed itself in many ways. The school year for Black students in Mississippi was shorter than for white students, whose academic year started the day after Labor Day and went through the end of May or the first week in June. The starting date for Black children was determined by when their labor was needed in the cotton fields. In 1945, the school year for Black children didn't begin until November 27, because 1945 was a banner year for cotton. We had already celebrated Thanksgiving that year before our first day in school. The school year for Black children typically ended in early May, but that year, Black children were deprived of three months of schooling—legally—by the state of Mississippi.

At the time I started school, Mississippi did not offer kindergarten for either Black or white students. The starting age for school was six, and the student's grade designation depended upon the book level to which the student was assigned. Books for Black students were seldom new and, for the most part, were the hand-me-downs from the local white school. I can recall being sent over to the white school to collect used books for my classmates and me.

In many, many counties through the Deep and mid-South, the highest grade it was possible for a Black student to attend was the eighth—or even the sixth—because there was no Black high school. And there were no plans for one.

Six-year-olds entering school were assigned to a pre-primer book until they were able to fully read it and master the lessons within it that introduced the letters of the alphabet and basic number facts. Many students required the full school year to accomplish this. Once they mastered that book, the student was promoted to the hardback primer, which was the next reading level up. Some students could also take a full school year to learn that level and be promoted to first grade. Under the Mississippi system, a child could be eight years old before reaching the first grade.

I knew how to read before I started school, and I was eager to let everyone know. I had learned to read by leafing through my older siblings' books and asking them what the words were. I was inquisitive, and my youngest sister, who was seven years my senior, to her eternal credit, instead of looking upon me as a nuisance, helped me with my reading. The only books around our house were schoolbooks, the Bible, and mail-order catalogs, so I would read those along with the *Pittsburgh Courier*, a Black weekly newspaper that my dad brought home whenever he returned from his out-of-town work. Although I was very competitive, I didn't quite have the height to excel in athletics, hard as I tried. But where my competitive nature really made itself manifest was in the classroom. From my very first day in class, my teachers were surprised to discover that I already knew how to read. I loved the feeling I got from impressing my teachers, exceeding their expectations. And that feeling never got old.

I was promoted from the pre-primer to the second grade by the end of my first year in school, which meant I entered the second grade at age seven, while most of my classmates were eight years old or older. News of my ability to read and do math spread throughout the school, which, at the time, offered classes only through the tenth grade. When I was in third grade, it was not uncommon for teachers from the fifth or sixth grade to ask my teacher if they could borrow me for a few minutes to come to their class and help a student who was having trouble with math or reading. I would eagerly accompany the teacher and showcase my reading and math skills before these older students. At the time, I thought it was an exciting thing to be doing; it made me feel important and special. But in retrospect, it was an awful thing for the teachers to do. I was, in effect, being used to shame and embarrass other students, and my "help" didn't necessarily improve their academic performance. It also contributed to my sense of entitlement. I learned to expect to be first in my class and to have opportunities others did not have, irrespective of whether I had earned them.

I always wanted my grades to be perfect and to be first in my class. During my first year in school I once tore up my paper and cried after looking at my 98 percent test score. When the teacher asked me why I was crying, one of my classmates said, "Miss McEvans, he's crying because he didn't get 100 percent on his test." She sat me on her lap, put her arms around me and tried to tell me that 98 percent was an excellent score on a

At age eight.

test. In fact, it was the highest score in my class. But it wasn't perfect. And I wanted a perfect score.

This attitude persisted until the fifth grade, when I received my comeuppance and an important lesson about making a difference from my teacher, Mrs. Johnson. Each year, our school produced a play, and that year,

Mrs. Johnson was in charge. She selected students from the fifth and sixth grades to try out for the various parts. Of course, I expected to be asked to read for the leading male role. I was so disappointed when Mrs. Johnson asked me to read for a lesser role that I told her if I couldn't play the lead, then I didn't want to be in the play. In the past I had been able to get my way in such situations, but it didn't work this time. Mrs. Johnson called my bluff, and I was not in the play at all. I never again challenged a teacher in that way. I continued to be competitive, and I made sure that I did my schoolwork well enough to remain first in my class throughout my school years in Mississippi. But my fifth-grade experience with Mrs. Johnson taught me that I didn't always have to have the lead position in a group to make a difference. It also taught me humility and respect for others. It was important for me to learn, at that stage of my life, that not everyone could be first, and that not being first didn't make me any less of a person. Looking back on it now, I see clearly that in some respects, my behavior with Mrs. Johnson was a form of bullying. I remain eternally grateful that she saw through the sense of entitlement I had developed—and burst my bubble.

———

As the Greyhound bus rolled along, I hardly paid attention to the world passing by outside my window. My mind was completely fixated on wondering about what kind of life awaited me in Portland. *Are the white people there going to be any different than the white people in Mississippi?* Black people in the South were often told that life in the North is so much better. But now that I was getting closer and closer to an opportunity to assess the matter for myself, I was wondering how, specifically, this might be true. I wasn't naive. I knew that Black people were still discriminated against in various ways up north and that many white people harbor racist views. I understood that some white people in Maine would look down their noses at me, but my hope was that I'd get to experience what it feels like to live without all the daily tension and fear around race that I'd grown used to in Mississippi—where whites were heavily invested in preserving their place of privilege, and our place at the bottom, through the sheer weight of all that racist tradition and the constant threat of violence.

These thoughts triggered an extremely unpleasant memory. I hated to cry, and so I didn't cry easily or often. But I couldn't help it that my body and soul kept a faithful record of every hurt, every insult I'd ever had to deflect or absorb. And that well of accumulated insult and injury ran very deep. As a consequence, there were some memories I just could not repress—all those incidents that had delivered a hard enough punch to the gut that they made me drop my guard and break out in tears. Whoever first said, "Sticks and stones may break my bones, but words can never hurt me" was dead wrong. Words that are meant to make you feel stupid, ugly, unworthy, and small, if well chosen and timed just right, can cut more truly and deeply than any knife. But words hurled at you that are meant to completely negate your very humanity—these strike a cruel blow to your spirit that can knock you flat for a long time, maybe even a lifetime, if you hear such words often enough. So it is that the memory troubling my mind as I traveled North was about a bitter moment of a kind I hoped I was now leaving behind forever.

—•—

A mean-spirited white man with an even meaner tongue had once made me cry and run a long way home for comfort. But as soon as I walked in the door, the pain I was feeling dragged me down to an even lower rung of hell, because I had to summon the strength to repress all that pain and hide it from view. I couldn't tell Momma *why* I was crying, because I understood there was nothing she could do about it. And I didn't want to make Momma feel bad and guilty about not being able to do anything about it— to protect me from this bitter, angry, racist fool. In fact, I thought I would probably be blamed for what happened, a common occurrence for Black people. Our social conditioning under Jim Crow inclined us to blame ourselves for whatever negative reactions might be hurled at us by white people. I had done nothing but show him the utmost deference and respect. His vile and vitriolic response toward me was exactly the opposite—and yet, thanks to the twisted etiquette of the Jim Crow world in which we both lived, I fled that room wondering *what I did* to make this white man so angry.

I was a paperboy delivering the *Delta Democrat Times* in my hometown. I really liked the job, and I had earned top honors for securing new subscribers to the paper. My reward was a gold-plated Bulova wristwatch, which I really never got to wear very much because it was too big for my skinny wrist and kept falling off. Eventually, I lost it.

But that day, I was excited about winning the watch, and I was still beaming with pride and satisfaction. On Sunday morning, I delivered the paper to the Gulf Service Station, like always. I held on to the paper and waited to give it directly to the white service station owner so that I could collect, because he owed me for several weeks' delivery. The newspaper office required paperboys to make collections on a weekly basis and then turn the money over to the route manager. That morning, there were several white men in the station talking, and I was waiting for a pause in their conversation so I could ask the owner for what he owed. I was taught not to interrupt adults when they were talking—and under no circumstance should I interrupt adult *white* people when they were talking. So I just stood there and waited.

After a good long while, the owner turned to me and said, "Nigger, is something wrong?"

I said, "No, sir. I just want to collect what you owe me for the paper."

He flew into an instant rage. "Nigger, get your black ass out of here and take that damn paper with you ... and you can stick it up your black ass for all I care."

When I heard that, I took the paper and ran. And I never stopped running until I got home. The next day I contacted the route manager and told him I was quitting my job. Momma never knew why. And I was glad she never questioned me about it. It would have hurt her to hear it, and it would have hurt me to tell it.

As my thoughts returned to the new world I was about to enter in Portland, I figured that whatever else might await me, white people in Maine couldn't *possibly* be as evil as white people in Mississippi. But Mississippi had been the only world I knew up until then. I allowed myself to consider for a minute what a momentous thing it really was to be leaving the state of my birth behind. I think I always believed I would leave Mississippi someday. I never saw myself growing up and fully coming into my manhood there. Part of that growing sense of certainty was probably intuition. But part of it was surely the fact that I grew up in the middle of the Great Migration, a time when millions of Black folks left the rural South for the industrial North and West. Everybody had family and friends who'd pulled up stakes and left for somewhere. My friend Joe Louis and I would be out in the field picking cotton, talking about where we'd go when we left Mississippi. The best part of the fantasy was when we'd imagine how we'd come back and showboat our success, wowing everybody we'd left behind back home.

The bus stopped in Bristol, a city that straddles the Tennessee and Virginia border, and from there pushed on to Washington, DC, the still-segregated capital of the nation. It was frustrating to us that we weren't in the District long enough to really see or do much, but we *were* able to catch glimpses of the Washington Monument and the US Capitol—somewhat magical glimpses, just at that golden hour of the day before sundown when nearly everything seems to take on a special glow. But already it was time to board yet another bus, this time for New York City.

As we moved to the back of the bus for seating, Sporty and I were thinking how odd it was—odd, and terrible—that here we were in the nation's capital, but this was still very much a Southern town. Once seated, we got philosophical for a while about the illogic of segregation and the stupidity of the rules that propped it up. "Why is it that they make us ride in the back of the bus," we wondered, "but then, we have to sit in the front coaches on the train?" Safety certainly didn't seem to have anything to do with it—in a collision, passengers in the back of the bus would no doubt be better protected from severe injury or death than those up front. But even when we were younger, we'd already clearly seen that Jim Crow laws were nonsensical because they were based on nonsense: first, the idea that one race is superior to another and that therefore a natural hierarchy needs to be preserved; but more fundamentally, they're nonsense because, scientifically, there's no such thing as race at all.

I was keeping close track now of where we were, because I was obsessed with knowing when we crossed the Mason–Dixon line. I knew that this must happen not long after we crossed the northern boundary of the District of Columbia. I doubted the driver would suddenly announce, "We're crossing the Mason and Dixon line. All Black folks are free to take any available front seats." But still, I wanted to know when we crossed, because even if that line meant nothing to him, it meant something to *me*.

I was curious. I wanted to know if I'd feel any different on the other side. But night had fallen and I was very tired, so the next thing I remember was pulling into the bus terminal in New York City. I had missed the big moment I'd constructed in my head, and we had eaten up both boxes of food, so I was hungry too. We had less than one dollar between us, and four hundred miles still to go.

The one big plus left for us was that we could be first in line when it was time to board the bus from New York to Boston, so we could take the front seats right behind the driver. Shortly after our arrival, we ventured out of the bus depot to take in a good look at the New York skyline. We'd never seen anything like it in our lives. My neck was stiff for the rest of the ride from looking up at all those tall buildings.

After we got settled again on the bus and were once more underway, looking out at all that water as we crossed the East River triggered a frightening memory for me about a time when I'd almost drowned.

———

When something happened to us as children that resulted from our misbehavior, we didn't expect to be consoled, especially by our father. I was six years old, walking with my mother and three of my brothers as we returned from a visit with a neighbor who lived across the bayou. It was easy to reach the neighbor's house during dry weather. We'd simply walk across the bayou's dry bed. But to get there following a heavy rainfall, we had to traverse a wooden walkway about thirty feet long, one foot wide, and four feet above the bayou's surface. It had rained heavily the day before our visit, and the water was high enough to lick the underside of the walkway.

Its narrow width meant we had to cross the bayou single file. Momma and my brothers walked ahead of me.

Somebody should have brought up the rear and kept an eye on me. But they didn't. Instead of staying on the straight and narrow, I let my curiosity get the best of me. I was dying to know the depth of the water under the spot where I stood. I used an old window shade roller I had been carrying with me since we first left home. The walkway had no railing, so it was easy for me to simply kneel down and place my roller into the water until I could feel it barely touch bottom. At least I was pretty sure I'd felt it touch bottom. I extended that roller until the muddy water was all the way up to my armpit, but still, maybe that was mostly water weeds I was touching.

Even though I could feel myself dangerously close to losing my balance, I did what I nearly always did at that age: I pressed my luck until my luck ran out. I reached until I tumbled right over the edge into the water, which was probably four feet deep. It may or may not have been over my head—I was so panicked that I'm not completely sure now. But I know I was struggling mightily to find the bottom with my feet and keep my head above water. When my head went beneath the water once, then twice, all I could think about were the stories I'd heard about drowning—that if you go under that third time, your time is up. You drown.

Thankfully, after I came up the second time and went down for the third, my brother Orlandrous, four years my senior, jumped in and pulled me up. I don't remember exactly how my father responded when he heard about this incident later, but I'm sure he must have given his usual reply: "Well, now you know not to do that the next time."

When we finally arrived in Boston about midmorning, and about a hundred miles from our final destination, we called Portland to let my sister know we would be hungry when our bus pulled in. Over the next fourteen months of living with my sister Leola, my whole world would change forever. I would fine-tune some of my survival skills and learn some new ones. I would leave childhood behind and take a giant step into manhood. I would begin to learn who I really am.

2

A New World

Leola and her husband, Otis, picked us up at the Greyhound bus depot in their 1946 Hudson for the short ride to their apartment, a third-floor walk-up near the waterfront. It had two bedrooms, an enclosed back porch, and indoor plumbing—an amenity that wasn't installed in our home in Mississippi until a year after I left.

The space was small for the number of people living there, which included my sister Leola and her husband, my sister Sylvia and her husband, plus Leola's and Sylvia's two boys, ages one and two, respectively. When my brother and I joined the mix, the crowding got more extreme and sleeping arrangements even more problematic. My two sisters, their spouses, and their children had the two bedrooms. Sporty and I shared a sofa bed in the living room, and when there were guests, invited or uninvited, the kitchen and enclosed porch became sleeping quarters as well, weather permitting. The close quarters took some getting used to for me. Back home in Mississippi, the house wasn't large, but both the front and back yards certainly were. Us kids spent most of our time outside, especially when the weather was nice. Now, I was inside most of the time, and kids played on paved sidewalks and in the streets. I was beginning to wonder what I had gotten myself into, but I figured if I could make it through the summer, maybe it would work out for me to go join my dad and older brother, who were now living in Chicago.

Holding Down the Fort

Leola had not fully explained what her expectations were for me. I arrived in Portland the third week in May, and the summer camping season began in June. I didn't know Leola was the cook at a summer camp located over fifty miles north of Portland, which meant she would live at the camp and come home only on her days off. Those days generally came at two-week intervals, when a new group of campers arrived. Otis worked five or six days per week on the waterfront.

My sister Sylvia worked as a live-in maid, and she had a day off every week or two. Her husband, Clarence, was a handyman for the same family—when he wasn't working other jobs. That meant the two boys, Monte and Roufkes (RAW-fus) were at the apartment all the time. My job, as I would learn from Leola, was to be responsible for all household chores, including cooking, cleaning, and childcare, while she was away.

Back home I had virtually no household responsibilities. I didn't have to clean the house, cook, or care for the children. All of that was Momma's preserve. So I was used to having all kinds of free time on my hands, especially during the summer. Suddenly, living at my sisters' house, I felt like every minute of my day was tightly scheduled. This was really going to take some getting used to. Thinking about the summer in Maine had been a pleasant diversion before I actually arrived—but now, as the reality of what it was going to be took shape, I could see nothing but endless, joyless drudgery ahead. And the thought of it landed with a dull thud in the pit of my stomach, leaving me queasy. What had I gotten myself into?

Sporty was able to get a job at a waterfront fish factory, and he wouldn't be confined to the apartment, but I had some responsibility for him, too, because I would be cooking for everyone. At age sixteen, I was suddenly expected to step up as an adult—to be responsible for the daily care of a family of four adults, including me, and two small children. And I wasn't sure I could handle it. But Leola saw me as intelligent and industrious. She had decided that I was to be the one in the family who would go places and do things—that I would go to college and become a doctor. I survived that summer and was able to run the household because Leola was a big believer in structure and routine—and she had created a foolproof template for me to follow. She made a list of all the household chores that needed to be done, *when* they needed to be done, and sometimes even *how*. I knew I could manage taking care of the boys because I had been around my sister Irma and five of her seven children, and I had often helped her. The daily cooking would be my big challenge. Leola had anticipated this. On a kitchen bulletin board, she posted the menus for each day of the week, and it was understood that there would be no deviation. I was to follow the menu to the letter, because we had already done the weekly shopping. For example, we had pork chops on Saturday, chicken on Sunday. Friday was always fish with macaroni and cheese.

I had cooked pork chops and chicken before, but I'll never forget my first time preparing macaroni and cheese. It was Leola's first Friday at summer camp, and I checked the kitchen bulletin board. The menu for the day was the usual fish with macaroni and cheese. "A piece of cake," I thought. "This will be easy." The fish, of course, would be fried. No self-respecting southern Black cook would think about doing it any other way. As for the macaroni and cheese, I was thinking that should be easy too. I'd never attempted this classic favorite before, but how difficult could it be? Grab yourself an appropriately sized saucepan, add a cup of elbow macaroni, add milk to cover it, shred cheddar cheese on top, and place in the oven to bake until done. After a reasonable amount of time, take the saucepan from the oven and serve with the fish.

Well, I did all of that, but when I took the saucepan out of the oven, the cheese had baked into the uncooked macaroni on top, creating something as hard and inedible as it looked. It was a mess, and as I went over and over the steps in my head, I couldn't understand what I could possibly have done wrong.

Later, when I told Leola the story, she smirked and asked me if I had thought to precook the macaroni: boil it, drain it, and *then* put it in the saucepan, before adding the cheese and placing it in the oven to bake. No. I had missed that one important step. Live and learn. Next time, my macaroni and cheese turned out much better.

I also learned a lot about myself during the summer of 1950. I could take care of myself and others too, for example. Thankfully, Monte and Roufkes were little trouble, even though in Portland they couldn't run around outdoors freely like they could have back home in Mississippi. But running a household was hard work and not something I wanted to do beyond the summer. I had decided I really didn't like Portland either. I couldn't see myself staying there for any long stretch of time. Part of my unhappiness and malaise was just about sheer loneliness. Sporty was the only other young person I knew, and while there was one other Black family in the neighborhood, they weren't very friendly. I spent all of my time around my sisters and the boys.

Sometimes Leola and Otis would have a house party and invite their friends, but there were never any people my age there. Beyond that, I didn't like the parties because there was usually a lot of drinking, and I never liked being around alcohol or people who drank heavily. Making myself scarce while the revelers were there wasn't an option because the party was always going on in my sleeping space. And I couldn't always go to bed immediately *after* the party had ended either, because whether Leola and Otis recognized the pattern or not, the aftermath of a party often led to intense arguments between them. And much too often, the aftermath of a fierce argument was equally fierce physical violence, which always frightened me.

I certainly understood that sometimes couples fight, and that sometimes a fight can devolve into physical violence and abuse, but I had never experienced anything like this at home, and I was at a complete loss in knowing how to handle it. One night, I made the mistake of trying to pull Otis off of Leola. He turned his full fury on me, punching me as if I were a full-grown man, which made Leola feel both devastated and helpless since her impulse was to protect me like I had tried to protect her.

I was young and physically resilient. Bruises heal. But after that, I was more wary of Otis and his moods than ever before, and I always left the room whenever Leola and Otis were arguing. These uncomfortable memories are further complicated by the fact that, as I now recognize, Leola sometimes played the role of instigator, and that if a fight came to blows, sometimes she gave nearly as good as she got. But as for Otis's behavior from then on, I don't recall that he ever struck Leola again while I was living there. I'd like to believe that the thought that I might intervene again made him stop short of violence.

I knew I had a lot to learn about the complexities of a relationship between a man and a woman, and on some level I understood that being Black in America added a whole other overlay of complexity on top of those dynamics. But I did learn from this incident, and the things that led up to it, another valuable lesson that I would need later: that there are ways to deal with conflict without getting caught up in it. I had gained, too, the confidence-boosting knowledge that if push came to shove, and conflict just couldn't be avoided, I could take care of myself.

I also learned not to make facile judgments about people. I knew almost nothing about the story of Otis's life, but I intuitively understood that the deep well of anger that underlay much of his thinking and behavior came from somewhere. And even though those behaviors made me angry and more than a little scared, they also stirred in me some real empathy for him. After all, as I slowly but surely walked toward my own manhood—specifically, the walk of a young Black man in America—I was starting to become aware of my own well of anger, frustration, and grief, growing deeper by the year. And I wondered how whatever rage bubbled up from that well from time to time might affect my thinking and behavior in negative ways—might potentially incline me to lash out against people I loved. I hoped and prayed I could find ways to channel the energy of that rage into powerful, positive things: my people's fight for justice and my personal struggle to build the best possible life for my future family and myself.

Fortunately, my siblings and I had the best of all possible role models in our own father. He was a tough, no-nonsense man who had suffered a lifetime of indignities under Jim Crow but who had managed not to let the accumulated trauma and hurt turn him bitter like bile. He was living proof that big, calloused hands trained to work the hard soil could also be dreamer's hands, lithe and graceful enough to reach upward toward the stars, soft and gentle enough to rock a newborn to sleep. He was a man who wouldn't suffer fools, but who possessed a big and tender heart. And he always chose to lead with that with us kids and with our mother.

All this ruminating sparked another thought. I'd always placed a strong value on the importance of family. I had a moment of clarity now about what a double-edged sword this total embrace of family really is. Our families may, ultimately, be the source of some of our deepest, oldest wounds and personal dysfunction, but often they are also the source of our most important qualities and strengths—and our resilience too. Flaws, scars, shortcomings, and all, your people will always be a huge part of who you are at your core. I knew I didn't ever want to be without mine.

Sporty left Portland for Chicago when summer ended, but to my disappointment I couldn't go with him. Leola told me that I was going to stay in Portland and go to school there, because she wanted me to go to a good school. "Besides," she said, "there's no room for you with Daddy in Chicago." Daddy was sharing an apartment there with my brother Fred, plus Fred's wife and baby. Leola felt I'd be better off in Portland, and that was the end of the discussion. She wanted to keep Sporty in Portland and have him complete his senior year in high school, but Otis didn't particularly like the idea, and Sporty was against it too, so he got permission to leave.

High School

The day after Labor Day, Leola took me to enroll in Portland High, one of two high schools in the city. Deering, the other school, was located in a more affluent area. Portland High, only six blocks away in Leola's working-class neighborhood, was the larger of the two, with 1,600 students.

I felt anxious and a little uneasy on the day Leola took me down to the principal's office to register for school. We were the only Black people in an office full of whites. I had never been around so many white people in one place in my life.

I relaxed a little once it sank in that the staff were being friendly and welcoming toward us, and they seemed excited to enroll me for classes. But I was overwhelmed by the sheer size of the place. Sixteen hundred students! That was nearly as many souls as the entire population of my hometown in Mississippi, and nearly all of them were white. I was calm on the outside, but my body's natural fight-or-flight instincts couldn't have been revved up any higher. I wanted to ask if any Black students were enrolled at the school, but Leola had assured me I wouldn't be the only one. By lunchtime, I could finally exhale, because I could see for myself that this was true. It looked as though there were about a dozen of us. But I was the only Black person in each of my classes except history, where one other Black student was enrolled.

I ended up attending Portland High for only a single year, but I made great personal strides during that time. My academic skills took a giant leap forward. So did my coping skills, including my ability to overcome cultural shock, to confidently deflect or counter whatever racist attitudes were thrown my way, to trust and feel at ease around white people in general, and to compete with students who had been privileged to attend quality schools since they'd entered kindergarten. And I felt extra good about myself that I was able to achieve all this in a home environment that often wasn't conducive to studying.

I was old enough to understand why the civil rights movement had pushed so hard for the integration of schools. It was a strategic workaround for addressing the lie of "separate, but equal" in education. In the minds of dyed-in-the-wool racists, our motivation *must* have been that we wanted Black and white students in the same classrooms so that some of the white students' naturally superior ways would rub off on their Black fellow students. And I could see that part of the fierce resistance of oppositional white parents was because they didn't want what they presumed must be the naturally inferior ways of Black students to rub off on *their* kids.

But the actual logic behind working toward integrated classrooms was simple: the advocates of integration wanted Black students assigned to the same school districts as white students so that the same amount of money and resources would be allocated to Black students and white students alike. Period.

I also learned not to feel uncomfortable or intimidated about being the lone Black student in a class. The experience ultimately toughened me up and boosted my confidence, partly because I came to realize that getting to know me helped white students in my class to shed some of their stereotypes and misconceptions about Black people. And the more I thought about this, the more I realized that this is no small thing—that having more opportunities for positive exposure to each other is one of the things that would ease our collective pathway toward building a strong, multiethnic democracy that endures.

———

I did well in all my classes, excelling in machine shop and English. I found geometry the most challenging, but I did well enough to pass. Mr. Smith, my English teacher, did more than any other single person at Portland High to help me overcome my fear and lack of trust in white people. He was a tall, distinguished, gray-haired man in his mid-fifties, with the stereotypical look of an English college professor. He loved teaching, and he had high expectations for all of us. We had to report on four books that we'd read during the marking period. The reports could be a combination of oral and written. He'd noticed that I'd seemed a little uncomfortable in class—reticent to speak up. He pulled me aside one day and encouraged me to select books by Black authors and about Black people. He told me that if I didn't, none of the other students would, and he believed it was important that they be exposed to and learn about Black people in history and literature. He made me feel good about myself, good about being Black. I asked him if I could use my own story as one of the oral reports. He wondered how much of a story a sixteen-year-old would have to tell, but he agreed to let me do it.

When my turn to report came, I told the class about my linkage to slavery—about how I was only three generations removed from a bitter time, central to the American story, that most of them had only a passing knowledge of and regarded as ancient history. I told them of the stories I heard as a child from my great-grandfather Anthony Williams, who had been born a slave in 1840 and died at age 104 in 1944. My grandfather Mack Williams represented the first generation out of slavery. My father, Fred, was the second generation, and, of course, I was third—only the second generation born free. I was ten when my great-grandfather died. Suddenly, my fellow students understood that this was not ancient history at all.

It felt empowering to tell these white students and my white teacher that Black Americans had systematically been made to feel their history didn't count—that they had not made any significant contributions to the growth and development of either country or community. Most of them had clearly grown up sharing that assumption; for many, my presentation marked the first time any of them had been challenged to think about how this must feel to Black Americans. But I knew from an early age that history as it was taught then omitted the story of how the economy was built on slave labor and land stolen from Native Americans.

My great-grandpa Anthony often talked about how Black troops helped the Union Army win the Civil War. At the time, little of what he was saying fully made sense to me. But since then, I've realized how privileged I am to have heard so many accounts of the Civil War directly from his lips.

I stand truly in awe of the courage it took to volunteer for military duty during a time when the tactics of war exposed infantrymen to even greater risk of injury or death than modern warfare. Black troops *knew* they were likely to be disproportionately placed in harm's way. They knew that Confederates had a "take no prisoners" policy when it came to the formerly enslaved. And I stand in awe of the even greater courage it must have taken to continue to love and believe in a country that had given scant evidence that it would ever return even a little of that love to its Black citizens. Indeed, Black volunteers for the Union Army were fighting not only to end slavery and save the Union, but for the right to be seen and respected as full-fledged citizens in the land of their birth. The history my great-grandfather imparted to me helped instill a powerful sense of belonging to this country and a need to make sure I'm always in a position to make a difference.

From the age of six, maybe seven, I listened with rapt attention to Grandpa Anthony's stories: how he ran away from the plantation where he was enslaved to join the Union Army; how he fought in the Battle of Vicksburg. Some of his stories sounded so fantastical to me that they were hard to believe. My dad reinforced that sense of skepticism, often cautioning us kids to take most of Grandpa's stories with a grain of salt. The picture he painted for us was that Grandpa had at least as great a gift for embellishment as he had for storytelling.

This may well have been true, but years later I had an experience that made me reevaluate my grandpa's treasure trove of stories and begin to give them the benefit of the doubt.

Right up there at the top of the list of his all-time toughest tales to swallow was his recollection of the Battle of Vicksburg. He said that the wanton, fearsome slaughter of that fight was on such a massive scale that—literally—blood flowed in the streets: so much blood that a stream flowing through the edge of town ran visibly red with it; so much blood that for miles after that tributary entered the mighty Mississippi, even the Father of Waters looked, to everyone who saw it, like it was more blood than water. His description had always seemed just too extreme to be the literal truth. But when I had an opportunity as an adult to visit the Vicksburg Battleground National Park, I came across a plaque that supported Grandpa's contention, as did my reading of Christopher R. Gabel's *The Vicksburg Campaign: November 1862–July 1863*. Gabel quotes a soldier who said: "The creek was running red with precious blood spilt for our country."[1]

US census data verify that my great-grandpa Anthony Williams served with the Union Army from 1862 to 1865, and military service records confirm that a man whose name and age match his served in Company I of the 118th US Colored Infantry Regiment. Grandpa Anthony had helped liberate Mississippi's enslaved and save the Union, but he and nearly two hundred thousand other Black veterans soon understood that the end of the war was just the beginning of a protracted fight for freedom, justice, and full citizenship that would include many legal battles and that might well take generations to achieve.[2]

As I grew up and eventually came into my manhood, my knowledge of my Grandpa Anthony's bravery, and that of so many thousands of other Black men whose sacrifice helped save and build this country, became an anchor for me in this world—a linchpin of my identity. Their example was a constant reminder that I was called to be a soldier too. Wherever I saw injustice, it was my duty to confront it. Whenever I found teachers with the attitude that I couldn't accomplish something because of the color of my skin, I felt honor bound to prove them wrong.

In that spirit, enrolling at Portland High represented a culture shock for me, but I felt confident that I could handle it. I knew I could compete with these white kids, and that in this racially integrated environment I wouldn't be required to defer to them. Portland offered educational opportunities not available to me as a Black kid in Mississippi. It had a well-rounded and well-resourced athletics program. Members of the team didn't have to pay for their own uniforms, as would have been the case back home. Although I was small of stature (five foot six and 125 pounds), I loved competitive athletics and I wasn't about to let my size hinder me. In fact, I decided to try out for basketball! When I reported to the gym for try-outs, it was no surprise to find that nearly everyone there was bigger and taller than me. One of the other two or three Black students there invited me to join them in tryouts for track and field. I accepted their invitation, and I was soon very glad that I did. Not only was I able to earn a spot on both the indoor and outdoor track teams, but I lettered for indoor events that year. My timing couldn't have been better. Our team was able to set an indoor record for the three-hundred-yard relay that season, and I had the satisfaction and thrill of getting to be a contributor to that winning effort.[3]

The opportunity to be part of such a successful team was wonderful in and of itself, but the experience was made even sweeter by the fact that, in addition to taking on rival high school teams, we got a chance to travel and compete against college freshmen. It was through participation in these track meets that I got to visit a college campus for the first time.

Leola had been talking about her vision for me to become a doctor for years, but I remember that it was after visiting the campuses at Bowdoin and Bates that I first began to really sense college as a part of my future.

Only after living for a while free of Jim Crow attitudes and Jim Crow laws—of being able to do what I wanted and go where I wanted, and even to dream as big as I dared—did I begin to realize what an emotional, psychological, and spiritual drain that kind of overt racism had exerted on me. But it didn't take long for me to discover that ugly racial encounters could still happen anyplace, anytime. I didn't yet understand the dynamics of systemic racism, but I did understand that wherever there were white people, racial animus was always lurking just beneath the surface, ready to rear its ugly head without warning.

This was precisely the kind of casual, everyday racism that ambushed Clarence and me on a warm summer day in Portland when we were walking downtown on Congress Street. Clarence stood nearly six and a half feet tall without his shoes on, and he would stand out anywhere. A blonde white girl, about five years old, ran up to us, stopped in front of Clarence, looked straight up at him, and yelled, "Mommy, Mommy, look, two Niggers!" Her mother froze in her tracks, turned multiple shades of red, and profusely apologized. I simply replied, "Ma'am, that's alright. It isn't something I haven't heard before. Besides, she's only repeating what she's probably heard many times at home and elsewhere. Have a good day!" Clarence and I continued walking without looking back.

At least in Mississippi, the profligate use of the N-word was endemic, baked into a culture that was aggressively anti-Black, repressive, and terroristic. We understood that the word was a primal part of the racist toolkit, including its widespread use by young white children. Meant as a constant reminder to Black people that we had a place in their world and that this place was at the bottom, it reminded us that we should accept this place without question or complaint. And it's complicated, but I had also seen how many of us would use that same word to talk about each other, fueled by an unhealthy dose of racial self-hatred on the one hand and, on the other, an intuitive understanding that, like using snake venom to cure the effects of a potentially fatal snakebite, the word could be bent and twisted and worked like taffy to produce the kind of humor and irony that can sometimes actually help us heal.

I had begun to wonder how white people in the North could have developed the complex mythology that placed them comfortably above the fray when it came to race. How they could lay claim to a kind of blissful innocence about racism, given our nation's history with it and given the widespread prejudice so often casually expressed, even by people who protest, "But I haven't got a racist bone in my body," or "We've never used the N-word at our house."

It occurred to me that even with people for whom both these defensive statements are mostly true, a five-year-old kid learns that some people are "Niggers" from somewhere. If you don't see the racism all around you, then you won't see whatever racist beliefs and attitudes may live *inside* you either. Furthermore, if you see people act out their racist beliefs, but you never challenge them, or if you hear people casually spewing racist language, and you never challenge that either, then you are complicit in perpetuating that kind of poison. As a consequence, you may be shocked and appalled someday when your five-year-old embarrasses you in public as that word tumbles out of her mouth.

Soon the school year would be ending, and even though it had been a good year for me—an excellent year—my frustrations with Portland and the situation at Leola's apartment were growing, and I knew I needed to leave. Sporty had enlisted in the US Air Force and was no longer living with Daddy; suddenly there was room for me at Daddy's place. So I told Leola I was going to Chicago, contacted my dad, and told him I was coming. Shortly after school was out, I boarded a Greyhound bus headed west.

Greyhound was my favorite mode of transportation. I knew I'd especially enjoy traveling by myself this time. I could stretch out in comfort and enjoy the quiet, watch the world roll by out my window, and relish the rare opportunity these couple of days' travel would provide: I'd have the luxury of a good, long think about life, where I'd been, and where I was going.

3

CHICAGO

The trip from Portland to Chicago took about twenty hours, with bus changes in Boston and Cleveland. I didn't take much reading material with me because I knew that my mind and spirit needed to spend time daydreaming, reminiscing, and thinking about what my expectations were for life with my father. It would be a double introduction. I'd be exploring a huge new city, my first real metropolis, and I'd be getting to know my father all over again. Living there for a while would have changed him, I was thinking, in ways I couldn't quite imagine. He was probably feeling like a Chicagoan now. And I wasn't the same person after my time in Portland either.

It had also occurred to me that Chicago would be a city with an entirely different flavor because it was a place full of other immigrants and refugees from Mississippi, just like us.

After getting settled on the bus in Boston for Cleveland, it also occurred to me that this would be the first time in eight years that I'd be with Daddy when he wouldn't be leaving home for out-of-town work or to serve time in the military.

My father played an important role in my life, even though he wasn't around full time for much of my childhood. He was a powerful role model—strong and heroic. He took the difficult hand life dealt him as a Black man in Mississippi and didn't let it turn him bitter and mean. He was tender with our mother, and though he was always a strict disciplinarian with us, beneath his no-nonsense exterior there was a deep well of kindness and love for us kids. The Mississippi of our youth was a dangerous place for Black people, but under his roof, we'd always felt safe.

But there was trauma from which he couldn't protect us. The year I was born, we lost the family farm to foreclosure. This misfortune had nothing to do with bad management or irresponsibility on his part. It was the result of a court-enabled scam that was all too common in those times. The Black community called it "white larceny."

In those days, Black landowners in Mississippi didn't receive written notice when property taxes were due. It was incumbent upon them to keep track of these dates and to travel to the county seat to pay their taxes. When Daddy learned about the pending foreclosure, he traveled to Indianola with the necessary funds in hand, but county officials refused to accept his payment. The property was quickly foreclosed and sold at auction to a white buyer. Our family was prohibited from even putting in a bid for our own land.

The blow was particularly devastating because that land represented so much. My ancestors, only a single generation removed from enslavement, had worked hard and sacrificed to buy their own parcels of land. Land ownership meant taking a giant step away from the bitter past and a step toward self-determination, dignity, and a brighter, more prosperous future. But the sons and grandsons of Mississippi's enslavers were so terrified about the challenge such a future might present to their wealth and privilege that they fought to undermine it in every way they could.

As a consequence, many Black landowners throughout the South had their property stolen from them through means similar to the methods used against my family. This was a time in our history when, except for a few rare instances, our legal system refused to protect the rights of Black people. My family couldn't go to court to challenge the way in which they lost their land. No attorney would assist them, and even if there had been such an attorney, no judge would hear the case, because in Sunflower County,

Mississippi, the law still reflected the ruling in the 1858 decision handed down by the US Supreme Court in *Dred Scott v. Sandford*: The court ruled that Black people, as the descendants of enslaved Africans, were not citizens and thus had no standing to sue in federal court. And so it was that we had to swallow the bitter pill of losing our farm, knowing that we had no legal recourse through which we could hope to get it back. Overnight, the family went from being property owners and farmers to tenants and sharecroppers.

That experience turned my father against farming, because it was devastating to work so hard as a sharecropper, only to end up in debt each year. The majority of the Black farmers in Mississippi in the 1940s were sharecroppers, and sharecropping mostly benefited the white landowners. It was the easiest thing in the world for owners to cook the books in such a way that the costs of seed, fertilizer, other supplies, and equipment repair—all fronted to sharecroppers each season—almost always exceeded the net earnings they were owed, keeping them in perpetual debt. You couldn't put a man in a more demoralizing, hopeless situation. To men and women like my parents, sharecropping was just another form of slavery.

There was yet another chilling echo of slavery: if a family was in debt, as most were, it was illegal for them to leave. A family that left would be rounded up and returned to the landowner as if they were enslaved runaways. On the other hand, Black families could be *evicted at will.*

From the time I can remember, Daddy was away from home for part of the year, usually the winter months. There was no work off the farm available to Black men in Mississippi, so Daddy would leave for places like Kansas City, Helena, Little Rock, Pine Bluff, or Houston, where he would find work until the spring. Then he'd return home for crop planting season.

All the while that Daddy was away, he sent money home to support the family. That meant Momma was responsible for holding things together—but it was never just my mother who was around. There were always some other members of the extended family with us, like my maternal grandmother (Big Momma), an aunt, or my great-grandfather. All household members helped take care of the children, and this meant disciplining us as well. They all were licensed to spank, if they could catch us. I wasn't a difficult child who needed to be physically punished; the biggest challenge I presented was that I felt the constant drive to grow up fast. I wanted to do all the things the older kids were doing. I was a risk-taker, willing to try anything that made me feel grown—or to appear grown to others.

The Japanese bombing of Pearl Harbor on December 7, 1941, finally gave my father his way out of Mississippi. In 1942, at age forty-two, Daddy enlisted in the US Navy because, for him, it made economic sense. Even with the low salaries of enlisted men at that time, he could earn more in the navy than he could sharecropping—or in any other job available to him in Mississippi, for that matter. He served for most of his enlistment at Santa Rita Naval Base in Guam, in the South Pacific. In addition to his military pay, he received a monthly family allowance for each dependent, and he could claim a wife and five dependent children. It was this dependent allowance that enabled my mother to eventually build a house on the monthly allotment she received from my father.

When World War II ended in 1945, Daddy came home to Mississippi. But he was not prepared to return to life as a sharecropper, and no one would offer him work as a carpenter, a trade he had perfected over the years and enhanced in the navy. Unlike Daddy, Momma wanted to farm, even though we had built a house in town. She was so insistent on farming that she secured a plot of land from a local farmer to sharecrop. In 1946 Daddy took off for Omaha, Nebraska, for a job in a packinghouse where he could earn up to four dollars an hour, good money for a "colored" man.

My four older siblings had either left home or were in the process of leaving. Two of my sisters were married, and my oldest brother had gone to Chicago to find employment. My youngest sister was about to graduate from high school, and she had sworn she'd never work in the cotton fields again. That left Momma and her four young boys, ranging in age from ten to sixteen—including me. None of us knew anything about farming.

Naturally, Momma wanted Daddy home from Omaha because "the boys were too young" to be of much help. Daddy's initial reaction was that Momma had created this situation by refusing to move the family with him to Omaha. She had visited Daddy there once, and she didn't like it. Things moved too fast, she said. She didn't like the escalators or elevators she encountered in the department stores, and she insisted on using the stairs. She was a country girl through and through and couldn't understand why anybody would want to live in a big city. So she kept up her relentless pressure on Daddy to move back home.

To save his marriage and family, Daddy came back to Mississippi in the spring of 1947. But he was restless and not happy about having made this compromise. He'd missed all of us, but he hadn't missed farming one bit. His strategy for coping was to go out to the plot every day and pretend to farm. He'd stay on the farm long enough to get us to "lay-by" time, which is the period following planting the cotton and chopping weeds and grass from around the plants, enabling them to grow and then to blossom in late June to early July. When the blossoms fall off and the cotton bolls appear, the bolls ripen and open into cotton—a time when cotton plants require far less attention. This waiting period before the cotton is ready for harvest is generally a down time, and Daddy felt that when it arrived, he had done his bit and gotten us where we needed to be. Momma and the rest of us could complete the harvest now on our own, so Daddy left Mississippi in late summer 1947 one final time and headed for Chicago to join his oldest son, who had gone there to work.

The five of us did, indeed, complete the cotton harvest that fall, and we managed to get it to market. The next step was for the landowner to sell the cotton and give us our share from the sale. But Momma was told that there *were* no proceeds to share—in fact, he claimed she owed him. Young as we were, we understood that this was the nature of the cruel scam played on sharecroppers all the time. Sporty and I told Momma that what the landowner said couldn't be true because we had kept track of all subsistence allowances he had provided us, and the totals did not show that she owed anything. Based upon the price for the sale of cotton, we told Momma the landowner owed *her* money, which he was refusing to pay. So we encouraged Momma to challenge him.

She was reluctant because he was white, and in her generation Black people just didn't challenge the word of a white person in Mississippi.

Fred Williams Sr.'s US Navy portrait, 1942.

We were all so proud of her when she finally got up the courage to file legal action against him to make him pay what he owed her. And to make the eventual victory even sweeter, several other Black women from the area found the courage to follow her example and become plaintiffs too. The crowning glory of it all was that ultimately my mother and the women who joined her were victorious. My mother's share from the lawsuit came to almost a thousand dollars, which was real money in those days. News of the outcome quickly spread throughout the Black community across the state, giving us all a very proud moment.

I fully realize now what a truly remarkable accomplishment this was. An uneducated Black woman challenged a white man in court and won. How could that possibly happen when white people were still openly terrorizing Black people in Mississippi, forcing them off their land and lynching them with impunity? My speculation is that the courts didn't see the defendant as a "real" white man because he was an Italian American.

In those days, Italians and Jews were more or less lumped together toward the bottom of the social ladder in the Mississippi Delta—not relegated to as lowly a status as us Black folk, or Mexicans, or Filipinos, or Chinese—but certainly not regarded as white either. Frequently referred to as "dagos" (Italians) and "kikes" (Jews), they were treated with gross disrespect. This wasn't just a uniquely Southern thing either. Indeed, until the 1960 census, citizens of Italian descent were supposed to check "Italian" for their ethnicity on the census form, rather than "white." I strongly believe that if the landowner had been an Anglo-Saxon white man named Jackson or Johnson, Momma's case would never have been heard, much less decided in her favor.

Momma continued to be committed to living in Mississippi until all of her children began to leave. First my sister Sylvia graduated from high school and moved to Omaha to join our oldest sister, Leola, who was living there at the time. Next to leave was brother Orlandrous (four years my senior), who enlisted in the US Air Force at age eighteen. Brother Anthony (Sporty) and I left in 1950 for Maine, to join Leola and Sylvia, who had by then moved from Omaha to Cleveland, Ohio, and eventually to Portland.

This left Momma and my baby brother Gus in Mississippi. They finally left Mississippi to join Daddy in Chicago in 1951.

———

My bus departed the Cleveland, Ohio, bus terminal between midnight and 1 a.m. and arrived at the downtown Chicago terminal about ten in the morning. When I got off the bus and looked around, it finally hit me. I was in Chicago, and I knew in my heart that my life had just changed.

I was awestruck by the size of everything: the buildings, the streets, the traffic. I couldn't believe how many people were out and about on a Saturday morning. Everyone I saw was in a hurry, many of them running and disappearing belowground into what I later learned were subways, where trains ran underground. My brother Fred was waiting to pick me up, but I was still taking in the city—this marvelous "Sweet Home Chicago" that people sang about—this magnetic dream destination for Black Mississippians.

This great, Northern magnet for most of us refugees from the Delta had been widely talked up as a place where we could go to escape the discrimination that had so suffocated our lives back home. But I would soon learn this was not really true. Before long, Chicago revealed itself as a place where the face of exploitation and discrimination might look different, but where Black people were still very much exploited and discriminated against—both by white people and sometimes by our own.

I remembered that when I first arrived in Portland, population 75,000, I saw it, too, as a big town. And it *was*, compared to Shaw, Mississippi, population 1,800. But I could hardly wrap my head around the concept of living in a city of nearly three million souls.

I gathered up my luggage and followed Fred to his car, still gawking at all my new surroundings, wide-eyed. I must have looked so *country* to anyone who saw me. It's a good thing I was in the company of my solid older brother, because had I been on my own, I might've been an easy mark for somebody who was up to no good.

Fred and his family lived with my dad in a third-floor, walk-up, rear apartment on South State Street, about three miles from downtown. Unlike the Portland apartment, it didn't have a back porch or a dining room, only two bedrooms, a living room, and a kitchen. Before my arrival, the place was shared by Fred, his wife Ellen, their two-year-old son Clifford, and of course my dad. Four adults, including me, and a child sharing a two-bedroom apartment actually wasn't bad by Chicago standards, but by the end of the summer, my mother and brother Gus would be joining the household. Sleeping arrangements would radically change upon their arrival.

Before they came, everyone had a room with a door. After they came, Gus and I shared a sofa bed in the living room with no doors. Soon after, my sister Sylvia left her husband and moved in with her three-year-old son. Now, every room in the house had become a sleeping room.

Rollaway beds were brought into the kitchen, which now became the bedroom I shared with Gus. Sylvia and her son took over the sofa bed. None of us enjoyed any privacy at all, and the need for more space would worsen when Ellen gave birth to their second child, Ronnie. Ronnie's arrival meant that Daddy's four-room apartment would be home to ten of us—seven adults and three children—until finally, a year later, all of us were able to move together into a much larger place.

I had just turned seventeen when I made the move to Chicago. Dad reminded me that I was expected to find a job and contribute toward household expenses. I'd fully expected to work and help out however I could. I had *always* worked—back home in Mississippi, I'd worked in the cotton fields, had a newspaper route, sold vegetables door to door, and mowed lawns. In Portland, I'd worked after school, cleaning at a retail wallpaper store. I'd also sold ice cream from a cart that I pushed around from neighborhood to neighborhood. I was actually pretty excited about the prospect of finding myself some work. The problem, of course, was that I didn't know anything about Chicago yet, or where and how to begin my search for a job. I began by checking the newspaper want ads.

I was dismayed to find that even newspapers up here in the "promised land" were still accepting job advertisements that clearly stated "whites only." I saw many such ads, not only in the classified section of the papers but posted prominently in shop and store windows. I'd been hoping Chicago would show me a sign that life here was going to be different and better than the life I knew in Mississippi, but "whites only" was an old, familiar sign that I'd already seen far too much.

Just when the search was getting too demoralizing to bear, my dad let me know that he had talked to the people where he worked and they'd told him I could work there as his assistant. Daddy worked as a janitor in a cabinet-making factory on the Northside. Although he was a skilled carpenter, they would never hire him as a cabinetmaker because he was Black, at least in part because they knew he'd never be accepted into the cabinet-makers union. The building-trade unions were infamously discriminatory against both Blacks and women, so men like my father had no choice but to swallow their pride and settle for sweeping up behind the white male tradesmen.

My job was to help Daddy keep the shop clean. We had to continuously sweep sawdust from the floors and then dust down the machines at the end of each day. We worked nine hours a day, six days a week. My pay was $.65 an hour; my father's, $1.05. We wore face masks to keep from inhaling the sawdust. I found the job far worse than working in the cotton fields back home—and the pay wasn't any better. I vowed that if I survived the summer at this job, I would never do this kind of work again. I understood with clarity now that in order to make good on that promise to myself, I needed to get a college education. As for Daddy, he remained on that job for three or four more years, but he was eventually fired because he'd had the temerity to ask for a raise and vacation time.

This awful job made summer seem to last forever, but when it finally ended, I was never so glad to return to school, even though it meant being the new kid again. This would be the final year of my secondary school education. I'd be a senior at Wendell Phillips High School, and I was happy to discover that the school was only about seven blocks from our apartment—easy walking distance. It was tough for me on that first day of school because I had to get through it alone. There wasn't a single familiar face in sight.

As soon as I walked through the door, I felt overwhelmed by the sheer number of students in the building—3,500 in a building meant to serve

1,500—and all of them except for one were Black. It's a funny thing: in Portland, it had seemed overwhelmingly strange and intimidating to find myself in an environment that was almost entirely white. Even though my segregated world back home in Mississippi had made navigating environments that were all Black very ordinary and familiar, it was extremely strange and unexpected to feel a similar sense of culture shock at being surrounded now by surging crowds of my own people. I was a little like an immigrant, newly arrived from the old country and just beginning to get my bearings, surrounded by people my age whose parents or grandparents had been the immigrants but who had never experienced life in the old country themselves. Despite the shared experience of being Black in America, there was still a cultural gap between us that was deep and real.

Sporty, who had attended Wendell Phillips for a couple of months, had given me the names of a few students and suggested I look them up. Beyond that, I didn't know anything, although I had heard a few horror stories about violence and disorder at other Chicago high schools, including a recent fatal stabbing.

I did well in all of my classes at Wendell Phillips, but communicating with students outside of class was very challenging. At times, I felt like we were speaking different languages altogether. I'm sure I must have sounded awfully country to them, but for my part, I had a hard time making sense of the urban street language *they* spoke. One day, a student asked me if I owned a "short." The way I understood the question, he was asking me if I owned a cigarette butt. What kind of question was that? I later learned he was asking me if I owned a car. I felt equally astonished when I learned that *crib* or *pad* meant apartment or house, and *gig* was a job. Where I grew up, a crib was a barn or a place to store cotton or corn; a pad was something one put on the floor; and a gig was used to spear fish. Eventually, I began to learn the language, and as I did, I began to make friends.

I was old enough to question many things I hadn't thought to question when I was younger—especially things that related to the racial dynamics I saw all around me. For example, since I'd left Mississippi, I had yet to encounter a single Black classroom teacher, even at Wendell Phillips, where all but one of the students was Black. This would continue to be the case throughout my undergraduate and graduate education. In fact, after I left school in Mississippi throughout my education including graduate school I had only one Black instructor. And he was a field instructor at the University of Pennsylvania Graduate School of Social Work, not a classroom teacher. I began to reflect on what a powerful impact just a few Black teachers would have had on me—just to see someone who looked like me and had shared some of my cultural experiences up there in front of the classroom. By the time I left the University of Pennsylvania with my master's degree, I wasn't sure how or when I'd get the opportunity, but I was determined to somehow help ensure that ever-increasing numbers of Black teachers are recruited, retained, and supported.

Just before Thanksgiving of 1951, my father was hit by a truck while crossing the street. He was injured badly enough that he was out of work for six months. Money was always tight in my family, but it became even tighter following the accident. I needed to find a job if I planned on graduating from high school on time.

With the help of a friend, I was able to secure a part-time job as a bus-boy and dishwasher at the Young Men's Christian Association (YMCA) Hotel. That job turned out to be a godsend, because I made friends with many of the students working at the hotel, the majority of whom attended Wendell Phillips. Getting the job at the YMCA is an example of how Black people historically have relied on networking with family members and other Black people to survive. The Great Migration was built on the backs of Black people helping one another with finding work, housing, and friendlier surroundings. Working there illuminated for me the value of relationships and taught me that networking is a tool all of us need in our toolbox of life skills. Who do you know? How well do you know them? How well do they know you? Will they vouch for you? For the first time in my life, I used my network to achieve an important goal.

Better yet, some of the students I met became lifelong friends. After sixty years, I'm still connected to three friends from Phillips who helped solidify my decision to go to college.

That job was also important because it meant I could afford to participate in many of the senior activities at school. Even when I was assaulted by two men on my way to work and ended up in the hospital for three days with a concussion, my main concern was keeping my job. It was the first of two times my job was threatened by an event over which I had no control. This time, I reported to my supervisor what happened and was assured that I still had my job. I later was able to secure employment at the hotel for my brother Gus, a freshman at Wendell Phillips.

I made it through high school in great standing, and my circle of friends grew as I improved my communication skills. My job enabled me to afford the expenses of senior prom and also to buy a new suit for graduation. My family attended my graduation, and I felt a real sense of accomplishment. I was not the first member of my family to graduate from high school, but mine was the first graduation my parents had been able to attend. I would also be the first member in both my immediate and my extended family to attend college, which was a big deal. But I was literally on my own to figure out how best to make it happen. I didn't have any grand plan, but I firmly believed that it was my destiny to go to college and to finish a degree.

By the time I graduated high school, I had been accepted at Fisk University and the University of Illinois, Navy Pier, a two-year branch campus in Chicago that served many returning veterans. Fisk offered a tuition scholarship, but without any other financial aid, I couldn't afford to go away to school, so Navy Pier became my choice. I would have to work over the summer, earning enough to both contribute toward household expenses and save for tuition. I worked full-time, six days a week, at the YMCA Hotel, and by the end of the summer I had saved almost $300, which was more than enough to cover tuition, which was $130 for the year.

Although I had successfully completed high school and was headed to college, I had no specific career plans. My sister Leola had been trying to convince me for years that I ought to study to become a doctor. Although I really wasn't enthusiastic about pursuing a medical career, I understood Leola's real bottom line: she wanted me to graduate from

As a graduate from Wendell Phillips High School, 1952.

college with a degree or two and then go on to accomplish something great, something noteworthy, that would make the family proud. Our generation felt driven to "advance the race" and make our ancestors proud by achieving things they couldn't have dreamed of doing. By this point in my growth and development, I felt this aspect of our heritage deep down in my bones. I had heard the clarion call to do something significant with my life, and I was all in.

4

GOING TO COLLEGE

Although I graduated in the top 15 percent of my high school class, the truth is that I wasn't prepared for college. I never had the chance to consult with a college guidance counselor. Most of my information came from friends who were a step or two ahead of me, and I followed their lead. At first, I was full of questions about how to plan out the steps that led to becoming a doctor. As a Black kid growing up in Mississippi, aspiring to become a doctor was as good as it gets. Doctors were revered. I knew my services would be needed in my own community and I would be highly regarded. I had yet to learn much of anything about the range of other opportunities available.

College Struggles

My first year in college, 1952–53, was very challenging. I had no real guidance as to what classes to select, so I enrolled as a premed major and took all of the courses assigned to me, which amounted to nineteen credit hours in my first semester. On top of that, I was working, and I had no place at home I could study, since every room in the house was someone's bedroom. Academically, I was poorly prepared for the science and math courses I was taking, and I was only able to pass my math class because

I had a teacher who believed that any student who failed his course was a poor reflection on him. In the end, I managed to pass all of my courses, but my grades were not high enough to keep me off academic probation.

I transferred to Woodrow Wilson Junior College in Chicago for my sophomore year, focused on improving my grades so I could transfer to the main campus of the University of Illinois at Champaign–Urbana, 135 miles to the south, for my junior year. I did exceptionally well at Wilson because by then I had learned how to ask for help when I needed it. I used the powerful strategy of working with a study partner. This was easier for me at Wilson than it had been at Navy Pier because there were many more Black students in my classes and it was easier to find a compatible study partner. My grades at Wilson were outstanding, which vindicated my plan and made it possible to transfer to the main campus.

As I entered my junior year, it was time for me to declare a major. I knew by now I was not headed into medicine. Over time, I had discovered a strong interest in the social sciences—especially criminal justice. I had seen how Black people were disproportionately caught up in the system, and I wanted to understand every aspect of how the institutions that anchored the system really worked—our courts, prisons, and jails. I saw with clarity that if I were going to pursue a major in the social sciences, some level of graduate education was in my future. I had developed a passion for helping find ways to change oppressive systems, and I was beginning to recognize that the more I could learn about how institutions impact our lives, the better prepared I would be to help influence institutional behavior.

At the time, there were no financial aid packages to help cover the cost of student education. Fortunately, the cost of college in those years could be managed by a student with drive and dedication, even if his or her family wasn't in a position to help. One truly could work one's way through college. I had saved the $130 for my first year at Navy Pier, and my sophomore year at Wilson Junior College was tuition-free. The junior college system in Chicago was operated by the Chicago Board of Education and was prohibited from charging tuition. I was required to pay only a $20 registration fee each semester.

The summer after I had enrolled at Champaign–Urbana, I worked hard as an orderly at Illinois Eye & Ear Infirmary. In addition, I worked odd jobs whenever and wherever I could. I was determined to save enough money to pay not only tuition for the year but also room and board for at least a semester. I figured if I found a way to get to Champaign–Urbana, I'd find a way to stay there until I graduated.

And I did. The summer of 1954, I saved enough to pay for my first-semester tuition and a room at the university. During the year, I worked in the men's residence hall to cover the cost of my meals and stayed in university-owned housing, referred to as the parade ground units (PGUs). These were old army barracks built during World War II to house troops as they trained for deployment. Each barrack unit, heated by space heaters, housed eight students. Students were responsible for interior maintenance, including building fires in the space heaters during the winter. Space heaters were our only source of heat in Mississippi, so I knew a little about how to make a fire. But one of my roommates, Cyrus Johnson, had a skill set even higher than mine. He could build a fire that would last through the night, and all we'd have to do in the morning was stoke the coals. Cyrus and I became very good friends.

I arrived on campus a few days early, which gave me an opportunity to explore the campus community. I decided to visit a nearby bar and pool hall. When I entered, I was approached by a white student who invited me to play a game of pool. I accepted, thinking this would be a good way to kill some time and perhaps make a couple of bucks, since I had been playing pool since I was ten years old and had become quite good at it. As we racked the balls, an employee came over and told me I couldn't play because their establishment didn't serve Black people. I was forced to leave. I had known there was racism in Champaign–Urbana because there had been an incident the year before involving one of the University of Illinois star football players, J. C. Caroline. Caroline went into a local white barber shop seeking a haircut, and the barber cut a cross in his hair. This incident created quite a stir on campus, but it was not enough to end racial discrimination by local business establishments. Nor was it enough for the university to take action demanding the end to such discriminatory practices.

It would take the action of third-year law school student James D. Montgomery and a series of sit-in demonstrations by Black students at local white barber shops to end the discrimination. Montgomery had gone into the same bar and pool hall that discriminated against me and had the same experience. He brought legal action against them and won. This whole affair seemed to wake the university up a bit. Its administrators began to recognize that, as leaders of an institution central to this community, they needed to use the school's substantial economic and political influence to help end segregation in any of the public places that served students. And of course these efforts had a major, positive effect on the entire community, not just the student body.

The Importance of a Work Ethic

I had to work every year I was in college to sustain myself and pay my tuition and fees. Jobs were more accessible to me when I was going to school in Chicago, but I was now in Champaign–Urbana, where the University of Illinois essentially *was* the town, and I was without my Chicago network. Eventually, my roommate Cyrus came to the rescue and offered me an opportunity to earn some extra money at the Champaign Country Club, where he often worked serving big parties. Unfortunately for me, this became a one-time gig after I dropped a whole tray of six steak dinners worth over $60. Fortunately, it did not destroy the friendship.

I survived the loss of yet another job when I worked in the men's residence dining hall, which was paying for my meals. I was observed allowing a member of the football team to jump the line and take an extra dessert. The person who reported me assumed I was making a regular habit of this, which I was not—but I was guilty in this particular case. I've always been a small guy, and I was even smaller and more slender back then. I don't know how I was supposed to stop a 250-pound lineman from taking an extra dessert. The one time I tried, I was given "the look" as my fellow student continued to his table.

Some wrongs in this world are worth fighting for, even if it means you go to jail, lose a little blood—or maybe even your life. But in my opinion, in that moment the illicit claiming of one extra, sad-looking slice of cafe-teria pie did not rise to such a level. However, my supervisor was not at all sympathetic to my point of view on this and I was summarily dismissed.

———

Every job you ever take gives you a chance to learn something valuable, even if ultimately the job doesn't work out. Some jobs you take during your formative years, the kind of jobs you might take on in order to work your way through school, become every bit as central to your education as the most impactful coursework you ever do in class. My 1955 summer job stands above all others as an example of this. It taught me about street smarts and resilience, fear and rage, compassion and greed, caring and ne-glect, and even a little about entrepreneurship.

When the 1954–55 school year was over, I was obligated to earn enough money during the summer to pay my deferred tuition and fees *plus* all of my tuition and fees for the coming year. I started the summer with no real prospects, and I was getting a late start with my job search because I had remained on campus for a week after school had ended. It would be the first time I'd ever secured employment strictly on my own. This job seemed to come easily for a change: I responded to a newspaper ad. It turned out to be ideal for my circumstances at the time, and I was going to make money doing something I loved to do—drive a car. "This'll be fun," I thought. "Simple. Easy money." I would soon learn how misguided that initial assessment was.

Checker Taxi was advertising for drivers, no experience required, and it *didn't* say "only whites need apply," which very well may have been the case just one year prior. Yellow and Checker cab companies had been under pres-sure to hire Black drivers, so I applied at Checker Taxi and, to my surprise, was hired on the spot. And they wanted me to start immediately. I chose to drive the night shift over strong objections from my mother, who was afraid for my safety. I understood very well by now what a dangerous town Chicago could be, but I knew my way around, and I trusted my survival in-stincts well enough to shrug off the danger and embrace the adventure of it.

This was a job that helped influence my eventual choice of a career, because it was the first time I really saw and experienced the underside of the city. I witnessed opulence and poverty, caring and neglect, violence and degradation. I got in touch with the part of me that feels driven to help people in need—and to challenge those who just don't seem to care.

As things turned out, accepting this job and choosing to work the night shift were to my distinct advantage—no other job would have paid me enough to save over $800 in less than three months. My first week on the job was almost my last. I picked up a fare and I had no idea about how to get to the address. It happens. But usually things work out. Another cab rolls by, you roll down your window and ask for help; or your fare will guide you through an alternate route or two. But with this fare, things quickly went from bad to worse. I had a street guide and could look it up, but my passenger began to give me directions on a sure-fire shortcut. While trying to find my way, I had a head-on collision with another car, knocking my passenger off his seat and damaging the front end of the taxi as well as the other car. Fortunately, no one was injured, and after the police completed their report I was able to get my passenger safely to his destination. I apologized to him profusely and explained that I was a college student trying to earn enough money to complete my senior year at the University of Illinois. This impressed him and dramatically amplified whatever empathy he may already have been feeling. He even gave me a generous tip.

The next day, I had to plead my case with the vice president of personnel before I could report to a garage to check out a cab. I must have done a good job, because he only gave me a warning—though he told me that if it happened again, I'd lose my job. It didn't happen again.

To drive a cab is more than a job. For each individual driver, it's a business, and each driver has to learn how to think and behave like an entrepreneur. Not only did I have to learn my way around the city, but I had to understand the nightlife and know the locations of a number of special attractions that would appeal to visitors. I had to learn how to read a fare in a subtle way and develop a sense for what kind of nightlife I might suggest if they didn't already have something specific in mind. This was a tall order for a twenty-one-year-old who had just reached legal age, so I listened to other cabdrivers and asked questions. I learned which nightclubs paid cabdrivers for delivering customers to their establishments. It was up to the driver to know which clubs paid and to ask the doorman for the money. If the driver failed to ask, the doorman kept the money. I learned that the hard way. I also discovered that I could make more on short trips between downtown nightclubs and hotels. I always talked to the passengers, and I never failed to mention that I was a student working my way through college. Many nights, this feel-good story triggered more money from tips than I earned from the fares. Those tips were golden, because that was income I didn't have to share with the company.

Delivering customers to prostitutes became another source of income. I convinced myself I was not a pimp because I didn't have any prior connections with any of the prostitutes. Besides, it was serendipity, not any kind of intention, that made this income stream a possibility. My first job transporting customers began about 1 a.m. on a hot summer morning. I was parked in the Bismarck Hotel's taxi stand with my window rolled down. I was tired, trying to take a quick nap, and hoping for a fare that would take me south so I wouldn't have to deadhead—to return my cab with no fare.

I was suddenly awakened by a tap on my shoulder. It was a middle-aged white man who asked if I knew where he could find a girl. I hesitated before answering because I had heard other drivers say this was a typical police tactic—that if you replied in the affirmative, they would demand a payoff to keep from arresting you. Having sized him up, and feeling pretty sure this guy was not a cop, I told him I didn't know any specific girls but could take him to an area of the city where the kind of girl he was looking for could be easily found. The only area of the city I really knew was the South Side, and everyone knew that in Chicago, the South Side meant Black. The sly smile on his face told me he understood this when he asked, "Will they take me?"

"If you have money, they'll take you," I said.

He got in the taxi and I took him to the DuSable Hotel, in the heart of Bronzeville. When we arrived at the DuSable, I got out of my taxi and was immediately approached by a pimp who asked me if I was looking for a date. "No, but my passenger is," I replied. He told me to wait and he'd send a woman out to my cab. Soon a statuesque, very attractive Black woman sauntered over and got in the backseat with my passenger. She insisted that they go to a nearby hotel, the Manor House. When we arrived there, my passenger asked me to wait, which I agreed to do with my meter running. Every three minutes of waiting time would add an additional ten cents to the fare. I waited for over an hour before my passenger and his date came out.

When the two climbed in, I turned and looked directly at the woman because I wanted to get a better look at her. She was truly beautiful. She extended her closed hand over the front seat and opened it, slipping me a five-dollar bill. I took it and thanked her as I pulled out of the lot and headed back to the DuSable.

I dropped her off and began driving my passenger back to his hotel. We got as far as Cermak Road and Indiana Avenue when my passenger insisted on going back to the DuSable. On nights like this I sometimes made over $100 in tips, and there would be many such nights over the summer. I also learned that when a taxi driver made a referral to the prostitutes who worked out of the DuSable Hotel, they often got one-third of what she earned. That was a good deal for me, but not for the women, because pimps demanded their share too. The people benefitting the least out of such encounters were the women providing the actual "service."

It didn't make me feel good to know that I was part of that chain of exploitation. I wondered and worried about the women who were at the center of it all. How did they become involved in this business? How safe were they in their workplace? If they decided someday to walk away from "the life," what other kind of life might feel desirable—or even possible? Was there anyone or any institution out there to help them make such a transition?

By summer's end, I was glad I'd had the opportunity to work and earn my tuition, but I was also filled with gratitude that this was *not* my future— that as much as I felt empathy and respect for the folks who do this work, I was on a path in life that didn't end with a full-time career as a cabdriver. I left the job feeling genuinely excited to return to college.

This experience validated my choice of sociology for a major, with minors in psychology and history, moving me toward a career in a helping profession. I figured there have to be better options in life for people who find themselves marginalized and exploited, and I wanted to help create them. My dream became to build a career around helping people find pathways that led away from exploitation and victimization and toward dignity and self-determination.

I had become a member of Kappa Alpha Psi Fraternity, and I decided to live in Kappa House because it was far less costly than living in university-owned housing—mainly because no meals were provided. A time-honored work-around for this was that many of the brothers living in Kappa House worked at white sorority or fraternity houses in exchange for meals. We called the work "meal jobs." The brothers who worked them often brought food home to share with brothers who didn't have jobs. My membership in the fraternity expanded my network, which I used to secure one of those meal jobs for myself. I landed at a sorority where the head cook was aunt to one of my fraternity brothers. We were always looking out for each other like that.

Pledges to Kappa Alpha Psi Fraternity, 1955. I'm seated, second from right.

Graduation—A Family Affair

I had enough money to pay all my tuition and fees through the first semester, but paying for the final semester became a family affair. My brother Fred sent me five dollars a week. Sister Leola paid my graduation fees. Other siblings sent me money periodically to cover unanticipated expenses, and even my mom and dad, who had little to give, contributed. Because I was the first member of my immediate and extended family to graduate from college, my success was a family success. I became the family role model for my generation and other generations to follow.

My sister Sylvia and a cousin, Valarie, were challenged to find a place for the graduation party because my family didn't have enough space where they lived. They felt strongly that a real celebration was in order, not only because of what it would mean to me but also because of the message it would send to others in the family. Judge and Leola Hardy, our cousins, offered their place as a graduation gift to me. They had six children, all younger than me, and they wanted their children to aspire to higher education too. The party was special and we had a great time. Judge was as excited as I was and, just as he hoped would happen, his children shared in the excitement. I was the center of the family's attention, but it was also a big deal to these kids that they got to meet my college friends. Looking back now, I can understand how seeing not just me but a number of Black graduates gathered together in one room, celebrating each other, felt deeply inspirational to them. I think it helped them see the idea of going to college as *normal*. And sure enough, all six of them went on to earn college degrees.

I received a bachelor of arts degree with a major in sociology and minors in psychology and history from the University of Illinois in 1956, and I immediately enrolled in a graduate school summer internship in penology at the university. I served an internship in the Illinois state prison system at three of its prisons: Joliet Prison, Statesville Prison, and Dwight Reformatory for Women. I functioned as an intake worker for short periods of time at each of those facilities. I was also expected to design a research project that could be implemented at a later date as a partial requirement for a master's degree in sociology. My interest at the time was to eventually earn a doctorate degree in sociology in preparation for an academic career. I never pursued the doctorate, but the experience I gained through the internship would later serve me well.

Le maestro

As a college student in Chicago, 1956–57, in a photo I labeled "Le Maestro."

the cool one

As a college student in Chicago, 1957, in a photo I labeled "The Cool One."

them perform. Black entertainers could *work* at these nightspots, but th
weren't allowed to let down their hair and party there with friends. Bla
soldiers had to pool their resources and be creative about finding way
to get off base and have a good time. We had to organize ourselves an
travel together to cities like St. Louis, Springfield, or Kansas City for ou
entertainment.

I knew the military couldn't order changes in the communities where
bases were located, but the army *could* declare businesses that discriminated off-limits to military personnel. And since military personnel were
the primary sources of business for most of these establishments, I decided, near the end of my tour of duty, that I would launch a campaign to
persuade the military to use its considerable leverage in these communities
to wage war against the rampant discrimination faced by Black soldiers.

I began by writing a letter to the post commander describing the problem, encouraging him to place such establishments off-limits to all Fort
Leonard Wood military personnel. About the same time, I applied for
an early release to attend law school. I crossed my fingers and hoped my
letter to the post commander wouldn't affect his decision on my request.

I was never interested in earning a law degree; I was applying to law
school because it was my opportunity for an early release from the army.
I had the mindset of a draftee: serve your time, stay out of trouble, and
take advantage of any reasonable opportunity to shorten your stay. Social
work, not law, was my educational and career priority. Besides, all of my
friends were leaving, and I thought I might later return to law school and
augment my social work degree with a law degree.

The timing was complicated. I had to be accepted by a law school before I could officially apply for an early release. It was December, and my
regular release date was in April. To be released ninety days early, I needed
to be accepted at a law school by January 1, 1960—and I had yet to apply.
I needed to find a law school that offered evening classes because I was
going to have to work in order to afford school. The only law school in
Chicago that had a full-time evening program was DePaul University, so
getting accepted there became my primary mission. Over the Christmas
holidays, I took a three-day pass to Chicago so I could apply in person.

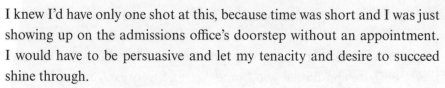

I knew I'd have only one shot at this, because time was short and I was just showing up on the admissions office's doorstep without an appointment. I would have to be persuasive and let my tenacity and desire to succeed shine through.

I took a copy of my transcript and my degree from the University of Illinois to the registrar at DePaul and told the receptionist I was there to apply for admission to the law school. She gave me the application and told me to complete it and mail it to the office and to have the university mail my transcript. When I told her I needed a decision *that day* because I was applying for an early release from the army, she insisted it simply couldn't be done. When I asked if there was anyone there who could make an exception, she said the dean was the only person who could do that. I wasn't about to relent now. I asked if the dean was in his office. When she told me he was, I asked to see him.

A few minutes later, Dean Richard Ward agreed to see me. I passionately told him my plans, emphasizing how much I really wanted to study law and become a lawyer. I also shared some of my life story, closing with my journey to become the first member of my family to graduate from college. He said my request was most unusual and outside of the process, but he acknowledged that he was swayed by the fact that I had already earned an undergraduate degree and completed a graduate-level internship, which he saw as proof of my capacity to do graduate-level work. He made an exception, approved my application, and dictated a letter stating that I had been admitted to DePaul University Law School effective February 1, 1960. He even gave me a copy to hand-carry back to Fort Leonard Wood. With that letter in hand, I was able to formally initiate my application for early release. I was released from active duty on January 27, 1960, and enrolled at DePaul on February 1, 1960.

I later learned that during the summer of 1960, the commanding general at Fort Leonard Wood had used his influence to bring an end to racial discrimination at the entertainment establishments near the army base. This was the first time I saw that concerted action by one person really *can* make a difference.

I completed a semester at DePaul, and I did exceptionally well academically. But my interest was in social work, and I had already applied for admission to the University of Pennsylvania School of Social Work (now the School of Social Policy and Practice) when I received my early release. That admission enabled me to return to my job as a caseworker at Cook County Department of Welfare, where I hoped to take advantage of an opportunity available through the department to earn my master of social work degree. The county wanted to increase the number of professionally trained social workers in the department, especially Black social workers. To help accomplish this goal, the department created a program that would pay for the graduate education of any employee selected to participate. I felt confident I could successfully compete and be selected. Once admitted to the program, the department would not only cover my tuition and fees, it would provide me with a $300 per month stipend to cover living expenses. *In addition*, if I selected an out-of-town school, the department would cover my travel expenses to school in the fall and back home at the end of the school year.

In exchange, I would commit to work one year for each year of education I received while a participant. The master of social work (MSW) degree was a two-year program, so I was committing to remain an agency employee for at least two years after graduation. My application for the program was approved, and I was granted a leave to attend the University of Pennsylvania School of Social Work. Now I truly felt I was on my way toward building the life and career I had begun to envision for myself. And the contours of that future life were becoming clearer and clearer.

6

PHILADELPHIA:
A GRADUATE DEGREE
AND A BRIDE

The Greyhound bus has always been there for me whenever life-changing experiences have required me to travel from one place to another. It was the sweet chariot that liberated me from the Jim Crow strictures of life in Mississippi, showed me my first glimpses of the wide world beyond Dixie, and carried me north to Portland, Maine. It was the zephyr that carried me cross-country to Chicago to reunite with my parents. And now it was the conveyance taking me onward to my life's next major chapter: to Philadelphia to further my education—and, though I didn't yet know it, to find a wife and start a family.

A Fortuitous Move

In September 1960 I boarded a bus from Chicago to Philadelphia. I had accumulated many traveling miles by bus but had never been to

Philadelphia, known as the City of Brotherly Love. We pulled into town very late, and it took me 'til midnight to check in to the Robert Morris Hotel. I was tired, but I needed to walk a little and stretch my legs. I asked the doorman if there was someplace close by where I could go have a beer. I didn't feel much "brotherly love" as he smirked at me and laughed. Was I serious? I didn't know it, but the Pennsylvania blue laws were then in effect, which meant that, by law, all bars and nightclubs had to close at midnight on Saturdays and couldn't reopen for business until Monday.

I knew only one person in Philadelphia, an army buddy from Fort Leonard Wood, Joe Blue. He would be a big help to me in adjusting to Philadelphia and building a social life.

My graduate education and training at the University of Pennsylvania School of Social Work included a two-year fieldwork internship at the Pennsylvania Prison Society. Founded in 1787, the organization provided services to prisoners and ex-offenders. My education at Penn helped me understand and value the role that institutions have as mediating forces in the community. Unlike Columbia University and the University of Chicago, which were known as "diagnostic" schools that followed the theories and teachings of Sigmund Freud, Penn was referred to as the "functional" school, based on the theories and teaching of Otto Rank.

Rank's theories about how community institutions can be a powerful and progressive force for good resonated with me, and they became foundational to my way of looking at the world. My studies helped me see that although I had been raised in a community that was dirt poor, the world I knew was actually quite rich in human resources because I was always surrounded by people who were resilient, caring, nurturing, and strong—just the kind of people who, given the opportunity, could help build and sustain institutions capable of nurturing, strengthening, and healing stressed communities. With the strong foundation I got in that MSW program, I launched on a career that has been connected with organizations—public, nonprofit, and faith-based—that delivered services designed to have a

positive and tangible impact on communities and on the quality of life of
the people who live in them.

———•———

The quality of my own life took a giant leap upward after I began to get
to know the young woman I sat next to in class. Mary Louise Sales had
gorgeous hazel eyes and the most beautiful legs I'd ever seen. She was
smart and funny, and the more I got to know her, the harder I fell. Unfortunately, the feeling was not mutual. I'm sure she counted a number of
strikes against me, but the two I knew about for sure were that I was from
Chicago and that I smoked. I wasn't sure where her distaste for Chicago
and Chicago people came from, but that was something I couldn't change.
I could quit smoking, though, and I did. She noticed. Whatever else may
have sparked her initial distaste for me melted away, and we began dating.
Suddenly, not only did I have a girlfriend, which was wonderful in and of
itself—I now had a whole new family who provided me a warm and pleasant place to go for the weekends. I had dinner every Sunday at her house
after we attended church together. I got to know her father and brother
well, and they made me feel welcome and at home. Her mother had died
earlier that year. I'd like to think that welcoming in and caring for a new,
de facto family member played some small role in their healing process. I
learned the social pleasures of playing pinochle and cooking and eating
popcorn, because those were among Mary Lou's family's favorite activities.

She and I were married in 1962, just two days before we received our
master of social work degrees from the Penn School. Two weeks later, we
moved to Chicago. The move was hard for Mary Lou, both because of her
negative prior impressions of the city and because Chicago was a long way
from her family and friends. We did manage to make multiple trips back
to Philadelphia, and we enjoyed visits from her brother and father during
our first year of marriage. But the commitment to remain with the Cook
County Department of Welfare proved to be challenging, so I promised
my new wife that after the required two years, I would seek employment
opportunities outside of Chicago, my broad target area being somewhere
along the Eastern Seaboard, between Washington, DC, and Boston.

Mary Lou and I were married in 1962.

My mother and me at the wedding.

I began my employment search in 1964, making three trips back to Philadelphia for job interviews that didn't pan out. I also applied for a supervisory position in New Haven, Connecticut. Finally, one day in September 1964, I came home from work and Mary Lou told me I had an important long-distance call from Minneapolis. I was to call Operator 18. At first I thought she was joking, because I didn't know anyone in Minneapolis. When she reassured me that the call was for real, I called Operator 18, and was connected with the executive director of Unity Settlement House, Elsie Weinlick, who invited me to come to Minneapolis for a job interview at her expense. I learned later that she got my name from a Minneapolis independent recruiter, Ashby Gaskins, who had heard about me from one of my fraternity brothers.

It was late September when an army buddy, Bob Johnson, joined me for the trip to Minneapolis in my 1962 Rambler station wagon. The drive was pleasant enough—until a tire went flat on us at 1 a.m. The night was cold and we didn't have heavy coats. I discovered that there's not much in this world that feels colder than frozen metal on a cold night. Once we successfully mounted that spare tire and got back on the road, I told Bob I sincerely hoped this wasn't any kind of an indication about how the rest of our trip was going to go. We needn't have worried. We made it to our motel without further incident and got a decent night's sleep. Later in the day, I went to my job interview and walked out feeling confident I had done exceptionally well.

Bob and I took time to tour the city, and we were impressed with the neighborhoods, especially because we could see how many people lived in single-family, detached homes. Most of the people we knew in Chicago lived in multiple-unit apartment complexes. In the neighborhoods we knew in Philadelphia, most people lived in attached row houses. We knew, of course, that Minneapolis had a long list of racial disparities and other issues to address, but we took note of what felt like an unexpectedly high number of Black families living in these single-family detached homes—living, we thought, something a little closer to the American dream.

That evening, as Bob and I were getting dressed for a social event to which we'd been invited by Mr. Gaskins, we heard a loud knock on our motel room door. When I answered, there stood two white men dressed in trench coats. They flashed their badges and announced that they were FBI agents. Bob and I froze, our pasts flashing in front of our eyes as we tried to think what we had done to warrant this attention. They told us they were looking for a Robert L. Johnson, not a familiar name to either of us. The agents had already checked our backgrounds and knew all kinds of details about both of us, which was more than a little unsettling.

They conferred with each other in hushed tones, and then, a few minutes later, they announced that we were cleared. The Robert L. Johnson they were looking for was a white man, and it seemed obvious to them that we didn't know him or anything about him. After they left, Bob and I agreed that this was a rare brush with law enforcement we could always look back on and smile—because this was an instance when, for once, it was actually *great* to be Black.

Once I returned home, I told Mary Lou I was confident I would be offered the job. I was upbeat about it and looking forward to saying *yes*. But I worried that she might be disappointed to be moving deeper into the Midwest and even farther from Philadelphia and the Eastern Seaboard.

So I was relieved to hear her say, "Well . . . it's getting us out of Chicago." The fact that she was okay with the move lifted my spirits, and one week later I accepted the job offer, telling my new employer I could commit to a two-year stint. Mary Lou was fine with that too. So it was that we pulled up stakes and moved to a city that had never even been on our radar screen before—a city we would eventually embrace as home.

7

MINNEAPOLIS: A DIFFERENT KIND OF ENGAGEMENT

This was the first major transition time in my life for which I needed to push aside my old, trusted friend the Greyhound bus in favor of my Rambler station wagon. I was a family man now—Mary Lou and I had an eighteen-month-old son. And our Rambler wagon was a family man's car: a sensible, safe, comfortable ride for the three of us. On a cold winter day in early January 1965, I loaded my little family and our most essential gear into the car and moved to Minneapolis, Minnesota.

It was cold when we left Chicago and even colder when we arrived in Minneapolis. The temperature never got above zero degrees Fahrenheit on the day we checked into the motel where Bob and I had stayed when I came for my job interview. The motel was home for a couple of weeks, and then we moved into an apartment in a newly constructed building, located about a mile from Unity Settlement House in North Minneapolis, where I would be working.

Immediately, Minneapolis felt different from Chicago—in many ways, it was more like Portland. In Chicago, Black people were concentrated in certain neighborhoods on the south and west sides of the city. They worked in the post office, collected the trash, and comprised much of the army of workers who kept the hotels, the factories, the department stores, the streets and parks, and the public buildings clean. Almost all of the public jobs were patronage jobs, which meant, essentially, that Black people were exchanging their votes for the opportunity to do this work. It was as if the city had offered Black folks an unspoken contract: "Okay. Y'all have moved here looking for a place in our ecosystem? Well, here's the place we're offering. You can like it or lump it."

But it didn't take long to notice that in Minneapolis, Black people didn't seem to work in *any* of these jobs. In fact, the longer and the closer I looked, it seemed clear to me that in Minneapolis, Black people were essentially invisible.

I pondered over why this should be the case. The public jobs in Minneapolis were held by white people, and since I didn't see Black people cleaning the streets and parks, I thought perhaps a significant number of them held professional jobs in the corporations and nonprofit organizations that were such a prominent part of the local ecosystem. I soon learned that this wasn't true either. A closer look revealed what I figured must be at least one piece of the puzzle: the very small size of Minnesota's Black population at the time. The 1960 US census data show that approximately 12,000 Black people lived in Minneapolis, less than 2.5 percent of the population. But even adjusting for the disparities in the numbers, Black people didn't seem to have their just share of the jobs.

Minneapolis, unlike Chicago, had never been a major destination for the millions of Black folk who left the South during the Great Migration. But we had emigrated to Chicago in large enough numbers that our presence simply couldn't be ignored. To soothe rising white anxiety over growing numbers of Black folk, Chicago's unspoken social contract had to address how the social pecking order should look. After all, the civic life of virtually the entire country was still heavily influenced by the legacy of Jim Crow laws and Jim Crow thinking. But in Minneapolis, given our small numbers, tucked away in a few segregated pockets—invisible—perhaps we were simply not on white folks' minds much at all. At least, not enough to amend the social construct to create a place for us, somewhere near the very bottom.

I pondered this while I explored and tried to understand the workings and the culture of my new hometown. I discovered that civic and community engagement in Minneapolis was at a whole different level compared to Chicago. In Chicago, community engagement was highly politicized, which is to say that very little change could happen in any Chicago neighborhood that didn't begin with the support of the political leadership. To get public support for any neighborhood improvement initiative, one had to climb, bit by bit, up the political chain of command: precinct captain to the city council member, then ward committeeman to the representative of the mayor's office. The initiative's approval would be directly correlated to the supporters' commitment to Mayor Richard J. Daley's political machine, a process that left little room for grassroots initiatives.

In Minneapolis, there was no strong political party in control of the community engagement process—at least not in the sense that people mean when they talk about machine politics. I could see that people truly felt they had direct access to their elected officials. I noticed a refreshing sense of optimism and ownership of the political process I'd never seen before. A citizen didn't have to check in with a precinct captain before contacting a council member, nor worry about getting prior approval to contact the mayor. The root of this difference lay in the cities' differing governmental structures. Chicago's mayor was, by charter, given a great deal of authority, and he was able to get things done by issuing edicts, like an autocrat. In addition, he controlled large numbers of city jobs, which he and his cronies could distribute among his supporters in accord with their level of support. By contrast, the Minneapolis mayor could hire only his own personal staff and one department head: chief of police. The civic culture in Minneapolis dictated that the mayor had to build coalitions and develop partnerships with public, private, and nonprofit sector institutions to get things done for the people of Minneapolis.

Chicago mayor Richard J. Daley, though he was also just a politician elected to public office, used the political clout and the capital resources given to him by city charter to effect the kinds of changes he believed to be in the best interest of the people of Chicago. Minneapolis mayor Arthur Naftalin, driven by the sincerely held belief that he was a *public servant* elected to public office, worked within a political culture that expected him to use collaboration and public persuasion to help transform communities. Richard Daley would never have been elected mayor of Minneapolis, and Art Naftalin could never have survived the politics of Chicago.

I never met Mayor Daley during the fourteen years I lived in Chicago. And had I remained there, I most likely would *never* have met him, because the kind of civic and community engagement into which I was drawn in Minneapolis could never have happened in Mayor Daley's Chicago.

I had been in Minneapolis only three months when I met Mayor Naftalin and began to develop a relationship with him and his office. I also met the mayor's wife, Fran, during my first month on the job at Unity House. She served on the board of directors of Eastside Neighborhood Services, a settlement house in Northeast Minneapolis.

I was given the luxury of ample time to do the nitty-gritty work of getting to know the community. I began to work with a couple of groups of adolescent boys from Franklin Junior High School, and I participated in a number of community meetings, including the Minneapolis Federation of Settlements, where I soon learned that the issue of duplication of services had become a major issue with funders and social policy decision-makers.

In 1965, there were at least seven independent settlement houses in Minneapolis, three of which—Phyllis Wheatley Community Center (PWCC), Unity House, and Wells Memorial Settlement House—were located in North Minneapolis within a one-mile radius. The United Way and other public and private funders were raising questions regarding the need for this many independent agencies providing essentially the same services, competing for dollars from the same funders. As a consequence, the Minneapolis United Way and the Community Health and Welfare Council of Hennepin County were encouraging the Northside settlement houses to consider some form of merger. Initially, I didn't get involved in these discussions, since I was neither an executive director nor a board member at any of these agencies. It was just as well, because I had my hands full just working with the two groups of teenage boys who were my responsibility. I spent that first summer on the job as the resident social worker at Unity Camp near Amery, Wisconsin. My wife and our two-year-old son, Chris, enjoyed that summer camp experience right along with me.

I came back from summer camp ready to reengage and contemplate my future in Minneapolis. My plan was to spend two years at Unity before returning to graduate school, where I would earn a PhD and become a professor at an eastern college or university. But by now I understood quite well that things don't always work out according to the plans we make.

Soon after I returned from summer camp, Henry Thomas, executive director of PWCC, announced that he was resigning to take the same position at Hallie Q. Brown Settlement House in St. Paul. I had already begun to identify the resources I would need to resume my graduate education, and I figured it would take me to the end of my two years at Unity to finalize my plan. I couldn't have conceived at the time what a momentous impact Henry Thomas's resignation would have on my life and career.

Our move to Minneapolis turned out to be good for me, and good for my marriage and family as well. Our experience in Minneapolis gave Mary Lou an opportunity to develop her own identity, to become known as Mary Lou Williams as opposed to Mrs. Theartrice Williams, which was still very much the tradition for married women in those days. Her work eventually included co-teaching a summer course on housing discrimination at the University of Minnesota, helping develop the first open school program in Minneapolis Public Schools at our daughter's elementary school, serving as an aide to Mayor Don Fraser, serving as a board member at the Citizens League, serving twelve years on the Augsburg University board of regents, and finally teaching social work for thirteen years at Augsburg University, where she helped build the graduate program in social work.

Although we were happy in Minneapolis, I wasn't yet convinced that we would be staying for the long haul. Mary Lou and I were still interested in getting back to the East Coast for more graduate studies. And then I received a special telephone call from someone I had not yet met—a momentous phone conversation that would change our lives and, in the process, transform us from people who'd thought we were just passing through to Minnesotans.

8

Beginning at Phyllis Wheatley

In late August 1965, Mildred (Min) Himmelman, a Phyllis Wheatley Community Center board member, called me at my home to invite Mary Lou and me to lunch at her St. Louis Park home. Neither my wife nor I knew Mrs. Himmelman, and she didn't reveal the reason for the invitation. She had also invited two other people: Dr. Anna Hedgeman, a well-known civil rights leader and top executive at the National Council of Churches; and Mrs. W. D. Brown Sr., the wife of a prominent and well-known African American physician in Minneapolis. I soon learned that I was invited to dine with these three powerful women so they could convince me to apply for the vacant position of executive director at Phyllis Wheatley Community Center.

They were unrelenting in their attempt at persuasion.

When I told them about the commitment I had made to stay at least two years at Unity, they dismissed that with, "We've discussed this with your employer, and she's supportive of our efforts." I thought to myself, "These women got some nerves ..." But it felt good to be wanted. Eventually, I decided that while I couldn't formally apply for the position, I would come if Phyllis Wheatley sent me a letter inviting me to interview for the

job. I told them they could work with Mary Lou to get a copy of my resume and any other necessary background information. Without batting
an eye, they complied with my requests, accomplished their mission, and
the Phyllis Wheatley Community Center board of directors appointed me
as executive director effective October 1, 1965, almost nine months to the
day after my arrival in Minneapolis. The next seven years at PWCC would
prove to be among the most challenging and rewarding years of my professional career—and my life.

A Significant History and Role

Phyllis Wheatley Settlement House was established in 1924 on the recommendation of the local Women's Christian Association (WCA). It was
named for an eighteenth-century enslaved woman who became a well-
known poet. Initially, the organization's focus was on creating a place to
accommodate the cultural, social, and recreational needs of "Negro girls."

The African American community leadership of the time saw the proposed focus on "Negro girls" as much too narrow, because cultural, social, or recreational spaces were not available to *any* of the approximately
four thousand Black people living in Minneapolis in 1924. But the Black
community had an even deeper, more fundamental need: an institution
that could position itself to fight for social justice—to oppose all the
many ways that anti-Black discrimination showed its ugly face—for the
long haul. In response to this critique from the community, the new center hired W. Gertrude Brown, who was an associate of settlement house
movement pioneer Jane Addams. The Black community simply had a
better understanding of its community's needs than the all-white WCA,
and W. Gertrude Brown was the right person at the right time.[1]

From its earliest days, Phyllis Wheatley differentiated itself from the
other settlement houses in the state, and most of the settlement houses
in the nation, because under Brown's leadership, social justice was unam-
biguously central to its mission. In contrast, up until this moment, the
central mission of the nationwide settlement house movement was to help
new immigrants find the smoothest possible pathway to assimilation into
American life and culture.

Gertrude Brown, about 1925. *Minnesota Historical Society*

European immigrants to these shores had been a big part of the American story since long before independence, but the country had never seen such a tidal wave of immigration as the one that arrived between about 1880 and 1920. Irish, Scandinavian, German, and other European immigrants came in large numbers to the East Coast and the Midwest to escape the harsh realities of grinding poverty, starvation, and crisis levels of civil strife. Many Jewish immigrants were among them, driven by the same pressures, but fleeing the murderous pogroms that swept across much of Central and Eastern Europe during this era. Their arrival was the primary driver for the settlement house movement, which aspired to provide a progressive, optimistic answer to a complicated, two-part question: 1) How do we welcome into our country over two million people from dozens of different cultures, speaking dozens of different languages, helping them assimilate well enough that they can forge a shared identity with each other and with the rest of us as Americans? and 2) Can we do this in such a way that we turn a crisis into an opportunity for America?

Gertrude Brown saw clearly that settlement houses serving predominantly Black neighborhoods had a parallel mission. For a generation and a half, Black Americans had also been engaged in a Great Migration, fleeing to safety and hoping for a better life, much as these other immigrants from Europe. On Black Africans' flight from "Dixie," they had to traverse a historical and cultural divide just as deep and wide as any ocean. But Brown could also see that there was no national sense of urgency about creating a smooth pathway into the heart of American life for them. In the world she knew, the old roots of anti-Black prejudice and animus ran too deep for even the most optimistic person to think that this social reality would change anytime soon. She resolved to make Phyllis Wheatley House a model for demonstrating what a community-based, nonprofit institution could accomplish in terms of providing a safe, nurturing space for Black people while also serving as a champion for civil rights, educational and economic progress, and dignity.

When A. Phillip Randolph's Brotherhood of Sleeping Car Porters sought a safe place to meet in Minnesota, on their way to organizing their first national strike in 1925, Brown offered them space over the strenuous objection of the Wheatley board of directors. Randolph's fledgling union went on to organize their Minnesota chapter in a meeting room at Phyllis Wheatley. Black victims of police violence who were fearful of retribution were given refuge at Wheatley House. Black students in need of remedial help with reading and math skills got tutored at Phyllis Wheatley. Brown raised enough money that Wheatley House could afford to hire Black women in a variety of jobs intended to develop leadership skills. Many of those Wheatley House alumni went on, as Brown had foreseen, to become educators, businesswomen, and skillful organizers in the struggle for Black civil rights.

Many large settlement houses throughout the country, like many large YMCA and YWCA facilities, managed a block of rooms that were rented to people who had a short-term need for a decent, affordable place to live. Black families who had difficulty finding an apartment that an owner would rent to them or a house that an owner would sell to them were housed at Phyllis Wheatley until they could find a suitable place of their own. Black travelers in need of lodging could find a room at Phyllis Wheatley when no hotel would accommodate them. When affordable public housing open to Black families was first proposed, it was Gertrude Brown and Phyllis Wheatley House that led the charge. A collaboration with the Minneapolis Housing Authority led in 1938 to the creation of the Sumner Field Housing Project, the first government-built public housing in Minnesota.

Gertrude Brown had rightly foreseen that, due to the rampant, unchecked racial discrimination of her times, settlement houses that focused on the needs of Black citizens would have to include more guest rooms than the others. Phyllis Wheatley was listed in *The Negro Motorist Green Book*, a publication developed by Victor Hugo Green as a guidebook to help Black people find lodging and other essential accommodations as they traveled through the South or across the country. From 1929, when the new Phyllis Wheatley House was opened, through the 1940s and well into the 1950s, Black students were not permitted to live in University of Minnesota dorms, and there were no accommodations for Black faculty either. Black celebrities visiting Minneapolis couldn't stay at any of the downtown hotels. Even high-profile graduates of the University of Minnesota like Roy Wilkins and Carl Stokes were unwelcome in university dormitories, and entertainers such as Duke Ellington, Hazel Scott, Ella Fitzgerald, and

Phyllis Wheatley Settlement House, 1936. *Hennepin County Library*

Count Basie stayed at Phyllis Wheatley House when they were performing in Minneapolis. Not a single top-tier hotel in the Twin Cities would allow even these internationally acclaimed stars to book a room.

By providing housing for Black students and faculty, Phyllis Wheatley became an important community partner in the educational advancement of Black students and in the launching of a number of academic careers. Throughout the thirties, forties, and fifties, Phyllis Wheatley Settlement House was the most viable and essential institution in the city's Black community, engaging entire families with its cultural, athletic, and recreational enrichment; early childhood education; and other program activities. It was the Black community's premier venue for large gatherings and special events. The historical significance of Phyllis Wheatley to the Black community of the Twin Cities is unparalleled, and it remains to this day a vital and indispensable community-based institution.

My appointment as executive director in 1965 came near the end of an era. The grassroots civil rights movement had won a long string of victories, its gains augmented and solidified by the Civil Rights Act of 1964. Suddenly, Phyllis Wheatley Community Center, as it was renamed in 1962, no longer needed to serve as a de facto hotel, because Black travelers could now book rooms at hotels that had previously turned them away. Black residents could attend cultural events and use recreational facilities that had previously been off-limits to them. But this new reality didn't diminish the important roles Phyllis Wheatley had historically filled as a beloved and trusted linchpin of community life.

When I first laid eyes on its facility at 809 Aldrich Avenue North, I was highly impressed. Here was ample gathering space for community meetings and special events. The sprawling physical plant occupied more than half of the block, with a large gymnasium, an auditorium, a dining room, an institutional kitchen, office space, and more than a dozen residential rooms. Many visitors commented that the place looked like a hotel. And indeed it did—a reminder in brick and stone of Phyllis Wheatley's historical importance as a place of residence and refuge.

I was the first executive director who did not live at the center. Before me, the executive director was called head resident. My office was in the space that had served as my predecessor's living quarters.

By the time I took the reins at Phyllis Wheatley, some of the most egregious forms of racial discrimination had been outlawed, but specific, persistent problems still presented major barriers to something resembling a reasonably high quality of life for Black Minnesotans. For example, there were still many instances of undisguised housing discrimination and police misconduct in the treatment of Black citizens. Phyllis Wheatley still had a major role to play in combating these and other persisting vestiges of Jim Crow, and not just in the policy arena but also in terms of offering assistance and advocacy to individuals fighting their own personal battles with one kind of discrimination or another.

A perfect example of the latter is illustrated by what happened when Henry Thomas, my predecessor at Phyllis Wheatley, offered a room to John Steele, a young man newly arrived from Oklahoma who, owing to his race, needed a place to stay because he'd been turned down flat by several landlords in a row. He was offered a room in exchange for helping around the center until he found employment that enabled him to pay a modest rent. He was still there when I became executive director, but he understood his housing was transitional and that he would be expected to move out once he was able to find a suitable place. Soon, John's brother-in-law from Oklahoma joined him, and they became roommates for a few months until they found a decent apartment together. By that time, they both were fully employed, and they were able to help several other family members relocate from Oklahoma to Minneapolis.

One of the family members who joined John in 1968 was a younger sister, Betsye. She came to Minneapolis as a recent high school honors

John Steele, the last resident at Phyllis Wheatley. *Vanessa Steele*

graduate in need of a job. Betsye had a burning desire to attend college, and we were happy to help her along toward her goal however we could. Fortunately, funding available just then from the Office of Economic Opportunity, a program of President Lyndon Johnson's War on Poverty, enabled us to offer her and a number of neighborhood youths meaningful employment for the summer. Betsye became a youth counselor at Phyllis Wheatley, working with elementary school kids. As her interest in attending college at the University of Minnesota intensified over the summer, we encouraged her to apply for admission. We assured her that we'd help her figure out how to pay for it if she was accepted.

Betsye applied and was admitted, but when we learned that the non-resident tuition was unaffordable, I discussed her situation with Katherine Parsons, a longtime Phyllis Wheatley board member. After meeting Betsye, Ms. Parsons committed to paying her tuition and fees for her first year. With the assistance of PWCC and Ms. Parsons, Betsye was able to complete her undergraduate education at the University of Minnesota. And she was not the last of the Steele family we were able to help in achieving their educational goals. Betsye was followed by her sister Patsye and brother Winzell. We connected Patsye with a program at Concordia University in St. Paul and Winzell with Augsburg College (later University) in Minneapolis, which was affiliated with the American Lutheran Church. A fraternity brother, Louis Zachary, was coordinator for the Concordia program, my wife was a member of Augsburg's board of regents, and I chaired a minority scholarships and grants program for the American Lutheran Church. With the support of the Phyllis Wheatley and Minneapolis community, Patsye earned her degree from the University of Minnesota and Winzell graduated from Augsburg.

Building Trust

In 1965, the agency was at a major crossroads. There had been much national discussion of how the racial climate of the country might begin to change should the Civil Rights Act of 1965 become law. Now, in the wake of its passage, funders had begun to raise the question of *whether or not the agency was still needed* going forward, since to some white people who counted themselves as allies, it had begun to appear as if full racial justice in America might actually be just around the corner.

The management-level staff of Phyllis Wheatley and I knew very well that we had a major job to do. Our board members needed to understand the depths of anti-Black attitudes and behavior that still existed in 1965— and to recognize that those attitudes and behaviors weren't simply going to melt away overnight because some federal legislation had been passed. We were up against the profoundly deep gap in empathy that persists to this day between Black and white in this country owing to the many aspects of our shared history that have gone largely unexamined, both in our educational curricula and in our national discourse about race and the legacy of slavery.

We also understood something else that some of our white allies did not: even if all racially prejudiced Americans lost that prejudice overnight, there was still a long road ahead in targeting and dismantling the systems of institutional racism that had long been suppressing Black access to capital, decent housing, equitable employment opportunities, a quality education, and equality under the law.

Finally, our happiness with the policy move toward greater racial justice was very much tempered by our knowledge of an important aspect of the nation's history that made us feel uneasy and extremely on edge: whenever the Black community makes significant progress toward equity, inclusion, and political power, such progress is always met with fierce, relentless resistance and backlash.

Though we tried to be optimistic, hoping that substantive and lasting change might really be accelerating, we remained vigilant, watching to see in what forms this resistance and backlash might appear. Critical decisions regarding policy and program priorities would have to be made that would impact Phyllis Wheatley staff and our partner relationships with other institutions, including funders. I looked forward to steering this beloved institution through whatever it took to meet these challenges. Whether I was fully prepared for these tasks remained to be seen.

I was naive and a relative newcomer when I assumed the role of executive director. Before any of these big-picture issues could even be considered,

I needed to establish myself as a competent leader and guide. But this was *my first experience with leading an organization*, and I had to learn on the job within what at times felt like a hostile environment. The top staff position in the organization was now being entrusted to a thirty-one-year-old who had lived in the city for less than a year. To make managing the organization even more challenging, I had been selected over two current staff members who had also applied.

I was able to establish an excellent and trusting relationship with one of the two. The other had to be dismissed after I was one month on the job, when she told residents the untruth that I had been brought in specifically to implement a merger between Phyllis Wheatley and the other Northside settlement houses. This false information was especially disturbing to the large number of seniors who lived in the nearby public housing project. As the person who spread this misinformation had been well liked by the residents, I had to work extra hard to build trust with them.

They say that one of the pitfalls of taking on a large and ambitious task is that, at the beginning, "You don't yet know what you don't know." That's a big part of what makes a steep learning curve so steep. There were moments when I felt almost completely overwhelmed as I contemplated how much I had to learn about running an organization.

For starters, I had never worked with a board of directors and I didn't fully grasp the nuances of how my role as executive director differed from theirs. I firmly believed that the power over most agency issues rested with me. It wasn't long before my board decisively corrected that misconception. At the very first board meeting I attended, things got off to a rocky start. Barely enough people showed up to constitute a quorum, and I was very upset, feeling that the board had let me down before I'd even had a chance to get started. I even questioned my decision to take the job in the first place.

Feeling as angry as I was disappointed, I sat down and wrote a scorching letter to the board of directors, reminding them of their responsibilities to the agency and the community. I scolded them for the poor attendance at that first meeting and told them I hoped attendance at future board meetings would improve. I mailed the letter without discussing its contents with anyone, including Mary Lou. I'm sure she would have encouraged me to not send it—or at least to rewrite it to seem less abrasive and intense.

Predictably, I'd soon wish that I *had* shared the letter with someone, because just a few days after I mailed it, a white woman who stood barely five feet tall and weighed about a hundred pounds soaking wet stormed into my office and slammed the letter down on my desk in front of me. "Young man," said Betty Salisbury, "How dare you send such a letter to me and other board members? This is a reprimand, and you have no authority to send such a letter."

After thoroughly raking me over the coals, Betty acknowledged that the board needed to be challenged, but she said I was going about it the wrong way. She told me that my first priority should be about building relationships with the members. Her first bit of advice about relationship building was that I should never send a letter to the board members criticizing how they were doing their job. She suggested that I discuss my concerns with the board chair or another board member and let *them* raise the issue of board performance. However, she added, because I had not been in my job long enough to know how the board was performing, she believed I was premature in my judgment. I needed to give myself time to get to know its members and their histories with the organization, and she graciously volunteered to work with me on that.

At the end of our meeting, I apologized for sending the letter, thanked her for her advice and counsel, and told her I would surely call upon her again for help. And Betty Salisbury and a few other women on the board, to their eternal credit, really did become some of my strongest, most loyal allies throughout my tenure at Phyllis Wheatley. Their support helped give me the time, space, and mentorship I needed in order to grow into the job.

Growing into My Role

The board of directors supported my decision to fire the staff member who had miscommunicated with our senior residents. The harder part of this challenge came when I had to hire a replacement. This staff member had worked exclusively with senior citizens living in the community, and I needed to replace her with someone who could work with the youth, whose growing numbers made them a larger and larger focus of our activities. I had seen a clear need to expand our after-school programming. The new youth programming coordinator would help recruit volunteers from the University of Minnesota and Augsburg College to work with youth in music and the arts. Other staff and volunteers could take on the work with our seniors.

I had met the person I wanted to hire shortly after we moved to Minneapolis. Mirza Jones worked for the YMCA in an after-school program at Lincoln Junior High, where many of the youth who came to Phyllis Wheatley were enrolled. Mirza was married to a colleague with whom I'd worked at Unity House. The challenge came from my board president, Irv Nemerov, when I told him of my decision to hire her. The person I fired was a Black woman, and Mirza was white. Nemerov didn't like the optics, and he believed the hire would be controversial in the Black community. I disagreed, and I told him so. The young people at Phyllis Wheatley worked with white staff all the time, and the majority of the volunteer staff were white college students from the University of Minnesota and Augsburg College. Mirza was well qualified and had a lot of great ideas about how to build a strong program for us. She already knew many of the youth from her work at Lincoln, and they were excited about the possibility that she might come to work at Phyllis Wheatley. I pushed back on Nemerov's objection and told him I needed to move forward, because we needed to have the new hire begin work as soon as possible. He asked me if I would wait until after he and I met with Cecil Newman, owner and publisher of the *Minneapolis Spokesman and Recorder*, and with Mary Kyle, Newman's counterpart at the *Twin Cities Observer*. These Black media figures were highly respected in the Minneapolis community, and their opinions really mattered.

Nemerov set up the meeting. I had heard about Newman and Kyle before our lunch at the 620 Club, but I had not yet met them. Both were members of the Phyllis Wheatley board of directors but had not been in attendance at the only board meeting held since my appointment. During lunch, I presented my rationale for moving forward with the hire I wanted to make. There would be other opportunities for me to hire new staff members in the future, and I certainly would be mindful of the need to seriously consider a Black person to fill the next position.

Children perform in a play at Phyllis Wheatley, about 1967.

They respectfully explained their concerns, which revolved primarily around what it would look like in the community to replace a Black person with a white person, especially since the community saw no signs that white organizations were regularly hiring Black people to replace white people. I told them I understood and respected their position—that Black organizations should make career opportunities for Black people a priority—but I held my ground and said it was important for me to be able to make this hire. I was happy to accept full responsibility for my decision, and if this put my job at risk, then I was willing to live with that. By the end of the lunch, they acknowledged that I had the authority to make the hire. There would be no interference, but they hoped I was making the right choice.

Following that meeting, I hired Mirza Jones as director of cultural enrichment programs, where she did an outstanding job for almost two years. That experience prepared me for a similar decision I would make years later, in another job.

Pressure to Merge

When I took the position at Phyllis Wheatley, there was high expectation in the community, and also among some board members, that there would be a merger of Phyllis Wheatley with other Northside settlement houses Unity and Wells Memorial. Some people believed that because I had worked at Unity, I would bring a strong bias in favor of the merger and that soon after my arrival Phyllis Wheatley would cease to exist as an independent agency identified with the African American community. I continually reassured the community and members of my board that I had not come with any such agenda. I was not there to merge or close the agency. I could understand why the African American community and members of the Wheatley board were anxious about the idea of a merger, as this move was being publicly proposed by such powerful entities as the United Way, the Health and Welfare Council, and the Minneapolis Planning Department.

My entry into the picture *slowed* the process, because I insisted I needed time to study the situation before I could make a recommendation to my board. In this tug-of-war with the United Way and other players, it seemed obvious to me that out of all the agencies and institutions involved, Phyllis Wheatley had the least amount of influence over the outcome. The way I saw it, my job was to change that.

Before I could seriously entertain any proposal for merger, I needed to focus on strengthening Phyllis Wheatley's programs and status in the community compared with its prospective partners Unity House and Wells Memorial. Phyllis Wheatley may have been held in relatively high esteem in the Black community, but it did not yet enjoy the same stature within the broader community. The United Way and the Health and Welfare Council certainly didn't believe that Phyllis Wheatley was on a par with other community-based nonprofit organizations of a similar size, and the budgets of these United Way organizations clearly reflected this perception.

Phyllis Wheatley's 1966 budget was $62,000, with $60,000 of that coming from the United Way allocations. Because Phyllis Wheatley was so dependent upon the United Way for its funding, it was very limited in the kind of fundraising it could do to grow its budget. I would need to change that too.

Enter DFL Politics

The most prominent people on the Phyllis Wheatley board derived their influence primarily from the public, civil rights, and nonprofit sectors. There were no giants of business and commerce on the board, nor did I think we were likely to attract such people. I had been in the Twin Cities long enough to appreciate how access to political power operated on a much more grassroots and democratic model than the autocratic, top-down model I'd known in Chicago. But I'd never been high enough in Chicago politics to have to learn how to be a player. Now that it was time for me to become a player, I needed a crash course so that I could get up to speed as quickly as possible.

My board chair, Irving Nemerov, made sure I got properly introduced to the state's top public figures. For example, he accompanied me on a planned special visit to the state capitol to meet Governor Karl Rolvaag—an opportunity I know I would never have had in Chicago. I was excited, but I didn't realize the implications of that visit until later. I clearly recall walking into the governor's office and being introduced to him by his executive secretary, James Rice, who was also a Phyllis Wheatley board member. Although Rice was on my board, I was also meeting him for the first time. The agenda of the meeting was unremarkable. Its real intent was to show me how important it was to have and maintain political connections. I was not feeling it at the time, but as I would come to realize, this meeting marked the true beginning of the very important mentorship in political engagement I received from Nemerov and Rice during the early days of my tenure at Phyllis Wheatley, an education that would stand me in good stead the entire rest of my public career.

I learned later that the reason for my introduction to the governor was to get me to support his fight for the 1966 Democratic-Farmer-Labor (DFL) party gubernatorial nomination. That was the year of the "big split" in the Minnesota DFL party, when Lieutenant Governor Sandy Keith challenged, and eventually won, the party's endorsement for governor in the DFL primary election. Rolvaag soundly defeated Keith in the primary, then went on to lose by a big margin to Republican Harold LeVander in the general election that November.

Unfortunately, I was caught in the middle of the Keith–Rolvaag fight. Two members of my board, high-profile elected public officials state senator Robert Latz and Mrs. I. G. Scott, a Hennepin County commissioner and a member of the governor's staff, supported Keith. Irv Nemerov, my board president, who was a friend of both Rice and Rolvaag and a strong DFL supporter, wanted Rolvaag. Pieces of the Keith–Rolvaag conflict eventually played out in a couple of board meetings during which Nemerov and Latz were close to physical blows. Many years later, I learned that the source of the conflict between Latz and Nemerov dated back to when Latz was a prosecutor in the attorney general's office, and he and Nemerov found themselves opposing one another in court. Latz had come out on the winning side.

This clash between Latz and Nemerov made my job as executive director especially challenging during board meetings. The ongoing tensions finally came to a head at the Fifth Ward DFL caucus meeting.

In 1966, the Fifth Ward held all of its precinct caucuses together at the Knights of Columbus Hall on West Broadway in North Minneapolis. I was attending my first political caucus meeting in Minneapolis—or anywhere, for that matter. My introduction to the ward caucus system, organized and coordinated by neighborhood volunteers, was mind-blowing. In Chicago, the kinds of policy issues I heard being argued all around me would have been the exclusive preserve of party bosses, not everyday citizens at the grassroots level.

When I arrived at the meeting, delegate slates had already been drawn up with supporters for Rolvaag and for Keith. To my surprise, I found my name on a slate of delegates for Rolvaag. Nemerov had placed my name there without my permission. When Latz saw that, he was furious, and I had to explain to him that I had not agreed to be a delegate for Rolvaag. In fact, my plan was to not be available as a delegate candidate at all, because I wanted to learn more about the process and how it worked. When I emphasized how important it was for me to work with Rice, Latz, *and* Nemerov as board members, they all understood my position and took my name off the Rolvaag slate of delegates.

I was then free to observe the remainder of the meeting, which became a bitter and closely fought contest. The struggle played out—literally—in a smoke-filled room. This was 1966, before any anti-smoking legislation had been passed, and most of the adults I knew were smokers. I had heard about smoke-filled, backroom politics—old-school politics as blood sport, à la Chicago or Tammany Hall—but I hadn't expected to see echoes of that style here in Minnesota.

Tensions were high as the counting of the delegate ballots got underway in the kitchen. Rolvaag's counting team was led by James Rice; the Keith team was headed by Robert Latz. That night, I had a view of the kitchen from my seat in the hall. I'd heard the story about how Rice had headed the Rolvaag team in his recount of the 1964 governor's election, and it was reported that Rolvaag won the recount because of Rice's skills as a counter. I had also heard stories coming mostly out of Chicago about how ballots sometimes went missing during recounts; some tales alleged that there were counters who literally ate some of the ballots. While I will not swear that I literally saw any counters eating ballots, I *did* observe Rice periodically taking his hand to his face and wiping it across his mouth *as if* he might be putting something into it. I pointed this out to a friend seated next to me, and we both wondered if there was at least an outside chance that this might, indeed, be what was going on. Whatever the truth of it, Rolvaag won the Fifth Ward endorsement that night.

The Keith–Rolvaag political conflict came early in my tenure at Phyllis Wheatley, and it taught me some key lessons in dealing with conflict. The first lesson was to avoid taking sides before clearly understanding the issues. The second was how to manage doing that: clearly communicate to all parties why you're staying neutral, offer constructive alternatives when asked, and do your best to maintain good relationships with the people on both sides of the conflict.

I was able to get across to my board that Phyllis Wheatley had strong community support because of the services it provided, not because of its board members' political affiliations. Phyllis Wheatley could not afford to be identified with any political party. We needed to remain free to challenge anyone who, in our judgment, didn't have the best interest of the community at heart.

We made a point of applying this principle consistently so that, over time, not only did the broader community come to understand and respect it, so did elected officials and activists from across the political spectrum. This fiercely independent stance helped solidify and strengthen Phyllis Wheatley's reputation as an effective and trusted community institution in the Twin Cities and beyond.

Doing Double Duty

The Fifth Ward DFL political caucus that had endorsed Rolvaag over Keith was held in March 1966, when I had been Phyllis Wheatley's executive director for just over six months. I had been there less than a year when, on August 3, 1966, Minneapolis was shocked by the first of two significant outbreaks of summertime street violence. A group of Black youth, frustrated over the chronic lack of employment opportunities, threw rocks and shattered the windows of several businesses along Plymouth Avenue in North Minneapolis. And while property damage was limited, the psychic and emotional damage was high. Local news outlets bent over backward to not characterize it as a riot because liberal Minneapolis would be embarrassed to have a disturbance labeled a race riot. Disturbances of that kind only occurred in places like Cleveland or Los Angeles.

After all the broken glass had been swept away and the initial shock had worn off, the mood in Minneapolis was pensive and sullen. A town that had largely considered itself somehow above the fray when it came to issues of race and poverty had lost much of its "innocence" overnight, discovering that, at least in this regard, perhaps it wasn't so different from Cleveland or Los Angeles after all.

The immediate spark of the violence—the issue of youth employment— was real and very deep. By and large, the only bona fide employment opportunities for local youth were for those enrolled in school. School *dropouts* were out of luck. And predictably, many of the youth involved in the street violence were dropouts. Phyllis Wheatley and other neighborhood centers in Minneapolis were some of the best sources for youth employment, at least during the summer. For example, Phyllis Wheatley employed approximately a dozen youth between the ages of fourteen and eighteen, part-time, during the summer of 1966. They were employed at the center through the Neighborhood Youth Corp (NYC), one of the War on Poverty youth employment programs administered through Minneapolis Public Schools.

The 1966 street violence focused a lot of public attention on North Minneapolis. Naturally, Phyllis Wheatley and other community organizations in North Minneapolis held numerous gatherings to discuss how to respond and take full advantage of at least the positive, potentially constructive public attention for as long as it lasted. I remember one meeting in particular that was held at a small neighborhood park at which both Mayor Naftalin and Governor Rolvaag were present, along with a long list of prominent business and church leaders. All made promises to take action that would generate more jobs for youth. Some businesses even made specific promises regarding the numbers of jobs they would commit to creating.

Unfortunately, when all was said and done, the only thing North Minneapolis actually received was media attention. There's no record of how many neighborhood youths gained jobs as a result of the commitments made in the park.

One specific, positive outcome of the 1966 street violence was the establishment of an organization called The Way Opportunities Unlimited, Inc., commonly referred to as The Way. The organization's first leader was Syl Davis, a former staff member of Wells Memorial. The Way did not receive United Way or any public funding. Most of its budget was raised from year to year through private fundraising campaigns. As an organization that had bubbled up from the grass roots, this lent The Way some street cred: the organization was "unbought and unbossed"—not beholden to either the political or the business establishment.

The Way gave voice to the deep frustrations of Black Northside residents with the slow pace of racial progress, taking consistently more radical positions on issues than did the older, more traditional community organizations also striving to create opportunities for Black people. Another aspect of The Way that made it controversial to many, both within and outside of the community, was that much of its focus was on Black power and Black empowerment—on self-reliance, rather than on coalition building or close cooperation with government agencies and sympathetic organizations that were predominantly white. This emphasis on self-reliance was also reflected in the free classes The Way offered on Black history and Black liberation.

In short, the organizational culture of The Way aligned it more closely than most others in the metro area with the historical Black Nationalist tradition, which has always said, to paraphrase, "Oppressed people can't ask or beg for their liberation. It has to be taken." Building agency and autonomy for our people was much more important to adherents of Black Nationalism than civil rights or equal opportunity, even though these goals were also embraced. The Way's perceived militancy sparked discomfort and controversy among white citizens across a wide swath of the political spectrum, including significant numbers of those who counted themselves sympathetic to our cause and considered themselves allies. There were those within the Black community who felt somewhat skittish about how The Way framed some of our issues too.

But those feelings were mediated. In Black leadership circles, there was an understanding that, as in any large community, our people have never been a political or cultural monolith, and there needed to be room in the ecosystem of Black-focused organizations for a diversity of thought and action regarding how best to address our historic struggle for justice, dignity, and equality. We knew these were perilous and challenging times for Black community organizations everywhere, and this reality required us to build and maintain as much of a united front as we could manage. Even if we sometimes disagreed on tactics and priorities, we always understood that collective survival and progress demanded that we have each other's backs and that we needed to stay focused on finding common ground.

In the summer of 1967, the crises to which all of our organizations and institutions needed to respond just kept relentlessly coming. It seemed to me that I might never get to experience the luxury of running something resembling business as usual at Phyllis Wheatley. It often felt as if crisis management was the order of the day, every day. But some crises were bigger, more explosive, and more challenging than others. On July 21, 1967, Minneapolis had its second outbreak of racially fueled street violence, a more widespread, violent, and longer-lasting incident than the first, resulting in considerably more property damage. This was the zenith of the "long hot summer" years of the mid-to-late sixties—a period during which simmering Black anger over the glacially slow pace of racial justice regularly boiled over into communal street violence during the summer months. The grim tally for 1967 records at least 159 such incidents across the country, including the disturbance in Detroit, with nearly seventy confirmed deaths—events that frightened Minneapolis, now that it had become abundantly clear that our city was in no way immune to the turmoil sweeping the nation. City leadership understood that there would have to be a more focused and truly meaningful community response this time. There was general consensus that the response had to be based on an honest assessment of the realities faced by our Northside community; that it had to be strategic, with both short-term and long-term goals; and that, ultimately, the process had to produce an action plan that was both concrete and realistic.

Immediately I was reminded, once again, how very different the cultural norms regarding civic engagement were in Minneapolis than in Chicago. There, political party bosses would have huddled privately behind locked doors after conferring by phone with a few wealthy and powerful citizens; plans would be made, then announced, and then implemented to some degree, all with precious little, if any, community input or involvement. But in Minneapolis, as executive director of Phyllis Wheatley I was expected to meet and interact with top officials in the public, nonprofit, and private sectors. This, of course, turned out to be an opportunity.

I'd already met the governor, and I had other elected public officials from county and city government on my board of directors. But I didn't expect, as more and more meetings were convened in search of a response to this crisis, to be invited to work closely with the very top-level business and corporate leaders of the region. In the world I'd left behind in Chicago, the movers and shakers behind the scenes, whose wealth and privilege had always given them a powerful voice in public policy, chose to *remain* behind the scenes—invisible and unaccountable. They gave their money to museums and other cultural institutions, or to universities. They vied to outdo one another with large, very public legacy gifts so that a building or a park or a scholarship might someday bear their name.

I soon discovered that what was brewing here in Minnesota was an interesting and encouraging experiment with the use of corporate wealth to tangibly enhance the quality of life for everyday citizens—especially the poorest—by funding initiatives meant to achieve such goals as improved access to well-paid jobs; better, affordable housing opportunities; and targeted support for minority-owned businesses.

Since 1964, the federal government had stepped up and embraced its role in pushing the nation forward toward racial justice through civil rights initiatives and anti-poverty programs. State, county, and municipal governments often offered nothing but resistance—either active or passive, or a little of both—to these federal initiatives. Representatives from the nation's faith communities had also been exercising leadership and allyship in the struggle for racial justice: marshaling support for civil rights and anti-poverty legislation; cajoling white people to confront their own often unacknowledged prejudice, laying much of the groundwork for today's anti-racism work; and challenging America to live up to its highest ideals. But leadership from the private sector—especially the corporate world—had been largely missing.

Corporate funds were still going to be funneled into beloved arts institutions and to the kind of charitable giving they'd traditionally supported, except that, as a group, many of the most highly visible corporations in the Twin Cities mutually agreed to substantially increase the amount they were giving annually as a percentage of corporate profit. Instead of continuing to echo the medieval tradition of *noblesse oblige* (the generally understood principle that people blessed with substantial means should feel an obligation to spend some of their money for the public good), leadership from the corporate community in my new hometown had come together to propose a commitment on the part of all the participating businesses to invest at least 5 percent of their pretax earnings in this way every year.

Five percent may not sound like a lot, but in theory any community with a substantial, prosperous business sector would see a significant increase in its overall quality of life if its largest businesses regularly contributed such an amount.

We can argue all day about the complicated place of private philanthropy under our current socioeconomic system and the ever-evolving ways in which well-meaning people attempt to answer the ageless question, "How can I help?" But up until my experiences that year in Minneapolis, attempting to learn and navigate the complicated evolution of the ways in which the civic culture of the Twin Cities has tried to answer this question, I'd never met with anyone who was directly involved with this new wave of corporate philanthropy. I was excited for the opportunity to explore what kind of collaborations or partnerships might be possible.

I was pleasantly surprised and felt like it was right on time when I received a phone call from John Cowles Jr. in late August 1967. And I was eager and cautiously optimistic for my opportunity to sit down and talk to him.

We'd never met. All I knew was that his family owned the *Minneapolis Star* and *Minneapolis Tribune* (separate newspapers in those days). Here was my chance to place a finger firmly on the pulse of what was going on in the hearts and minds of corporate leaders who had awakened to the need to do something in response to the urgent call of the times we were living through. At the very least, this would be a great networking opportunity and a chance to gather information that might in the near future prove highly useful to Phyllis Wheatley and other Black-focused organizations and institutions.

Frankly, I was as full of self-doubt as I was full of questions. I was still inexperienced and largely untried as an executive director—still a newcomer to the Twin Cities. If a meaningful opportunity to advance the work of Phyllis Wheatley or an allied organization bubbled up during our conversation, would I know enough to even recognize that potential opportunity when I heard it? Was I now resourceful enough to lay out and amplify what I heard so that I could help it progress from a good idea to an action plan? What qualified me to speak for anybody else in my community? Was John Cowles the least bit sincere about his stated desire to learn from me and from grassroots members of my community, or was this mostly an exercise in public relations on his part?

The very fact that his interest in sitting down with me sparked such questions in my mind was an excellent indicator of how terribly far we still had to travel, more than a hundred years past the start of Reconstruction, in terms of race relations. As the era of the "long, hot summer" escalated throughout most of the sixties, radio and television talk and news programs were full of Black leaders who had to sit and endure questioning that was sometimes absurd, often depressingly ignorant, and sometimes downright hostile, on the general theme of, "What does the Negro want?"

But this request felt like an opportunity to be part of the cutting edge of something new and potentially important. Cowles made it clear that although he was interested in seeing the entire nation make significant progress in terms of racial equity and justice, his burning, personal concern was laser-focused on thinking strategically about what he and potential allies could accomplish here in the Twin Cities and throughout Minnesota.

Despite all my reservations, I thought, *Nothing ventured, nothing gained. Let's do it.* My first meeting with John took me by surprise. He was younger than I had expected and very soft-spoken. At times I had to strain to hear him, probably because, to his credit, he truly was mostly interested in listening. He wanted to know about me and why and how I came to Minnesota. He was interested in hearing my assessment of what was happening in Minneapolis. And, of course, he was concerned about the past two summers of violence. He never explicitly said so, but I got the feeling he had thought Minneapolis was above all that. It had clearly shaken him to his core to discover that he'd been wrong.

I told him I thought that people in Minneapolis had been living under a false sense of security when it came to race relations. I said that when white Twin Cities residents look around, it probably seems to most that the quality of life led by the majority of Black citizens is fairly high. After all, public spaces and public schools were already integrated, through initiatives approved by the local electorate, without major pushback or violence. Redlining and racist housing covenants had existed here as they did nearly everywhere in America, but this legacy had not left sprawling urban ghettos like those that existed in larger cities like Chicago and Detroit.

I suggested to him that this was probably attributable to the relatively small Black population of the Twin Cities compared to those larger urban centers—not just in terms of sheer numbers, but in terms of the high concentration of impoverished Black people in those cities. I stressed that if the ratio of Blacks living below the poverty line compared to whites in Minneapolis became similar to what we saw in Chicago or Detroit, the racial tensions here would likely look much the same.

We talked for over an hour. I thanked him for coming and for listening; when he left, I wondered what he planned to do with the information. While the visit was as pleasant as it was interesting, I didn't really believe it was likely to lead to very much.

Slowly but surely over the next several years, I would discover that this first meeting was just the beginning of some long and fruitful collaborations that helped move us toward racial healing and justice.

Moving Forward

Phyllis Wheatley had sold its building to the Minnesota Highway Department shortly before I became executive director. The property was located close to the path of the new Interstate Highway 94, which was scheduled soon for construction. The building was not in the direct path of the highway, but it was near enough that it could be acquired if the owners wanted to sell it. Apparently, PWCC agreed to sell because the building was in need of significant renovation and the resources required for this were simply not available. In addition, United Way encouraged the move because it believed the center should merge with the other two Northside settlement houses, and the proceeds from the sale could be used to acquire another, more appropriate property that was less expensive to maintain. But after the 1966–67 street violence on Plymouth Avenue, the political winds suddenly shifted and there was general support for retaining community organizations that had Black identities and were controlled by Black people.

What had *not* changed for Phyllis Wheatley was the need for a new facility. The building that had so impressed me was in need of renovations. Fortunately, the Department of Housing and Urban Development (HUD) offered funding to cities that partnered with schools, parks, and nonprofits to build school–community–park complexes that could be managed by a nonprofit. The facility would be owned by the public institution because HUD was prohibited from allocating funds to nonpublic entities. Phyllis Wheatley faced two challenges: finding a local public agency to partner with and obtaining the local matching funds required to complete the application.

Any number of city or county agencies were eligible grantee applicants, but the most logical applicant was the Minneapolis Parks and Recreation Board. But before Phyllis Wheatley entered into negotiations with Parks and Recreation, United Way wanted to involve the other Northside settlement houses in the process. I insisted that the negotiations should be between Parks and Recreation and Phyllis Wheatley only, because the merger between Wells Memorial and Unity House did not include Phyllis Wheatley. The local match would be provided by Phyllis Wheatley from the sale of its facility to the Minnesota Highway Department.

Ultimately, the negotiation process did end up involving more than Phyllis Wheatley and Parks and Recreation, but the circle of other institutions that became involved expanded in a way that felt organic, collegial, and truly collaborative. That circle included the Minneapolis Public Schools, United Way, and the Minneapolis City Planning Department. Minneapolis Public Schools had an interest because the new facility would be constructed in what was then known as Grant Park, on the same site as a new elementary school then under construction to replace the old Grant Elementary School. Our new building would share a common wall with the school. The City Planning Department got involved because the new construction plans needed their approval. Finally, United Way was at the table because at that time they were the source of over 90 percent of Phyllis Wheatley's operating budget.

An application for a grant of approximately $500,000 to build Phyllis Wheatley a new home and let it serve as the hub of a community center–school–park complex was submitted to HUD. The grant application was approved, and a new replacement facility for Phyllis Wheatley was built at its current location in Bethune Park, connected to Bethune Elementary School.

The replacement facility for Phyllis Wheatley was built at its current location in Bethune Park, connected to Bethune Elementary School. *Hennepin County Library*

We entered into a forty-year lease with the Minneapolis Parks and Recreation Board, wherein we promised to assume responsibility for all programming from the site, while Parks and Recreation would be responsible for all building maintenance and operations. Phyllis Wheatley occupied its new facility in November 1970. The Phyllis Wheatley/Bethune School/ Bethune Park facility became the first such project built in Minnesota using federal funds.

As the 1970s began, the Black community was anxious about what the new decade would bring. Emotionally we were still reeling from the shock and despair sparked by the assassination of Dr. King only two years before and the violence that swept the nation in its aftermath. A Minnesota favorite son and civil rights ally, Hubert H. Humphrey, had lost his bid for the presidency in 1968 to Richard M. Nixon, who had won the election in part with a "Southern strategy" that successfully tapped into the anti-Black/ anti–civil rights animus of a great many white voters. And these voters had come from a wide swath of the electorate, not just the South alone.

In my office at the new PWCC, November 1970. *Minneapolis Star Tribune*

The war in Vietnam, against which Dr. King had so passionately railed, had continued to escalate and seemed like it was just going to grind on and on with no end in sight. Partly because of the massive resources required to fuel the war effort, by the middle of that first Nixon administration America had taken a giant step away from domestic social spending in general— but especially the kind of social spending that in any way resembled the anti-poverty, anti-discrimination activism of the Johnson administration.

That's what made the rise of our Phyllis Wheatley/Bethune School/ Bethune Park project important for its time: during a period marked by increasing urban blight and pessimism about the future of inner-city communities, we were able here in Minneapolis to work with our core constituency to imagine the kind of multipurpose community center the Northside needed and to then build the kind of consensus and collaborative action among institutions that was required to make that vision come to fruition. The new community center stood as a tangible reminder that when a community works together, it can accomplish great things.

9

ESTABLISHING THE URBAN COALITION

Once Phyllis Wheatley was settled into our impressive new space, it felt good to take stock of where we now stood as an institution. In our Northside community, we had become more visible than ever—a symbol of community pride and cohesion. And now, we were beginning to feel truly *seen* by the wider metropolitan community as well, our place in the ecosystem of human services better understood and respected. Phyllis Wheatley had come to be viewed as an institution with the ability to bridge the racial divide, one that had the respect of both the radical and conservative elements within our diverse Black community. The Northside remembered well that during the aftermath of the 1966–67 street violence, we were the one place in the community where people with varying points of view could safely gather to discuss their differences.

Unfinished Business

When John Cowles Jr. had come to visit with me in 1967, he listened closely and respectfully to everything I had to say about the needs of the Northside community and the needs, as I saw them, of the wider Black community in general. But he was more than a little cagey about how he intended to use any of the information, ideas, and opinions I shared with him that day. I would soon learn the real purpose of John's visit from Larry Harris, special assistant for urban affairs to the superintendent of Minneapolis Public Schools.

In August 1967, John was among a group of corporate, civic, and public officials who had been summoned by President Lyndon Johnson to press the need for a coalition of business and civic leaders that could address the critical needs of the inner cities. The nation had been rocked and frightened by violence over several consecutive summers, and social analysts were starting to agree that a decade of top-down, ham-fisted urban renewal may have done much more harm than good in terms of alleviating urban blight, lifting residents out of poverty, or in any other way improving their quality of life.

President Johnson was a big believer in and one of the greatest champions of the idea that government can and should do big things. But he knew that in order to continue to drum up bipartisan votes for his ambitious agenda, he needed to respond to political pressure from powerful people on his political right by demonstrating that he understood government shouldn't ever be the only driver of progress and social change. These factors and more made the public/private partnership an idea whose time had come. And what better place to try out a model for how such partnerships might work than Minnesota, which was already widely known and respected for its socially engaged corporate sector?

Mayor Naftalin, John Cowles Jr., and other Minneapolis corporate leaders were moved to explore appropriate responses to the president's call to action, but they didn't know where to start. When Mayor Naftalin encouraged John and Larry to lead a study to determine the need for a coalition-type organization in Minneapolis, Larry said he didn't believe the community would accept the findings of a study conducted by a white man on behalf of a group of rich white men trying to solve problems in low-income communities of color. But he and John Cowles agreed that if I would come on board as co-investigator, they would proceed with the work. I had questions about this initiative. Lots of questions. But I knew that jumping in with both feet at the very beginning would be the best way to exert influence over the direction this initiative would take.

I agreed to undertake the assignment as long as I didn't have to give up my position at Phyllis Wheatley. My board of directors was excited that I had been asked to assist with such an important, high-visibility project, and they granted me a six-month, half-time leave of absence with full pay. The arrangement also allowed me to keep all of my compensation from this new job. The board knew I was the lowest paid of all the community center executives in the city, so they were happy about this opportunity.

In the end, I did double duty, integrating my work for the newly formed steering committee with my role as Phyllis Wheatley's executive director.

A Coalition Takes Shape

Cowles and Naftalin had recruited top executives from fourteen of Minneapolis's major corporations to serve as a steering committee during the study process. Among this group were chief executive officers and vice presidents from major retailers like Dayton's, media outlets including WCCO and the Minneapolis Star and Tribune, Minnegasco, and companies with household names like Honeywell and General Mills. Larry and I would supply staff leadership throughout the process, which included providing orientation and education to steering committee members regarding issues and problems in inner-city communities about which they knew very little.[1]

Before we began, Larry and I told the committee how excited we were to be conducting a study designed to determine how to effectively engage the affected community in the coalition process from the outset, a critical element that was entirely missing from much of what passed for "urban renewal" in those days. It was important for these corporate leaders to understand from the very start that the steering committee would not have the option to use study findings to assert that there was no need for an urban coalition.

Larry and I understood that these business leaders had to be convinced that a much more cooperative model of shared leadership than they were accustomed to was possible, involving stakeholders from communities these men knew hardly anything about. We also understood that part of our role was all about convincing people from low-income communities of color that these corporate executives were sincere in their efforts and that this was not just another attempt to use poor people and minorities to stroke their public image and make their philanthropy look good.

On September 12, 1967, Earl Ewald read from a prepared statement at a meeting at North High School that began,

> A group of 14 Minneapolis businessmen, of whom I am the temporary chairman, thinks it urgently important to study the possibility of creating some kind of Urban Coalition here in Minneapolis, to provide a total community focus on problems of poverty and race.... A careful study of the practicality and need for an Urban Coalition will require a small but highly qualified staff; and for that purpose, we are hoping to employ on a temporary and part-time basis Mr. Larry E. Harris, Director of Urban Affairs for the Minneapolis Public Schools, and Mr. Theartrice Williams, Executive Director of Phyllis Wheatley Community Center.

Unfortunately, the statement also included this language: "I should make clear that none of us is absolutely certain that some form of Urban Coalition is either practical or necessary.... To determine whether some form of Urban Coalition could provide that help is the purpose of this study."[2]

Although Larry and I could now officially begin the tedious, challenging, and sometimes frustrating research, we believed this statement put our credibility and the credibility of the corporate community at risk. There was no way we could spend nine weeks studying the issues and conclude that an urban coalition was neither feasible nor practical.

In order to maintain the integrity of the process, Larry and I decided we would always work as a team, and for the sake of transparency, document our every move. We would conduct all interviews with community, public, labor, nonprofit, religious, and other participants together to ensure that the people we interviewed would not because of race have one truth for Larry and another for me. We understood that this was an important part of the foundation we needed to build if the urban coalition was going to become an entity capable of "speaking truth to power."

To these ends, our study was laser-focused on how to create the kind of organization that could have a significant and positive impact on issues of race and poverty in Minnesota. This meant we needed to hear from the people and organizations that were engaged on a daily basis with thinking about and working on such issues. The study would reach out to a wide range of key informants from nonprofit, public, civic, civil rights, social, labor, fraternal, and faith-based organizations. Our long interview list included a representative from the governor's office, the president of the Minneapolis City Council, the mayor of Minneapolis, the chairman of the Hennepin County commissioners, and the president of the Minnesota AFL/CIO.

As we began our discussions with the key informants, we wanted it to be crystal clear to everyone we interviewed that we were very intentional about listening and that we would use our careful, respectful listening to make sure we were being faithful interpreters of what each key informant wanted to express to the committee, understanding that it was our job to make sure that these participants, from significantly disparate backgrounds and not used to talking to each other, would be mutually understood.

Because many of the low-income people and advocates for the poor we interviewed were deeply skeptical of this effort and didn't trust the business establishment, part of our task was to help them process their skepticism by discussing the circumstances and conditions under which this coalition's approach to problem-solving had the potential to be much more impactful and effective than top-down initiatives coordinated by government agencies. Our ability to demonstrate to our target population that our commitment to listening was a genuine and deep part of our culture as an institution—creating a sense of *certainty* that they were being both seen and heard during this process—gave us a powerful tool in terms of creating credibility and legitimacy.

Meanwhile, Larry and I were meeting weekly with the steering committee, chaired by Earl Ewald, to report on our progress. Six to eight members of the committee attended those meetings on a regular basis. The full committee would be present to receive our final recommendations.

Confronting Biases, Overcoming Objections

The committee members brought diverse life experiences and biases to the work that strongly affected what they understood or believed about the issues we had been convened to study. Of course, one of our earliest struggles was to come up with the *language* required to hold a deep and mutually respectful discussion, much less to move those discussions along into the phase where we could collectively strategize about what it might take to implement a few impactful solutions.

But the biggest preliminary stumbling block we needed to overcome was that *not all of the committee members were fully committed to an urban coalition as the appropriate strategy*, although members who weren't fully on board never proposed a constructive alternative.

Fairly early on, Earl Ewald determined that a decision to move forward with our project had to be unanimous. Earl asked Larry and me to visit with John Pillsbury Jr., because he was one of the committee members who remained most resistant to embracing the concept. In Earl's eyes, it was especially important that John support the initiative because his family was so prominent in Minnesota business and politics, and as the public became more and more aware of the committee's work, this made John one of its most visible members. John's great-uncle had been the eighth governor of Minnesota, and his grandfather was a cofounder of the Pillsbury Company, one of the state's best-known enterprises—not just in Minnesota, but around the world.

The day Larry and I sat down with John, we gave him our best tag-team presentation on the real-world consequences of race and poverty in Minneapolis and, as urgently as we could, laid out the necessity and opportunity for collective planning and action toward alleviating them. We spoke in glowing terms about what a rare and special opportunity the committee now had to bring all segments of the community together to work toward constructive solutions to our problems.

We did our best to provide him some context so he could see the bigger picture—that America was at a critical tipping point at that moment, a moment in which we could choose to make serious strides toward "a more perfect union" or choose instead to close our eyes and walk away, as

America had done toward the end of Reconstruction in the aftermath of the Civil War. In that tumultuous period, the principal institution established by the federal government to help shepherd the throngs of formerly enslaved folk toward full citizenship was the Freedmen's Bureau. During its brief, fractious life, the bureau managed to put a serious dent in Black illiteracy through an aggressive, ambitious effort at building and staffing schools for Black students throughout especially the South but also wherever in the North and Midwest there were large concentrations of Black folks. The bureau also steered Black war veterans toward land grants and/ or training opportunities for which they might be eligible and aided the widows of the fallen when they had difficulty navigating the bureaucracy of the War Department in order to claim the pensions they were owed. The bureau was well on the way to accomplishing a great deal more, owing mostly to the energy and passion that many of its staff brought to their work. The Freedmen's Bureau was never funded with anything close to the levels its leadership requested from Congress, and the campaign of relentless hostility toward it never let up, until in 1872 Southern congressmen succeeded in starving it of funding altogether and it closed shop, leaving a great and important order of national business unfinished.[3]

Even though many of the programs that were part of President Johnson's Great Society were beginning to prove their effectiveness, the Black community could clearly see in 1968 that the political winds had shifted, much as they had during Reconstruction. Nearly all the pieces of the federal initiatives specifically designed to remediate disparities between Black and white Americans were in grave danger of being severely cut or eliminated altogether, disparities in household income, access to capital, access to decent housing, access to a quality education, and fair, unbiased treatment in the justice system, among others.

African Americans had responded to the shuttering of the Freedmen's Bureau by doubling down on what these brave, resilient people had already been doing anyway: taking care of each other through extended family networks and through our oldest, proudest, self-made institution—the Black church. A rallying cry made popular in the 1960s actually comes from this effort at grassroots community building in the 1860s—"each one, teach one." Black churches set up schools for learners of all ages, creating and sustaining a stupendous leap forward in the Black literacy rate. As a result, dozens of Black newspapers with intensely loyal readerships quickly proliferated across the country. Families pooled their limited resources to "make a way out of no way" and seed small businesses, but the energy, goodwill, and ability to eliminate or at least shrink barriers to Black success offered by the Freedmen's Bureau was sorely missed.

At the crossroads moment where we now stood in 1968, with government walking away from the table as a partner for change, it made sense to turn to the potential partner who was walking *toward* the table. By lending leadership and resources to this ambitious local initiative, our committee had a golden opportunity to offer up to the nation a model for how a community-driven, urban coalition approach to addressing major problems could work. By the time we were done making our case, John Pillsbury Jr. had agreed to support the steering committee's position.

But he was not the only skeptic we had to convince. We visited with public officials, labor leaders, and civic and civil rights leaders, and we found a significant level of skepticism among them all, as well as within the communities they represented. We were often asked, "What do *we* get out of it?" For example, in our discussions with labor leaders like David Roe (AFL/CIO) and Dan Gustafson (Minneapolis Building and Construction Trades Council), we focused on how business leaders were proposing to be involved in alleviating some of the worst harms of historical racism, including persistent poverty. We encouraged them to see that large labor unions had a potentially major role to play in such an effort, too, by removing barriers to membership for Black workers and other workers of color. We understood that their relationships with many of the businesses involved in the project had often been adversarial. But by asking them to become part of a group—with their adversaries—to help solve major community problems, we hoped they would choose not to be outdone by them.

In the Black and Native American communities, we had to confront the fundamental issue of trust owing to our deep, shared history of broken promises and exploitation. To these populations, business leaders involved in this fledgling organization represented the very apex of the white power structure. Why should they expect anything good to come out of creating such an organization?

Dr. Martin Luther King Jr.'s 1967 book *Where Do We Go from Here: Chaos or Community?* includes a stinging critique of capitalism. Elements of his critique, written not from a Marxist perspective but rather a Christian theological one, were not widely known by the general public at the time, but they were being preached from the pulpit here and there and they were the subject of discussion and debate in the Black community, at least among the clergy, the leadership of the civil rights movement, and academics. Harry Belafonte remembered King saying, shortly before his death, "Capitalism does not permit an even flow of economic resources. With this system, a small, privileged few are rich beyond conscience, and almost all others are doomed to be poor at some level. That's the way the system works. And since we know that the system will not change the rules, we are going to have to change the system."[4]

Much of the cynicism we heard was about the community's clear-eyed assessment that the granting of full civil rights to Black Americans and some sort of modest economic New Deal for America's poor was not necessarily a direct threat to the economic supremacy of the nation's 1 percent, but serious talk of reparations for slavery and some manner of fundamental redistribution of the nation's wealth certainly was.

Many white Americans of goodwill had been stirred by Dr. King's words during his iconic speech on the steps of the Lincoln Memorial during the March on Washington for Jobs and Freedom in 1963, when he talked about the dream he had for the Black community, and for America. The Black community treasured and remembered those words too; but they *also* remembered how he'd said, "We've come to Washington today to cash a check." And as the Urban Coalition began work on preparing its report, the community was still waiting.

Skeptics in the community who saw the corporate sector as deeply complicit in the creation and perpetuation of racial and socioeconomic disparities found it exceedingly difficult to believe that suddenly, important members of this sector had taken a strong, urgent, and authentic interest in dismantling them. A few of the doubters probed to see if they could discern what manner of hidden agenda might be at work.

I couldn't really blame them. Activists from poor communities of color have always seen with clarity how many problems in America are joined at the hip to race and poverty. Deep-seated, systemic discriminatory practices in employment, education, housing, criminal justice, and elsewhere have complex, interconnected roots—and therefore, no simple solutions.

A critical question that hovered over all our efforts in this ambitious initiative was this: even if their intentions were sincere, would these corporate leaders stick with the fledgling coalition long enough to see positive results regarding at least *some* of these issues? Every partial or limited victory is still a victory. Larry and I stressed that because this group of committee members was willing to risk their reputations and that of their corporations in exploring this initiative, they had a strong incentive to stay engaged and work for success, especially since our whole process was very public and highly visible. These corporations had committed their top leadership to this effort. Everyone involved was hyperaware that a large and growing number of people here and around the country were watching to see if what we were building could be used as a model, and we didn't want to let them down.

One of the factors that encouraged community representatives to show up and "speak truth to power" was that this time it was corporate leaders, not just politicians, who were listening. These corporate members of the coalition represented an important part of the power structure that had always been, in the eyes of most poor folks, a mysterious player somewhere behind the scenes. Everyone understood that these corporate participants were from or at least adjacent to the class of people to whom even the most powerful politicians turned for the donations that funded their every campaign for office. So there was a sense of cautious optimism that, with their active participation at the table, there just might be a chance to break the all-too-familiar cycle of "business as usual: talk, talk, and more talk, but no action."

Larry and I understood, although most of our coalition recruits from the community did not, that these corporate representatives were also quite anxious to get to know and understand representatives from the low-income communities targeted for assistance and that their interest was neither superficial nor entirely altruistic. Our core target community had precious little collective knowledge of the degree to which Minnesota's economic and cultural elite had always thought of Minnesota as someplace special and unique, largely immune, because of its affluence and its exceptionally strong and cohesive civic culture, from many of the social ills that dogged the rest of the nation.

It was a novel experience—and also a real shock—for them to hear personal stories from Black and Indigenous Northside residents about being traumatized by egregious police misconduct and about encountering overt discrimination in crucial areas of life: from both sellers and landlords when attempting to purchase or rent a home, from banks when attempting to secure a mortgage, and from the criminal justice system at every stage—arrest, charging, bail, jury selection, and sentencing. The corporate leaders knew they would never have heard these stories if they had not volunteered to take part in this process.

Most of the leaders who were now at the table were also deeply dismayed to discover how deep-seated racial bias, segregation, and long-term discriminatory practices had helped create and perpetuate disparities that were among the worst in the nation in household wealth, educational achievement, and equal access to quality medical care for the Black population here in Minnesota. And they were embarrassed not to have known all this. They were anxious to roll up their sleeves and see what concrete initiatives they might be able to help design and implement that could move the state closer to their long-held image of Minnesota as an ideal place to live, work, and do business for everyone.

Shock Waves

On February 29, 1968, the National Advisory Commission on Civil Disorders, known as the Kerner Commission, appointed by President Johnson to investigate the causes of the 1967 riots and recommend ways to keep them from happening again, released its report on race in America. It said that the United States was steadily "moving toward two societies, one Black, one white—separate and unequal." And then, just over a month later, the assassination of Dr. Martin Luther King delivered another kind of shock to the system that left us all reeling. Profoundly painful as the moment was, there was also a sense that the communal feelings of pain and crisis created by his murder just might persuade people to find the political will to finally finish the work of the country's post–Civil War Reconstruction and build an America in which we're all equal stakeholders.[5]

The recent spate of street violence that had occurred along Plymouth Avenue had brought the rest of the country's experience home, and the anxiety and feelings of helplessness and despair were still quite raw. Civic-minded people here and everywhere were taking a deep dive into the report of the Kerner Commission, looking for at least a few answers.

Dr. King had called the outbreaks of urban violence, "The language of the unheard." William S. Pretzer, senior curator at the National Museum of African American History and Culture, has summarized one major finding of the report in this way: "Commonly sparked by repressive and violent police actions, urban uprisings were political acts of self-defense and racial liberation on a mass, public scale. Legislative successes at the federal level with Civil Rights and Voting Rights Acts were not reflected in the daily lives of African-Americans facing police misconduct, economic inequality, segregated housing, and inferior educations."[6]

As the first conversations between community and corporate members of the fledgling coalition began, corporate members were asking, "What can we do, right now, that will make an impact?" They got an earful.

Predictably, one of the first demands laid before them was for aggressive hiring and promotion initiatives at their companies, and throughout the wider business community, for Black people and other people of color. There was a call for significant aid to Black businesses, including a program to step up the solicitation of bids for everything from construction and cleaning services to catering; facilitating easier access to capital; and mentoring.

These goals were quickly embraced. They seemed very doable and would require minimal expenditures, and our corporate partners seemed eager to get moving on these demands and fulfill them. This was noted by the community and appreciated.

But we understood that it was important for our credibility's sake to manage expectations. We were careful not to promise that our efforts were going to fundamentally change the world as we all knew it. But we *did* promise that once the Urban Coalition was fully up and running, stakeholders would begin to see and feel tangible progress on some of the issues that had been doggedly hindering them from enhancing the quality of their lives and making progress toward their American Dream.

We were also entirely aware that many community folk were going to remain highly skeptical about where and how far this effort had the potential to go. But we closed the deal with many of them by raising the question, "Wherever this process ultimately leads, would you rather be on the inside helping make the decisions that could bring about change, or remain on the outside, agitating for the change?"

We described our plans for an organization in which power would be shared in such a way that no one group could dominate another in the decisions made. In this organization, leaders from low-income communities of color would be equitably represented on the board of directors, along with representatives from business and labor. The organization we were designing would provide a seat at the table for people who had never been there before, and they would be there as full participants.

We expressed the opportunity to them by saying, "Here, for a change, is a process where you not only get to help decide on the menu, but on how the meal will be prepared and who will be served."

In the end, we did indeed get the degree of community-wide buy-in that our model required, and we were able to commence an ambitious round of meetings and interviews with a very diverse group of servant leaders representing many different constituencies. We felt reasonably confident of success as we began, because both we and everyone else involved knew the foundation of our work was well-earned *trust*. If all that preliminary work we had done can be likened to the plowing and planting of a field, now it was time to see how the crop would grow and, looking ahead, what would be required of us in order to ensure a good harvest.

Presenting Our Work—Launching the Coalition

After more than a hundred meetings, interviews, and discussions with various community and organization leaders, we were ready to present our report and recommendations to the steering committee. Mayor Naftalin and key staff members, including Josie Johnson, staff members from The Way, staff members from Phyllis Wheatley Community Center, and a good many Northside residents were in attendance to hear about what we had been doing and where all this effort was heading. All fourteen corporate leaders were present for this meeting, at which we made our recommendation to establish the Urban Coalition with the following objectives:

1. Focus on problems of poverty and race in a positive way;
2. Increase communications among all segments of our community;
3. Educate the community to the need for action;
4. Help agencies evaluate their programs;
5. Help agencies obtain funds to expand or implement programs;
6. Initiate programs when no one else can do the job;
7. Seek new ways of involving business and labor in programs;
8. Involve the suburbs in these problems;
9. Support racial and economic integration throughout the total community.

We knew that many in the audience would understand that if implemented all these objectives might be helpful, but they were waiting to hear *how* implementation was going to happen. In all candor, we were still working on the how. A big part of the answer would lie in our ability to make the Urban Coalition as fully representative of our target community as we possibly could. We heard time and again during our community meetings that we needed to ensure all voices would be heard, especially since the study itself was born as an initiative of the corporate community.

When the urban renewal projects of the late fifties and early sixties got underway across the country, older inner-city neighborhoods were not supported, were not revitalized. Instead, they were torn down to make way for interstate highways and blocks of large-scale public housing. Many of these projects were implemented with little to no input from the low-income, predominantly Black and brown populations that were most directly affected.

Here in Minnesota, Rondo Avenue, the largest and oldest predominantly Black neighborhood in the state, was divided in two and largely demolished in the early sixties by the construction of Interstate Highway 94. Just a couple of years later, the center of what had been the largest identifiably Black neighborhood on the south side of Minneapolis was largely destroyed to make way for Interstate Highway 35W. From the late fifties onward, this pattern of destruction and displacement had become common from coast to coast as white policymakers planned and carried out the dramatic expansion of the national freeway system.

The routes for this burgeoning, land-hungry spider's web of high-speed roads were designed to cut the most efficient possible pathways to the nation's urban centers of business and political power, which meant that somebody needed to be displaced—a lot of somebodies. A disproportionate number of the nation's poor inhabited what had come to be called "inner-city" neighborhoods—precisely the neighborhoods that got slated for bulldozing. Massive changes were made to these neighborhoods by huge public infrastructure projects that had absolutely no assistance plans for the affected communities: no improvements to local schools or parks, no new resources for the improvement of public safety, no aid for small businesses, no renovation of existing housing stock, and no provision of resources that could help low-income residents purchase a home.

We worked hard to ensure that the birthing of the Urban Coalition here in Minneapolis would be just the opposite kind of experience for residents and neighborhoods. We reasoned that the best way to demonstrate our commitment to a truly grassroots approach would be to provide a seat at the table for as many different voices as possible, and we were able to convince the steering committee that establishing an uncommonly large board was the way to get it done. Establishing a sense of balanced representation was a must. Although the corporate leaders were providing the resources to help start the organization, their representation on the board could not be out of proportion compared to other segments of the community.

To achieve this kind of balance, our report recommended that members of the board would all be representatives of organizations, and that each organization would choose its own representative. In addition, corporate members on the board would be limited to seven, with the expectation that these representatives would be either the CEO of the corporation involved or someone who directly reported to the CEO. A board president would be selected from among the seven corporate representatives—a provision Larry and I pushed from the very beginning, because we believed corporate leadership had to be highly visible within the organization and carry major responsibility for generating the operating budget. We knew full well that if the Urban Coalition became heavily dependent on either state or federal dollars, we (or whatever key staff came along after us) would someday be compelled to spend more than half our time lobbying and fundraising instead of implementing the organization's programs.

Despite what may seem like a balance of power heavily weighted toward the corporate participants, the Urban Coalition would be structured in such a way that the corporate board members could not control how the board voted on issues. They would have to collaborate with other board members to achieve any desired outcome. Larry and I also recommended that board members be selected from three general categories of organizations that were representative of the broader community: (1) business, labor, church, and community-at-large; (2) public and nonprofit service agencies; and (3) residents from neighborhoods with high concentrations of poverty and from racial and cultural minority groups. Twenty voting representatives would come from each of these broad categories, creating a sixty-member board of directors.

This was the only way, we believed, for the total community to feel represented, a reality that reflected and reinforced what our fledgling institution had truly become: an Urban Coalition. Eventually, the board grew to be even larger than the recommended sixty members as organizations petitioned for representation and several at-large members were added.

The creation of the Urban Coalition was formally announced in February 1968. The steering committee continued to meet to address a range of startup issues, including the selection of the Urban Coalition's first executive director and, even more important, its first president. This person would come from the top leadership of one of the fourteen founding corporations. Stephen Keating, CEO of Honeywell, Inc., agreed to become the first Urban Coalition president, while the discussion about an executive director continued. The committee believed it was important to name someone local—someone who could hit the ground running and quickly gain the confidence of both the corporate sector and the community at large.

Frequently during these discussions, one or more of the members would refer to needing someone with skills, background, and experience similar to Larry's. Comments like these were made so often that it invoked thoughts for me of Ralph Ellison's novel *The Invisible Man*. Even though everyone involved could clearly see that Larry and I had been fifty-fifty partners, equally sharing every aspect of the work during the entire process, and that our skill sets were remarkably similar, these white men were talking as if I hadn't been there at all, as if I weren't standing right there in front of them even at that very moment. I knew I had to speak up about it.[7]

One day at a meeting, I announced to the committee that the way they were discussing the search for an executive director made me feel invisible. "I did not take on this assignment just to add color," I began. "I brought skills, experience, and expertise on a par with Larry and am unwilling to take a back seat to anyone when it comes to this kind of work. I see myself as an expert. I have a job, and I have every intention of returning to my job. I like what I'm doing at Phyllis Wheatley, and I think I'm good at it. But I'm speaking up because you need to know how what you're saying makes me feel. For some of you, this is the first time you've ever worked with a Black person who was expected to give you advice and counsel on matters of interest or concern. You are now thinking of embarking on a course of action where that may be the rule and not the exception, and I wanted to let you know how I feel about how you're approaching this issue."

After I'd finished, the room was absolutely silent for a long, awkward moment. When the silence finally broke, it was to the sound of a long string of apologies from everyone on the committee. Some told me they needed to hear what I said and that, coming from me, it meant a great deal more to them than it might have otherwise. Larry also commented that he was glad I had said what I said. He'd been uncomfortable with them constantly referring to him as the ideal candidate too.

By the middle of March 1968, W. Harry Davis, a well-known Black leader in Minneapolis, was selected to be the Urban Coalition's first executive director. Harry was a member of the Minneapolis Civil Service Commission, president of the Phyllis Wheatley board of directors, active with the Minneapolis Urban League and the Minneapolis NAACP, and well-liked and highly respected by the broader community.

The Urban Coalition leadership didn't want their efforts complicated by a controversial hire, which probably would have been the case if someone outside of Minneapolis had been brought in. Harry didn't have all the background and experience some steering committee members had wanted, so recognizing that he might need support in managing the organization, they offered to lend him staff to provide mentoring and advice and to supply any other critical resources that might be needed from their respective corporations. In return, Harry was expected to help bridge the credibility gap between the corporate community and the communities that the Urban Coalition was designed to serve.

The Urban Coalition's most impactful years were also its most controversial. It was a brand-new institution that had emerged from the midst of controversy and conflict, and to be effective it had to learn how to operate within that context. Larry and I continually stressed to the coalition leadership that they would have to learn to be patient and persistent as the organization took root and grew.

Among the more frustrating challenges for the coalition's corporate leaders was conducting board and task force meetings open to the public. They understood the credibility and integrity of the organization depended upon its openness and transparency, but few of them believed that board meetings open to the public could have productive outcomes. For that reason, the coalition decided early on that most of its work would be conducted in specialized ad hoc task forces dedicated to creative problem-solving in such areas as housing, minority business development, and criminal justice.

The Urban Coalition leadership also resisted having the organization become one that delivered services to the community. They saw that the coalition's unique role should be to serve as a catalytic agent, using their power and influence to spark meaningful change. The fact that much of the coalition's work was accomplished in relatively small ad hoc groups meant the organization could respond quickly to issues that bubbled up in the community, making decisions about how to respond without having to wade through a potentially long and weighty bureaucratic process. The Urban Coalition quickly become a laboratory that championed and actively modeled the idea that diverse groups of community shareholders can be successfully brought together and work to find common ground on critical issues that need practical solutions.

It began to matter less and less that the corporate sector had initially taken the lead role in founding this institution. The community—as broadly defined as the word "community" can get—now felt it had the keys and was in the driver's seat. Participants understood from the outset that finding their way to practical solutions for complex issues would be extremely challenging with so many organizations juggling so many competing issues at the table. But as President Johnson liked to say, "A good idea doesn't care who had it."

Anyone who doubts that diversity can be an organization's greatest strength—its superpower—might well be won over if they had the chance to watch one of our ad hoc committees navigating some thorny, complex problem and identifying a potential solution or two. It was often precisely the different perspectives present at the table—sometimes radically different and not easy to reconcile—that allowed for a much deeper, more nuanced understanding of an issue, which in turn led to a more comprehensive, smart, out-of-the-box kind of problem-solving than would ever have emerged otherwise.

And in this important regard, it was very much in the coalition's favor that its membership made it, by far, the most diverse organization not only in the city of Minneapolis but anywhere in the entire state. There was no other place in all of Minnesota where people from such diverse backgrounds and experiences could come together and vigorously argue the issues of the day in their own style and vernacular, knowing that they were in a safe place to do so, and that their viewpoints would be respectfully heard and discussed.

Seldom was there a dull moment at large coalition board meetings, as representatives from disenfranchised communities—African American and Native American, for example—came to air their grievances and press for instant action to resolve long-standing problems around issues in education, employment, or housing. At the end of such meetings, which were definitely not for the faint of heart, those on either side of an issue often left dissatisfied and highly frustrated. Sometimes, debate around the table got so overheated that newcomers feared violence might be about to erupt. To everyone's credit, it never did.

But frustrated participants often left the table questioning themselves about the value of their efforts and wondering if anything would *ever* change. It could feel sometimes like we were just spinning our wheels—revisiting the same topic, using the same language over and over—with no forward motion. What these participants sometimes didn't see was the dynamic that these vitriolic meetings nearly always had the potential to create the fertile ground from which real change could grow once issues were identified, clarified, and then referred to coalition task forces for action.

Sometimes the act of referring issues to a task force generated further debate and accusations that this was just a cynical tactic meant by coalition leadership to table an issue indefinitely, rather than really deal with it. And to be fair, sometimes a tabled issue would indeed die in committee. It would take time, a great deal of trust-building experience, and reflective assessment for members to recognize that this was not always the case. Sometimes, tabled issues really did get the fuller, richer discussion they deserved, and powerful solutions to problems emerged as a result. Because of this hard-fought, hard-won reputation for serving as an honest broker, participants in the Urban Coalition's process began to see and appreciate the institution's impact, particularly during its first five years.

The community got an early start in presenting its issues to the Urban Coalition at a July 24, 1967, community meeting held at Phyllis Wheatley

House to address the aftermath of the street violence earlier that month. Attendees discussed the impact on human rights, employment, education, housing, community services, and law enforcement, and residents called on the city of Minneapolis to take immediate action to address those issues.

When nothing had changed by the end of the first six months, Gleason Glover, executive director of the Minneapolis Urban League, wrote letters to George Vavoulis, Minnesota's employment commissioner, and to Stephen Keating, Honeywell president, who was also serving as first president of the newly started Urban Coalition. Glover's letter, mailed in January 1968, expressed concern about the lack of action to resolve any of the problems residents identified at that July 24 meeting. "As we approach the summer of 1968, which from all indications might be the most violent yet, the Minneapolis Urban League feels that the City of Minneapolis must now begin to initiate affirmative action in the aforementioned areas if we are going to avoid another summer of racial disturbance," wrote Glover. His expectation was that the Urban Coalition could make a difference in addressing the issues presented at the July meeting.

Glover's letter would not be the only time a collection of issues was presented to the Urban Coalition with an expectation for definitive action. The next set of demands for action came at a special meeting of the executive committee on April 6, 1968, two days after the assassination of Dr. Martin Luther King Jr. The executive committee met over two days (Saturday afternoon and Sunday) to develop a response to fourteen "Recommendations from the Black Community," which it delivered at the April 10, 1968, board of directors meeting, well attended by forty-nine board members and four staff.[8]

I believe Minneapolis avoided street violence following the assassination of Dr. King—violence that Chicago; Washington, DC; Detroit; and other cities experienced—because of the presence and work of the Urban Coalition. The coalition was very proactive, convening meetings aimed at strategizing community action to prevent street violence. As a result, resources were made available to establish street patrols with communications equipment so the patrol could identify potential hot spots and notify the appropriate officials. Organizations like The Way, Phyllis Wheatley Community Center, and Wells Memorial Community Center on the Northside and the newly formed Sabathani Community Center on the Southside were placed on twenty-four-hour alert following the assassination. These organizations made staff available to deal with unfounded rumors and to work with youth to help keep them off the streets.

The Urban Coalition Responds

In the immediate aftermath of Dr. King's assassination on April 4, 1968, the community was in shock, struggling to manage a flood of emotions ranging from numbness to abject rage or despair. The community didn't yet know how this newly born Urban Coalition might be able to meaningfully respond. Many of those who had always been skeptical about the coalition and its intentions, like the strongly left-leaning activist Matthew Eubanks, waited with a tangible sense of extremely low expectations. Much of the community was watching and waiting for his reaction—his reaction, and that of the leadership at The Way. They didn't need to wait very long.

Before the board was halfway through the reading of its official response at the meeting on April 10, Matt Eubanks and several activists who had accompanied him into the room turned around and stormed out. This may have been the first coalition meeting during which an angry, frustrated faction got up and left, but it was only one of many.

On April 12, the *Minneapolis Star* ran an article under the headline, "URBAN COALITION CRITICIZED: Negroes Not Satisfied with Reply to Demands." The article reported on a statement issued by the group, which read in part: "[The Black community feels that the response by the Urban Coalition] did not reflect the serious conditions that created the urgency for the submission of our demands. At the same time ... the black community would like to believe that the Urban Coalition had good intentions in preparing a reply within the time allotted. [However, the Urban Coalition did not reply to some of our most critical demands and did not specify a general timetable for implementation]."

ys
e-
—

ll
t

ed:

"Full consideration of the proposal to eliminate tuition for underprivileged black high school students;

"Establishment of guidance counseling and recruitment agencies especially geared to the needs of black students;

"Establishment of a board to review the policies of the Athletic Department towards black athletes;

"Serious consideration of the possibility of using Martin Luther King's name for the new West Bank library;

"Representation of black students on all major university policy determining groups; and,

"Educational curriculum at the university to reflect the contributions of black people to the commonwealth and culture of America."

University officials who viewed the demands called them possible, with the exception of the specific request to rename the library.

The West Bank library, due to open next fall, already has been officially named after former university president O. Meredith Wilson.

The naming of any university building after a national figure would constitute a departure from established tradition, which has seen all buildings named after persons with a university connection.

The student demands will be reviewed by Moos' task force, which is scheduled to start deliberations next week.

The group will have about 25 members representing students, faculty, administration and the community. Its members are to be announced Monday.

The task force is to present its recommendations to

EASTER SEAL?—Enjoying an outing in the mild spring weather, this Como Zoo seal seemed ready for the big turnout expected on the Easter weekend.

URBAN COALITION CRITICIZED

Negroes Not Satisfied With Reply to Demands

By JOHN GREENWALD
Minneapolis Star Staff Writer

Members of the Black Community Steering Committee decided Thursday night that the Minneapolis Urban Coalition's reply to 14 demands presented last Saturday "did not reflect the serious conditions that created the urgency for the submission of our demands."

"At the same time," a statement issued by the group said, "the black community would like to believe that the Urban Coalition had good intentions in preparing a reply within the time allotted."

The coalition responded Wednesday to the committee's 14 demands to improve conditions for the city's minority-group residents.

Last night's statement was read by Syl Davis, director of The Way community center, following a closed meeting of about 25 committee members in the center, 1913 Plymouth Av. N.

"We feel that the Urban Coalition did not look very hard at some of the things that could be done immediately," Davis remarked.

He said a steering committee task force would meet today to outline action on demands which, according to the statement, "are not yet met."

One unmet demand is a call for the opening of "meaningful jobs and management and executive positions" to members of the minority community, Davis explained.

He did not elaborate further on what the committee meant by "demands which are not yet met," nor did other members of the group who were contacted later last night.

The steering committee is an informal minority-group organization composed of the heads of a number of social service agencies, professional persons, and community residents.

Thieves Ransack 2 City Churches

Two South Minneapolis churches were burglarized early Thursday, police reported.

There was no apparent loss after burglars ransacked the offices at Resurrection Church, 5355 38th Av. S., but thieves made off with about $50 in cash from Lake Nokomis Lutheran Church, 5011 31st Av. S.

* * * *

Statement by Negro Community

Following is a statement issued by members of the

---

voters in the public school district to add grades 9 to 12 to their public educational system.

Monsignor Henry B. Geisenkoetter, pastor of St. Michael's Parish, said "the parochial high school is being closed solely in order that the district school may have enough students to prevent annihilation of the district by means of a merger."

The Rev. Raymond Lucker, superintendent of education for the Archdiocese of St Paul-Minneapolis, said residents of the school district were faced with a 1967 state law which forced them to operate a complete 12-year program by July 1, 1970, or merge with another district.

He said if they continue to operate the Catholic school and did not build their

PFC. RICHARD E.
WILLIAMS
Marine killed in Vietnam

* * * *

Marine, GI Die in Vietnam War Activity

Marine Pfc. Richard Williams, 20, son of Mr. and Mrs. Richard N. Willian

---

Minneapolis Star, April 12, 1968.

To fully appreciate the challenges facing the Urban Coalition in responding to such a complex set of demands, one need only review the action the coalition took in preparing its preliminary report, which was developed during two meetings and reported on in an April 9, 1968, article by Dick Cunningham in the *Minneapolis Tribune* headlined, "Coalition Panel Supports 14 Demands by Negroes." Cunningham wrote that the Urban Coalition executive committee members expected their report to be approved by the full Urban Coalition board and that it would be up to the Black community to decide if their response was sufficient.

It's difficult to assess progress in the middle of a crisis. Three to five days certainly wasn't enough time to determine how effectively the Urban Coalition had responded to the demands, especially since some of those demands had no measurable response or any real way to connect to an action the Urban Coalition might have undertaken or planned to undertake to address any of the outcomes that were agreed upon as goals.

Urban Coalition—The Movement

Surely, the success of a movement is determined by what it leaves behind at the end of its era. The Urban Coalition survived for thirty-five years, but for its first five years, which were both its most active and its most controversial, it was in many ways more like a movement than an organization. One major reason for seeing it through this lens is that its leadership model was so unusually diffuse and democratic, allowing for ideas to bubble up from anywhere within its large, highly diverse family of organizations, institutions, and ad hoc groups. And after an idea that seemed strong to many had bubbled up and had been well argued and thought through from multiple points of view, an urgently needed program that otherwise might take months of planning plus subsequent months of fundraising and staffing before it could be implemented could be developed as a concept, planned, funded, staffed, and running in only a few weeks. All that was needed was a thorough, clearly expressed presentation before an Urban Coalition committee or task force and then a winning argument before the coalition board.

An example of this process is the creation of the grassroots, neighborhood public safety patrols—the Soul Patrol and the AIM Patrol—that sprang up with Urban Coalition backing and financial support starting in 1968. The original impetus was to create volunteer patrols in the poorest neighborhoods in town, the neighborhoods most likely to see outbursts of violence in the event of continued civil unrest. The idea behind the patrols was simple on its surface: having highly motivated citizens present as witnesses during volatile moments could help nip unrest in the bud before it escalated into a crisis with the potential to set a whole neighborhood aflame.

Neighborhood activists quickly saw the value of this approach, but they also saw that the patrols could facilitate a much broader goal—an opportunity to prove that through people power, the patrols could engender a greater, more tangible sense of public safety than the Minneapolis Police Department was able to ensure on its own. This, too, may *sound* simple, but it has layers of profound complexity.

Observers across the country had noted that one of the most common sparks for urban conflagrations of the period was an egregious incident of perceived police misconduct on the street—a beating, a shooting, a murder—that seemed completely unjustified in the eyes of whoever had witnessed it. Even though these were the days before the internet, a camera in nearly every cell phone, and the twenty-four-hour news cycle, word spread with stunning speed from person to person, and rumors, often deeply flawed or outright false, spread even faster. In response, the initial crowd gathered at the site of the incident could quickly grow to a larger crowd, restive and angry. A police presence would rapidly flood the area in reaction, dramatically increasing the odds that new violence between police officers and community members would occur.

Whether this occurred or not, there would almost certainly be an outburst of violence against commercial property throughout the affected neighborhoods, marked by the breaking of windows and opportunistic looting and arson, which prompted an even larger police presence, mass arrests, and too often the killing of residents involved in the violence—and bystanders—by the police.

So, among the priority goals for a volunteer neighborhood patrol was to keep an eye on the police—a need which low-income communities of color across the country were feeling every day, not just during moments of crisis. During the initial round of meetings with communities, Urban Coalition board members had been shocked to hear how many low-income people of color reported that, to them, comprehensive public safety meant more than enhanced police protection from criminal activity; it also meant having systems in place that would protect community members *from* the police.

Somebody needed to be out there on every major corner making sure that if police misconduct occurred, there would be a trusted witness or two at the scene to observe and document exactly what happened. But an additional and important plus to having neighborhood observers on the scene was, of course, that their presence might also serve as a powerful *deterrent* to any potential misconduct. Deeds usually done in darkness abhor the light.

The intent was to work *with* the police as much as possible. Patrol members carried walkie-talkies through which they called the Minneapolis Police Department if they saw something that might require an armed response. Patrol members often now got to be the *arbiters* of what kind of activity warranted a call to the police.

Street corner drug dealing, fights between residents that could have rapidly escalated, erratic behaviors on the part of a resident that may have been sparked by mental illness—these kinds of incidents and many more were often effectively handled by neighborhood patrol members. They knew the people involved, they knew their families, and they could use this knowledge to intervene or de-escalate or call a relative.

As a result, neighborhood residents felt safer in their homes. Women who worked night shifts reported a sharp and sustained downturn in the number of times they got harassed on their way to work or on their way home by "johns" looking for sex. Patrol members, many of whom had felt helpless in the face of both rampant neighborhood crime and police misconduct, began to feel a real sense of agency, self-respect, and respect from the community for the very public role they were now playing.

The first public funding for the American Indian Movement (AIM) came through the Urban Coalition in the form of funds for a patrol (sometimes called the AIM Patrol, sometimes called the Red Patrol) at various high-activity corners along the major corridors of Franklin Avenue, Twenty-Sixth Street, and Lake Street in the Phillips, Central, and Powderhorn neighborhoods. This was controversial, because in many ways AIM and the Black Panther Party shared much in terms of their basic worldview. But the AIM Patrol met with the same kind of success on the Southside that the Soul Patrol was having to the north, working the same kinds of high-activity corners along Plymouth Avenue and West Broadway in Minneapolis's near Northside.

The initial skepticism about this approach on the part of many in law enforcement quietly changed to support for the strategy of community policing because this cadre of trained volunteers took some of the daily burden of answering low-intensity service calls off their shoulders and clearly had the effect of keeping small problems on the street from becoming bigger ones that would require their intervention. The everyday rapport that existed between residents and patrol members was obvious and tangible. It provided daily evidence for the argument that police officers ought to live in or near the communities they serve, and that building authentic relationships with residents based on mutual trust and respect is the only pathway to working collaboratively with communities toward better public safety. The patrols built bridges that hadn't previously existed between the police department and community members—a win-win for everybody.

Fortunately, Minneapolis didn't experience street violence again that summer, but much of the country did. There was a heightened sense of urgency that much work needed to be done to get through the rest of the year, but there was widely shared opinion that the neighborhood patrols deserved a big share of the credit. Operating under the Urban Coalition umbrella gave them a great deal of autonomy, which allowed them to continue to work creatively toward realizing and continually refining neighborhood-centric visions of what public safety could look like.

An ounce of prevention really can be worth a pound of cure. Urban Coalition funding for both the Southside and the Northside patrols came to $200,000 a year those first couple of years. There has been no such organized volunteer patrol presence on the street since the turn of the new century. The City of Minneapolis spent $70 million to settle claims for police misconduct from 2019 to 2023.[9]

10

URBAN COALITION
LEGACIES

The Urban Coalition was extremely active from 1968 to 1971, creating programs like the neighborhood patrols and helping secure needed resources for the startup of the American Indian Movement (AIM). But even during those earliest years—the "movement" phase—the Urban Coalition also began building institutions aimed at doing effective, long-term work on some of the big issues negatively affecting the quality of life in our poorest neighborhoods.

In 1969, the Urban Coalition established the Greater Minneapolis Metropolitan Housing Corporation, whose name was later shortened to the Greater Metropolitan Housing Corporation (GMHC). That organization grew directly from a study done by the coalition's Housing Task Force that clearly identified an urgent and growing need for affordable housing throughout the metro area. Initial funding for GMHC was provided by the Urban Coalition, with contributions of $200,000 each from fifteen Minneapolis corporations over a period of five years. Today, GMHC, with some of those original sponsors still providing support, is the premier organization that builds and funds affordable housing in the Twin Cities. By the end of 2017, GMHC had provided loan commitments of $73,690,006 for development of 25,725 units of affordable housing, with a development cost of over $2.3 billion.[1]

In 1971, the coalition's Business Development Task Force recommended the creation of the Metropolitan Economic Development Association (MEDA) to address issues of rapidly rising poverty, crime, and unemployment in new and improved ways. The coalition believed that supporting the creation and development of minority-owned businesses was a positive and achievable approach to leading Minnesota minorities into mainstream economic life and to providing them with equal opportunities to access capital and grow their businesses. The original financial commitment to MEDA was $227,000, which came from private foundations, individuals, the Office of Minority Business Enterprise of the US Department of Commerce (today the Minority Business Development Agency), and over seventy Twin Cities–based corporations. That funding has exponentially increased since then. By 2011, MEDA's annual budget was over $2 million. With a mission to help entrepreneurs of color to succeed, in 2023 MEDA disbursed $18 million in services to over 250 clients, $10 million of which was in new loans. MEDA's impact has also seen exponential growth. Each year, MEDA-supported companies generate billions of dollars in sales. From 2015 to 2018 the US Department of Commerce recognized MEDA's Business Center as the top-performing center in the nation.[2]

In 1971, the Urban Coalition established Operation de Novo, previously known as the Hennepin County Pre-trial Diversion Project. The coalition's Criminal Justice Task Force had identified a number of social factors that were highly predictive in terms of who was most likely to commit crime and get caught up in the criminal justice system. Funded by a $400,000 grant, Operation de Novo was a program for people identified as being "at risk," working to disrupt those factors and to keep the target group from ending up incarcerated.

The program was patterned after the Manhattan Court Employment Project in New York and Project Crossroads in Washington, DC, out of the coalition's concern for poverty and racism, particularly in relation to how these factors affected criminal behavior. The New York and Washington programs were consistently demonstrating positive effects on rearrest rates among participating offenders by diverting cases from prosecution for a specified period of time. During that time, counselors and others worked to help place the charged offenders in employment or other services. If the placements were successful, all charges for the arresting offense were dismissed. Initially, Operation de Novo clients were limited to people convicted of misdemeanors and gross misdemeanor property offenses, but later services were offered to first-time felony property offenders and low-level drug offenders (primarily users and not dealers).

Upon demonstrating success, Operation de Novo was incorporated as a nonprofit in 1974, and over forty years the agency developed a national reputation as a leader in the field of court diversion services. By 2013, Operation de Novo had worked with 15,310 clients since opening its doors in 1971, 72 percent of whom successfully completed the program. In 2016, upon the recommendation of Hennepin County Attorney Michael Freeman, the Hennepin County commissioners selected a different vendor to provide pretrial diversion services.[3]

Powerful Networks

The Urban Coalition was a rich network of powerful individuals and institutions that provided immeasurable opportunities to its membership. Its impact on the community should be measured not only by the actions it took as an institution but also by the opportunities it offered as a network through which people of different racial, cultural, and economic backgrounds could meet and interact.

Where else in all of Minneapolis could a mother who was a welfare rights advocate sit next to the CEO of a major corporation and command equal attention and respect? Scenarios like this happened frequently during the early and more productive years of the Urban Coalition. And the networking opportunities flowed in both directions. It was important that people who represented wealth and power in the community be afforded the opportunity to directly engage with people representative of the citizens most adversely affected by some of the decisions they made in their chambers and suites.

Those meetings and interactions led to a range of largely undocumented outcomes that were meaningful to the people and communities involved. For example, the Urban Coalition provided Peter Dorsey, head of the Dorsey-Whitney law firm, and Clyde Bellecourt, president and founder of the American Indian Movement (AIM), with an opportunity to meet and discuss the issue of legal representation for Native Americans in criminal court. They probably would never have met under normal circumstances, because, of course, they ran in completely different social and economic circles. They certainly would not have met (as they did) at the Minneapolis Club. But, as a consequence of their relationship and interactions with others—people like the well-known civil rights attorney Doug Hall and Syl Davis, executive director of The Way, the Minneapolis Legal Rights Center was founded. The Legal Rights Center became an important institution because it provided an alternative to the chronically overworked, understaffed Office of the Public Defender for many Blacks and Native Americans. Retired Chief US District Court Judge Michael Davis and Minnesota Attorney General Keith Ellison spent some of the formative years of their legal careers as attorneys there.

Another Urban Coalition board member, Father Joseph Selvaggio, who served a small Catholic parish in South Minneapolis, took advantage of networking opportunities to help start a nonprofit that assisted low-income residents with finding affordable housing and jobs. Project for Pride in Living (PPL), established in 1972, now has a multimillion-dollar budget and employs over two hundred people.

I am convinced that historically, the Urban Coalition is one of the most under-recognized organizations in Minneapolis history for the contributions it has made in addressing issues of race and poverty in Minneapolis and the region. I am proud of the role I was enabled to play in the creation of this institution because the board at Phyllis Wheatley Community Center saw fit to lend my services to the effort for a while.

Another Kind of Networking Opportunity

In December 1967, near the end of my tenure with the Urban Coalition, Mary Lou and I received a handwritten invitation from Sage Cowles (wife of John Cowles) to a pre-Christmas party at their Wayzata home, which later became the Spring Hill Conference Center. We didn't know what to make of the invitation. I knew we were invited because of my role in the Urban Coalition, but the invitation asked us to bring our children, Chris and Jeff, ages four years and nine months, respectively. We were pleasantly surprised and accepted, of course, but because the children were invited we weren't sure as to what kind of party it would be or how we should dress. Mary Lou suggested that we dress formally and have the children do the same. She felt that since we didn't know these people, we didn't want to be embarrassed by turning up in inappropriate attire. She said she'd rather be overdressed than poorly dressed. So dress we did.

I'm holding Chris and Jeff, 1967.

I had never driven into Wayzata before. I got lost and had to find a pay telephone to make a call for directions. As we drove up to the house, we could hear the music of a live band. We were greeted at the top of the driveway by an attendant, who opened the doors for me and my wife, took the keys, and parked the car. As we mounted the steps, we were greeted at the front door by Sage Cowles, dressed in a beautiful floor-length evening gown and accompanied by a woman wearing a white nurse-like uniform who took our two children to the playroom.

As we entered the grand house, we saw immediately that Mary Lou had made the right call. *Everyone* there seemed to be dressed to the nines. Many were wearing formal attire. Only later did we fully understand that we had been invited to the party of parties, attended by the Who's Who of Minneapolis society. All of the family names we had heard about—the Daytons, the Pillsburys, the Wintons, the Bemises, the McMillans, and so on—were there.

The only other Black people at that party were Charles (Chuck) and Josie Johnson. At that time, Chuck worked as a senior scientist and mathematician for Honeywell, and later in his career he would become the first Black person to hold the position of vice president. Besides work as special assistant to the mayor and many involvements in Black community life, Josie was a member of the Junior League and the League of Women Voters. Later, she would be selected by the state legislature to be the first Black person to serve on the University of Minnesota Board of Regents. Josie subsequently became a vice president at the University of Minnesota, a position from which she retired.

I rather breathlessly told Mary Lou what a stellar opportunity we now had for some potentially powerful networking. She wasn't as excited about this aspect of the evening as I was, but she understood that for me, the gathering offered a chance to serve as an ambassador of sorts for Phyllis Wheatley, and for the Northside. I went off in one direction, and Mary Lou in another. I spotted a couple I had met during my work with corporate executives early in the process of creating the Urban Coalition, so I waded through the crowd toward them. Mary Lou decided to move about primarily among the women there. By the end of the evening, between us, we must have talked with everyone at the party.

While Mary Lou held forth with the women, I enjoyed the most fruitful part of my evening after becoming deeply engaged in a long, freewheeling discussion with a group of the men who were present. One of them was Douglas Dayton, chairman of the 1967 United Way fund drive and uncle of Mark Dayton, who would eventually represent Minnesota in the US Senate and would later serve as Minnesota's fortieth governor. I shared with him some of my concerns about the United Way and how it operated. I told him I was disappointed with the 1 percent increase in allocations that Phyllis Wheatley had received from the United Way for 1968, explaining that over the previous five years, United Way's allocations to Phyllis Wheatley had an accumulative increase of approximately 2 percent, which was below the current inflation rate of 4 percent.

Phyllis Wheatley received over 90 percent of its budget from the United Way, which placed serious restrictions on the kind of fundraising it could do. "My inclination," I said to Dayton and the others, "is not to accept the allocation and tell the United Way to keep it until they're able to do better." I indicated that I really would like to appeal the allocation but was unaware of an appeals process. Dayton said he was also unaware of an appeals process, because the issue had never come up before. Nonetheless, he encouraged me to write a letter to the chairman of the United Way Allocations Committee, describe my issue and concern, and be specific about my allocations request.

As we drove home that night, Mary Lou and I reflected on the party and wondered why we had been invited. Fifty years later, in a 2013 interview with Sage Cowles, I talked to her about that party, to see if I could finally put this long-standing question to rest. Unfortunately, Sage couldn't recall any specific reason for the invitation other than that she wanted us there. I shared with her for the first time my discussion with Doug Dayton about the United Way and its 1967 fund allocation to Phyllis Wheatley. She was pleased that I'd had the opportunity to meet Dayton and share my concerns. Years after the party, another friend and colleague suggested that Sage may have invited me in order to introduce me to a network of powerful people that would not have been available to me under any other circumstances. It would be up to me as to how I would use that network.

11

WEARING TWO HATS

Back at the office, I immediately began to work on the United Way appeal. I realized I would need to make a strong case for an increased allocation, so I did my research on the demographics and economics of the community. I had data on employment, crime, and housing conditions. I also cited the past five years of United Way fund allocations to Phyllis Wheatley and described our program, the number of people we reached, and the role we played during the aftermath of the 1966–67 street violence. I also cited the role I was playing in working with Larry Harris to establish the Urban Coalition. In my letter, I requested an $8,000 increase in Phyllis Wheatley's allocation, which would enable us to hire a full-time community organizer.

After I had prepared my letter, I called Harry Davis, our board president, and informed him of the plan. He wasn't enthusiastic, because he thought it could backfire. And he reminded me that United Way was trying, once again, to push Phyllis Wheatley into a merger. His reaction changed when I told him of my conversation with Doug Dayton, who had encouraged me to appeal. Eventually, he and the entire board agreed to support the appeal.

When Harry and I appeared to make our case before the United Way Allocations Committee, we referred to my letter and added that we were disappointed by how the United Way had treated Phyllis Wheatley in its allocations. We thought it unseemly that the United Way would fail to recognize the value of an organization such as Phyllis Wheatley during these times of crisis in our city. We were a well-established community organization that had worked for years to help improve conditions in the Black community. We had been able to bridge racial and cultural gaps and bring people together to help solve a range of community problems like no other agency in the metro area, which made us exceedingly valuable.

We felt disrespected and underappreciated, and we were now asking the United Way to take the first step in recognizing the great work that we had done in the past and were continuing to do during times of crisis. We closed by thanking the United Way for its past support, and said we hoped to hear from them soon.

The next day, I received a phone call from William Humphries, who informed me that the Allocations Committee had approved my appeal, and the full amount of our request had been granted. The outcome of that appeal would change the nature of our relationship for the remainder of my tenure at Phyllis Wheatley—and the United Way stopped pressuring us to merge with the other Northside settlement houses.

My part-time tenure with the Urban Coalition ended in February 1968, so Phyllis Wheatley would now be my full-time commitment. I continued to be involved with the Urban Coalition as a volunteer, and I was added to the board of directors as a vice president and member at large. This meant I would attend coalition board meetings, be on the executive committee, and work on task forces. I served as a member on multiple task forces and even chaired the Health and Welfare Task Force.

The Network Response to Street Violence

The Urban Coalition was a remarkable organization in many ways, but some of the expectations that people had for it were unrealistic. Some people believed that having high-powered business, government, and civic leaders together in one organization should be enough to quickly change the community and make it a more equitable place to live and do business. Others believed it slowed progress by providing the people with the *real* power some cover for not acting. The people who lived in the community—particularly the racial minority and low-income populations—continued to bring their issues to the Urban Coalition and expect quick solutions. This spelled inevitable disappointment for a number of reasons.

By the time the coalition began operating, many people were waiting for an opportunity to bring their issues there for some manner of immediate action. But the board configuration alone—a combination of "minority and low income persons, business, labor and religious figures, and representatives of public, private and social service agencies," according to a December 8, 1967, *Minneapolis Star* article—suggested that responding quickly to tough community issues would be challenging. Most of the time, this turned out to be the case. I would still argue that the Urban Coalition offered a faster process for getting new projects up and running than organizations that operated with a more traditional top-down decision-making structure.

Corporate Partnerships

The Urban Coalition also put out the call to Minneapolis corporations to make more summer jobs available to youth. For example, Cargill, Inc., a large privately owned Minneapolis-based corporation, offered twenty or more summer jobs for youths to work on its research farm near Elk River, Minnesota. When transportation to and from the farm proved to be a problem, Cargill offered to provide it and hired Leon Trawick, an athlete and recent graduate of the University of Minnesota, to coordinate the program.

I offered Phyllis Wheatley as the transportation pick-up and drop-off site. Phyllis Wheatley would also help recruit young people for the jobs. This program, available over the summers of 1968 and 1969, helped shape the lives of some of its participants in significant ways. James Marshall, one of the youths in the first summer program, went to work for Cargill for several years following his graduation from the University of Minnesota. Leon Trawick went on to graduate from the University of Minnesota Law School and became a practicing attorney in Minneapolis.

During the summer of 1968, Cargill expressed an interest in learning more about the issues of race and poverty in Minneapolis and invited me to be the luncheon speaker at a meeting of its board of directors. I was flattered by the invitation to speak to such a group of distinguished business leaders but didn't know very much about Cargill except that it was a big privately owned corporation and its board members were also employees of the corporation. This was long before the internet, and I had no way to quickly research them and learn more about the business. So my challenge was about what I should say to such a group of rich white men.

Shortly after I was named executive director at PWCC, I had learned an important lesson about speaking to an unknown white audience. One of my board members invited me to be the featured speaker at Westminster Presbyterian Church in downtown Minneapolis. My wife, who is a lyric soprano, was invited to sing, so while she practiced her performance, I carefully prepared a well-documented, fourteen-page presentation on the issues of race and poverty in Minneapolis.

That day, Mary Lou preceded me with a beautiful rendition of her song. I noticed that out in the audience, which seemed to have an average age of well over sixty-five, many attendees were wearing hearing aids. After she hit the first note, I saw many hands go to their hearing aids, presumably to turn up the volume to hear her beautiful voice. When she finished, it was my turn to get up and deliver my speech. As I came up and placed my fourteen-page speech on the podium and began, I again observed the audience adjusting their hearing aids. But this time, I was sure they were turning them down or off, so they wouldn't have to hear me. After this experience, I learned how to be more impromptu and draw upon my audience to help formulate my remarks.

I asked the board members to introduce themselves and tell me about their role in the company. They all were department or division heads. I wanted to know if any of them had a Black employee who reported directly to them. None did. Next, I asked how many of them could spend an entire day without encountering a Black person in any aspects of their lives. All could do that. I posed the same question for a week, a month, or even a year. When they all gave affirmative answers to that question, I suggested that they were isolated from what was happening in Minneapolis or any other city in which their corporation did business. If they were interested in being a part of the solution, they'd need to learn more about what was happening beyond the comfort of their own homes, as well as their work and social environments, because it was unlikely they would encounter much diversity there. I suggested they look for opportunities to bring about increased diversity within their respective spheres of influence—that they broaden their company's recruitment and hiring practices to encourage the hiring and promotion of more minorities. I closed by suggesting they each set a goal to hire at least one minority person as a direct report in their department or division.

After the meeting, I remained to talk individually with several of the board members. They all thanked me for my remarks, and they all said they would look for ways to improve their recruitment and hiring of minorities. One board member admitted that this was the first time he had ever been in a meeting where the featured speaker was a Black person, or where a Black person's expertise on a given issue was being called upon. His only associations with Black people had been the people carrying his bags or serving his food. He said, further, that he'd *never actually had a conversation with a Black person before*. When he said he was embarrassed that such had been his experience thus far in his life, I suggested he now had an opportunity to do something about that.

During that time, many of the issues confronting the Urban Coalition were issues that affected Phyllis Wheatley in equal measure. My status and visibility as a leader in the Black community had grown as a consequence of my role in helping to start the Urban Coalition. My network of influential people within the Minneapolis corporate community had also expanded, and I could feel in my bones that this exposure had lessened the pressures to merge Phyllis Wheatley with the other Northside settlements.

Wearing two hats may sound like a potentially insurmountable challenge for an executive director. But my duties with both organizations had become so compatible that I can confidently say neither organization suffered from any lack of attention from me, and for my part, both hats were an entirely comfortable fit.

12

CRISIS AT
THE UNIVERSITY
OF MINNESOTA

It was 1969, and I had been the executive director of Phyllis Wheatley for less than four years. We were no longer under intense pressure from the United Way to merge, because I had been successful in appealing Phyllis Wheatley's 1968 United Way allocation. The organization was gaining recognition in the community for doing good, effective work, and I was hearing from people I had never expected to meet. My work in helping to establish the Urban Coalition had also increased community visibility and credibility for both Phyllis Wheatley and me.

But building a strong, unique public identity for a Black organization during these contentious times was tricky business. Because much of the white community was anxious about how the march toward racial justice was going to play out and fearful about the prospects for more violence, there was a pronounced tendency to seek out and latch onto the Black voices that sounded least strident and threatening to them. Many in the white community came to see us at Phyllis Wheatley—and specifically me—as that less threatening, more moderate voice, especially compared with the spokespeople of more outwardly radical organizations like The Way and others, even though there was never really much daylight between our organizations in terms of what we all wanted. Along with this came the highly uncomfortable personal baggage of being thought of as representative of the *responsible Black community*.

We at Phyllis Wheatley, and I personally, as spokesperson, tried our best to shrug this off and stay focused on the goals we shared with other grassroots leadership. But this false dichotomy between "moderate" and "radical" was a heavy, emotionally exhausting burden to carry; a constant reminder that the power brokers and gatekeepers of the white community with whom we had to negotiate inch by wretched inch the terms of our "progress" didn't really even see us—any of us.

But being viewed as the "responsible" Black voice who should be at the table meant, more often than not, that I would be the first Black person invited to serve on an organization's board or committee, or to participate in some public activity, or to consult in a crisis. It was precisely for the last that I received a telephone call one mid-January night from Fred Lukerman, assistant vice president at the University of Minnesota.

The previous week, on January 14, a nearly all-Black group of students had barricaded themselves in Morrill Hall, the administration building that housed the office of the university's president, Malcolm Moos, vowing they would stay until the university agreed to a list of demands stemming from their grievances over its abysmally low number of Black students and Black instructors, lack of attention to their quality of life on campus, and the near total lack of attention to the Black experience in the university's curriculum.

After being promised that their grievances would be respected and given serious consideration, the students presented three written demands to President Moos when they left Morrill Hall peacefully on January 15:

1. That the University A) host a Black Conference whose purpose was to bring national resources to Minnesota to assist in the design of an African American Studies program that would be in sync with the best examples of such programming that could be found anywhere in the

country; B) that the university defray half the cost of the conference, estimated in the written document to cost a minimum of $8,000;

2. That an African American Studies Department leading to a BA degree be established by the fall quarter of 1969, with all plans and progress toward this end to be submitted to the Afro-American Action Committee (AAAC), which would have control over the committee that would establish the department; and

3. That a Martin Luther King Scholarship be created, and that the budget for the scholarship fund be placed in the hands of an agency within the Black community, leaving to that agency the determination of who should be eligible to receive it.

The most pressing demand was for the creation of an African American Studies Department.[1]

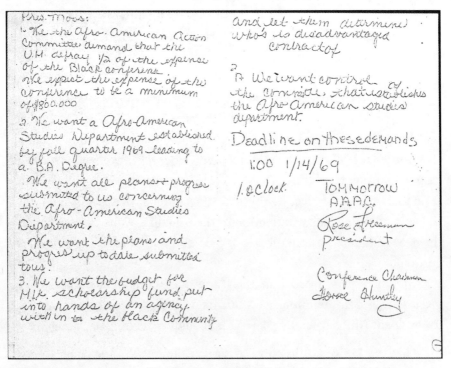

The list of demands presented to President Malcolm Moos by the students who occupied Morrill Hall, January 1969. *Morrill Hall Takeover, 1969. Information files collection, ua01158, University of Minnesota Archives*

The victorious students. Left to right: Rosemary Freeman, Horace Huntley, and Warren Tucker, Afro-American Action Committee members. *Alphabetical Files, A–Ad, 1941, 1964–1972, Afro-American Action Committee (AAAC), box 1, folder 1, 1968–1971, University of Minnesota Archives*

President Moos promised to name a University of Minnesota Morrill Hall Investigation Commission to explore what may have led to the incident and what happened during the occupancy. This, then, was the specific request that Fred Lukerman delivered, at the president's request, on or about January 16.

I agreed to serve. The commission was established on January 20, 1969. I was one of three community members appointed; the other nine members were staff, faculty, and students. My two fellow community members were Irving Brand, an attorney and senior partner at the Maslon, Kaplan, Borman, Brand and McNulty law firm, and Hugh Galusha, president of the Federal Reserve Bank of Minneapolis. The commission was cochaired by Warren Ibele, professor in the Institute of Technology and associate dean of the Graduate School, and Roy Williams, third-year student, University of Minnesota Law School.

Three of us who served on the commission were Black: Daniel Jackson, a student in his senior year; Edward Ellis, assistant professor for the School of Public Health, and me.

Our charge was set out in a letter from President Moos:

> *The objective of this investigation is to pull together from all available sources a factual account of that demonstration and the events which led to it. The Commission is requested to analyze available information and to gather additional factual materials which may be available. I am confident that the University staff, faculty, civil service and students who can contribute to this fact-gathering process will do so frankly and fully. The purpose of this Commission is to prepare a report that will facilitate making a determination whether charges should be brought, and, if so, what charges should be brought against individuals and groups for misconduct or violations of demonstration policy or civil law. The report will be used to guide our decisions as to any further action to be taken to protect the interest of the University and may be made available for the guidance of personnel responsible for developing charges before those University tribunals having authority to make findings concerning misconduct and discipline in both individual and group situations. The report will not constitute findings of fact for such tribunals nor abridge the requirement that appropriate evidence be developed before them.*

The commission's charge was discussed thoroughly during the first meeting. Some members, including me, were concerned that our work could be used to identify and punish students for participating in the demonstration. I let the commission know that, as a community member, I hadn't signed on for that kind of role. The university would have to find alternative ways for gathering information that it could use in punishing students for demonstrating. And just as importantly, there wasn't a single word in the president's charge to us about listening or responding to the students' demands!

I did my best to understand just exactly where we were in the process of establishing what we had to do, and I realized I would have to be patient and wait for the best opportunity I could find that would allow me to serve as an effective advocate for the Black students who had risked so much, not just for themselves, but for those who would come along after them.

Our discussion of this key issue led to an appropriate revision to the commission's working definition of the charge:

> *The Commission understood its charge to be an investigation of the facts and not, in any way, a finding of fact or determination of guilt or innocence of persons or organizations involved in the occupation. In the course of discussing the charge the question arose as to whether the Commission should comment on or evaluate evidence presented to it. Clarification of this point was sought by an exchange of views with President Moos, who requested the Commission to analyze, organize and evaluate the material presented to it, short however, of judging the responsibility of individuals or groups.*

It was of paramount importance to me that the anguish and discontent that led the students to occupy Morrill Hall be taken every bit as seriously as the university's concern over its bruised public image, not to mention any desire that may have existed on the part of some in the university community to punish participants as a deterrence to such actions in the future.

After the commission had satisfactorily iterated its interpretation of the charge, we proceeded with our work. We held our first meeting on January 22 and concluded our work on March 11 after conducting some twenty-two meetings, totaling seventy hours and forty-five minutes. All our meetings were tape-recorded, and minutes were produced.

We decided from the outset to conduct closed meetings for the following reasons:

1. The urgency of completing this investigation at the earliest possible date consistent with a thorough study.
2. To protect individuals against rumor and hearsay.
3. To provide for an organized, unanimous account of the events.

Since the objective of the hearings was an administrative investigation and not a judicial proceeding, the commission considered that there was no obligation to permit confrontation of witnesses nor to require representation of persons and groups involved in the occupation.

The pace of the work was extremely challenging. The twenty-two meetings we conducted were held within a forty-eight-day period and there were some weeks during which we met daily. I was present at every meeting, as were nearly all the other commission members.

I'd been pleased and flattered to be invited to serve on such an important commission. I was confident that, before our work was over and done, I could make a difference for Black students in terms of the quality of their overall experience at the University of Minnesota. After all, I was already well aware of how challenging it was for them. I knew a number of Black students personally and as director of Phyllis Wheatley I had helped some of them meet their scholarship needs. I in fact knew some of the students who had participated in the takeover, but I had not communicated directly with any of them during the time of the occupation. I thought a lot about what specific things I could bring to the table as an advocate for these students that other members of the commission could not.

It quickly became glaringly apparent to me that, symptomatic of the yawning racial divide in the country as a whole, the nine white members of the commission had very limited experience with Black people. In those days, university faculty members could go through an entire academic year without having a single Black student in class. Their faculty colleagues were overwhelmingly white as well. The communities in which they lived were likely to be just as lily-white. I had to conclude it was entirely possible that these nine members of our twelve-member commission could easily live through an entire lifetime without ever having a meaningful encounter with a Black person.

So I thought it would be important for me to help them to more fully understand the kind of experiences and worldviews Black students brought with them to the university. Otherwise, these commission members would have a hard time comprehending the larger factors that affected the students' decisions to participate in the demonstration. Beginning their inquiry with a better understanding of these Black students' lives would help the commission in its analysis of what happened and why.

Although the students made three demands to the president as conditions for ending the demonstration, my special focus became the demand for the establishment of an African American Studies Department leading to a BA degree, because it was the only one that would lead to measurable institutional change at the university. The call by Black students to establish such a department had now forced the university, for the first time, to directly address the issue of how best to include the contributions of African and African American people in its curriculum.

Without a thorough understanding of the history of slavery and reconstruction, how could white Americans even begin to understand the meaning and context of the historic struggle for civil rights that was unfolding all around them, remaking America right at that very moment? Dr. Lonnie Bunch III, secretary of the Smithsonian Institute and founding director of the National Museum of African American History and Culture in Washington, DC, has asserted that, "One can tell a great deal about a country by what it chooses to remember.... One can tell even more by what a nation chooses to forget." If we accept this assertion as true, then the clarion call for the creation of African American Studies Departments at universities large and small can be readily understood as a timely and necessary step toward helping build an American culture that chooses to remember—not just the bits of its past that comfort and that edify and reinforce cherished national myths, but the failures, contradictions, and shameful chapters of our national history that we had been consistently choosing to forget. This is the agenda that critics on the contemporary right like to call "woke." It is as foolish and ignorant as it is intellectually dishonest and misleading to label scholarly efforts to promote a more complete, honest, and nuanced telling of our collective history as "revisionist history." What they call "wokeness" arose as an answer and an antidote to the fact that too much of the standard history curriculum on which we, our parents, and our grandparents were raised should be rightfully called revisionist history.[2]

The twin folly of willful ignorance and deliberate forgetting ultimately serves nothing and no one. Those of us who embraced the students' vision of a strong African American Studies program sought to use this moment as an opportunity to cajole and encourage our white colleagues to step up and become strong allies in this quest—not just because they could see how Black Americans might want to gain for themselves and their children a deeper understanding of the profound contributions made by their ancestors to this country, despite the privation and suffering they'd had to endure, but because they could also see how knowing these things would be powerful, healing knowledge for them and their own children.

It quickly became clear to all that the occupation of Morrill Hall had not happened in a vacuum. Even my Black colleagues and I had not been fully aware of just how much turmoil around these issues, along with the basic issue of access to higher education, was engulfing the campuses of colleges and universities across the country.

Black students at the U had, in 1967, arranged for Dr. Martin Luther King to visit the university and give a major speech. His outdoor talk on the mall of the St. Paul campus was attended by a crowd of over four thousand. Later that year, the students brought in Stokely Carmichael for a speech, so that the perspective of the burgeoning Black Power movement could be shared as well. Suddenly, all the urgent, powerful movement toward liberation and dignity for Black people that was happening elsewhere in America and the world felt like it was happening here in Minnesota too. That was the point.

Immediately after the assassination of Dr. King on April 4, 1968, Black students who were members of the AAAC decided to seize the moment and submit a set of demands to President Moos detailing the grievances that had made the university feel like such an essentially hostile place for them. They deputized committee member John Wright to draft a position paper including their demands and submit it to President Moos. For the most part, Moos understood their demands and found them reasonable. They included calls for much more aggressive recruitment of Black students and faculty, significantly more scholarship aid for students of color, counseling and support for Black students, and the creation of an African American Studies Department. But the university did exactly what universities generally do in circumstances like these: they established a commission—much like the one on which I was then serving—to study the issues raised and report back to the administration when their work was done.[3]

This was the true spark that would lead to the takeover at Morrill Hall. After nine months of apparent inaction, the students decided to go ahead and "get into some good trouble," as the late Congressman John Lewis would say, by launching their occupation.

But we on the commission discovered that elsewhere around the country, including here in the Midwest, universities had already been challenged to step up and do much more to dismantle systems that have undergirded and perpetuated racism. In 1964, at the Wingspread Conference Center in Racine, Wisconsin, the Big Ten universities had held a conference called the Third Inter-University Conference on the Negro. One major outcome was a call to its member universities to commit more resources of all kinds to its impoverished and minority students. Following that conference, University of Minnesota president O. Meredith Wilson appointed Professor David Cooperman to head an ad hoc committee, the Cooperman Committee, on the role of the university in social problems. The Cooperman Committee urged the university in 1966 to become more involved in inner-city communities by establishing a Community Program Center "to increase the involvement of the University with the community and its problems through utilization of the wide range of resources of the University." In April 1968, shortly after the Cooperman report was reviewed in the press, President Wilson appointed another committee, a task force headed by Professor Warren Cheston, to consider the same question as the Cooperman Committee, but on a broader basis.[4]

The positive intent behind these two reports might have provided just enough momentum to help us turn the trauma of the Morrill Hall incident into real progress toward the creation of an African American Studies Department and to begin an admittedly ambitious, long-term campaign to find creative, meaningful ways in which the U could partner and share some of its considerable resources with the Black community, the Native American community, and other seriously underserved, low-income communities of color. But there's an old saying in the Black community: "Damn what they say—watch what they do." It soon became apparent that, despite the promising and well-intentioned talk, institutional inertia alone was going to frustrate any hopes for rapid change.

The Cheston task force became distracted during the fall of 1968 by issues of minority employment on university construction projects, which had been raised primarily by white students—Students for a Democratic Society (SDS) members—and not Black students. The Black students, most of whom were members of the AAAC, grew tired of waiting for action on their demands for the creation of a comprehensive African American Studies curriculum and a department to implement and carry it forward. Consequently, they stopped attending meetings—and the task force made no special effort to get them back. The channel of communications the president had hoped to open through this forum had failed to meet his expectations. Throughout the fall of 1968, there was virtually no participation by Black students in the task force meetings.[5]

It was not until December 1968 that any proposals relating to instructional programs in Black Studies were brought to the task force. And at that point, the Cheston task force determined that the university was already offering enough courses at the lower and upper division levels for students to piece together interdisciplinary majors in the area of comparative minority cross-cultural and human relations studies. Adding insult to injury, the task force's attitude toward the students was generally dismissive, suggesting that their demands were naive and largely unrealistic. After months of study and discussion, the task force's primary recommendation was that yet *another* committee should be formed that fall: an interdisciplinary faculty–student committee that would address the issue of making the university's curriculum more inclusive of the Black experience.

But this goal was expressed in terms that were both general and vague, because the task force had not fully understood that the Black students wanted to help birth a department that would facilitate their full participation in the new Black scholarship just then beginning to sweep the globe as more and more African nations achieved independence from the European colonial yoke. Black scholars from Africa, Europe, the Americas, and the Caribbean were leading a dramatic movement away from the colonial model of world history that had completely centered on Europe and Europeans toward a model that looks at the African diaspora as an equal player in an Atlantic history that includes the nations and cultures existing on both sides of the Atlantic. Black students were swept up in the headiness of the Pan-Africanist fever that was sweeping the diaspora and working to define the African American place within it. Anti-apartheid activists in South Africa and African American civil rights activists were learning and singing one another's freedom songs.

Professor Hy Berman, a member of the task force, was interviewed in the *Minnesota Daily* on January 9, 1969, and he reported that the committee's work emphasized developing a graduate program focused on comparative racial and ethnic study, rather than Black or African American Studies. The references to an "interdisciplinary major" and "comparative ethnic studies" represented university jargon unfamiliar to the Black students who were challenging the university. This response was dismaying because it seemed so completely tone-deaf. Testimony by a member of the Black community pointed out to the task force the reasons why the issue of African American Studies was so urgent in the Black student movement at the university and on campuses across the country: "Black students need not merely to be admitted or even supported financially and morally by an institution; they need to establish an identity with some academic unit within the intellectual community."[6]

To their eternal credit, the stakeholders at the University of Minnesota who had gotten involved in the work of the Morrill Hall Investigation Commission really did begin to take the students seriously, roll up their sleeves, and work collaboratively with the students and AAAC. The faculty and staff members who had been asked to serve were important campus leaders, highly respected and trusted by President Moos, and they did not let him down. The president had indicated at the outset that he wanted a comprehensive report to help him better understand what had led the students to take such drastic action. Despite the trepidation and distrust felt by many of the students as the process began, to their credit the students took full advantage of the opportunity they were given to describe the frustrations that had led up to their decision to occupy Morrill Hall, and as the fact-finding mission ground on, they could see that they were being heard. Ultimately, the work of the commission and the report it issued to President Moos provided just the catalyst that was needed in order to establish an African American Studies Department at the university.[7]

Although the white members of the commission had begun with very limited knowledge and understanding of what kinds of issues and barriers Black students were struggling with both on and off campus, they proved that they could listen and learn. The white commission members benefitted from my presence and that of my two Black colleagues on the commission, as we collectively discussed and analyzed all of the testimony of the various witnesses, especially from Black students and Black community leaders who spoke from their hearts.

Finally, with its university and community connections, the commission represented an informal resource to the entire university and its ecosystem as it continued to struggle with issues of race and inequality on campus. We could literally feel the culture of the university community begin to change as the learning gained by the commission started spreading outward. Many of us began to feel a real sense of optimism that the work we had done would help university communities across America to recognize and address issues of race and inequality in higher education. The new department officially opened in September 1969.

Even after the commission wrapped up its work, I remained very much involved as the university pushed ahead with its efforts to create an African American Studies Department. My service on the Morrill Hall Investigating Commission expanded my professional network at the University of Minnesota and in the corporate community in significant ways. Hugh Galusha and I became friends, and he offered to help address any issues for which I believed he could make a difference.

During the summer of 1970, I asked him to help two fifteen-year-old girls from Lincoln Junior High who were a step away from being caught up in the juvenile justice system. He created two paid internships at the Federal Reserve Bank in a move that was unprecedented for that institution. There was stiff resistance. He had to convince his management team to give it a try, saying that he trusted me, and that my belief in these young women was good enough for him. The girls were excited about the opportunity but full of anxiety too. The Federal Reserve Bank was only a few miles away, but it felt like an entirely different world than the one they knew. Was this an environment where everyone they met was going to expect them to fail?

Were they going to be given the chance to do real work that might help them set their sights toward a career in banking, or were they going to be shunted off to some isolated corner doing trivial, meaningless tasks that led nowhere? Cathy Young, a social worker on my staff, anticipated their trepidation and assured them that she would be there to support them.

Their time at the bank was truly transformative for them, and people who had known them before were witness to their positive change in self-confidence, attitude, and behavior. Both completed high school, and one of them went on to college. This never would have happened if I had not met Hugh while we were serving as members of the president's investigating commission. One of the lessons he'd learned there was that every institution in this country has a stake in furthering equity and inclusion and is obligated to find its own path toward an ongoing effort in pursuit of these goals.

As a result of Hugh's efforts, the Federal Reserve Bank became a Phyllis Wheatley Community Center partner. At least two of the bank's employees became volunteers at Phyllis Wheatley and, when the word spread rapidly around Lincoln Junior High that two of its students worked at the bank, these students became role models for other Lincoln students.

I felt a keen sense of personal loss when Hugh died in January 1971, two years after we first met. Hugh's family established a scholarship fund at Phyllis Wheatley in his memory. Sadly, the fund has long since been exhausted.

13

A DIFFICULT LESSON

Following the assassination of Dr. King, I began to receive telephone calls and letters from individuals and organizations looking for ways to become involved. Most of them sincerely wanted to help make a difference. Some of the individuals offered cash contributions to support the center's programs. One call I received was from George Grim, a columnist for the *Minneapolis Star*, who asked me to name a specific project I would like to get done for Phyllis Wheatley or the community, and he would write an article about it and encourage people to support it.

He encouraged me to be specific and identify the amount of money needed to complete the project. I was easily able to do both because, about a week earlier, I had read in the *Christian Science Monitor* that the *New York Times* and Arno Press were collaborating to make available sixty-six volumes of American Negro History and Literature—a collection that had been out of print for many years. This literature included the autobiography of John Lynch, the first Black speaker of the house for the Mississippi legislature and the first Black US congressman from Mississippi. I thought it would be great if Phyllis Wheatley could acquire the full collection for our library. We would then make arrangements to share the collection with the community and with the public schools.

The cost for the full collection was $1,100. Within a single week after Grim's story appeared, we had received $1,800 for the project. We acquired the full collection, and I encouraged the University of Minnesota and Augsburg College to do the same.

Other calls were from people looking for specific partnership opportunities. The more frequent calls were from suburban white women who were looking for opportunities to meet with Black women to learn more about the community and how they could use their resources to help make a difference. I tended to avoid the requests from individuals and groups I didn't know. It seemed to me as though some were less interested in helping bridge the racial divide than they were in seeking out a unique, exotic experience that would give them something to talk about when they returned to their secure, segregated lives—or some sort of personal merit badge.

I did agree to work with one group of women from Edina Lutheran Community Church, because I personally knew a couple of them. They were looking for an opportunity to establish relationships and share experiences with a group of Black women. They had realized that none of them had meaningful relationships with Black women, and that if relations between the races were ever going to improve, this had to change. They were clear that they were after an opportunity to build authentic, reciprocal relationships—not opportunities for charity. They believed they had many things in common as women and that these commonalities would help them surmount whatever differences of race and economic class might divide them.

I agreed to help facilitate their effort, provided they would agree to meet with my wife and me first to discuss the proposal, the purpose of such interactions, and what kinds of outcomes they were expecting. After encouraging them to moderate their expectations, I agreed to recruit a group of Black women equal in number to their own group. The Black women would host the first meeting, and the second meeting would be hosted in the home of a white member. White members would help provide transportation for any of the Black participants who might need it. With these conditions in place, I thought I had covered all the bases. But I was about to learn a painful lesson.

Once the white women had agreed to those terms, I recruited a group of six Black women and visited with them, both individually and collectively, to discuss the proposal. I explained that the first meeting would be in a North Minneapolis home and the second meeting in a suburban home. And I assured them that what happened after that would be up to those involved. The Black women were uncertain about the value of such meetings but were willing to give it a try, primarily because they trusted me, and I had asked them to participate. I assured them I would be available for consultation and would assist in helping to arrange that first North Minneapolis meeting.

The Black woman who agreed to host the first meeting lived in Sumner Field, a low-income public housing project adjacent to Phyllis Wheatley Settlement House. The majority of the family units were two-story townhouses with well-manicured lawns located around a small park. In 1968, about 40 percent of Sumner Field's residents were Black.

The Black woman who'd agreed to host was getting more anxious by the day. These suburban women she was about to meet were middle-class, but she found it hard to imagine them as anything other than rich. She couldn't quite imagine what their homes must look like, but as she looked around at *her* home, she worried about being judged. Her furniture was old and broken down—so much so that even after a good cleaning, she thought the place still looked a bit sad and shabby. As the date for the event grew closer, her anxiety about hosting her suburban guests grew worse. The thought that they might talk about her in a negative way after they were gone really began to eat at her.

For that first meeting, all the women from both groups came and interacted, and I received feedback from both sides that the women engaged in a significant amount of conversation. The white women were complementary and somewhat inquisitive, but nothing out of the ordinary took place. They agreed upon a second meeting, which would be hosted by one of the white women who lived in Hopkins. Transportation would be provided for any of the Black women who needed it.

But *none* of the Black participants chose to show up for that second meeting. When I heard about this, I really began to question my decision to bring these groups together. I wanted to know from the Black women why things fell apart, so I asked the host of the first meeting to tell me what she felt had gone so wrong. "Truth is," she said, "I felt like I had absolutely nothing in common with the white women there. They made me feel unworthy ... like a failure." When I asked *how* they made her feel this way, she said that all they talked about was their husbands and children. And I'll never forget what she said next. "Mr. Williams, I couldn't talk about my own husband, who had just walked out on me for another woman. I couldn't tell them I had to go get my son out of jail, and how now I have to go to juvenile court for him ... and that I think my daughter may be pregnant. I can't share that kind of information with those white women. We *can't* be friends. We have nothing in common."

Finally, I understood. I should have paid more attention to the queasiness I felt when the women from Edina Lutheran Community Church first approached me about this. They had been right to recognize that the lives they'd been living placed them and kept them in a virtually all-white bubble—a bubble built by all the spoken and unspoken rules of a culture poisoned by white supremacy—where the only Black people they were likely to encounter in a typical day were there either to serve them or to clean up after them. They had been right to recognize that, in this moment of national crisis over race, it was necessary for white people of goodwill everywhere to step up and ask themselves what they could personally do to challenge and help tear down the barriers of race, class, and caste that divide us.

But what I could see more clearly now is that, for any progress to be made at all, we first had to agree on some common language to even talk with each other about where we needed to go. And in order to do that, we need to recognize how invested so many Americans have been in our mythologies about race.

I remember so well the reactions many Southern whites had to the civil rights movement. Tens of thousands of Black folks had been stirred to action: registering to vote in large numbers; participating in boycotts, marches, and civil disobedience. And white folks just didn't understand. Some even felt hurt and betrayed. The myth of race relations to which they had desperately clung was that colored folk were generally content with the way things were before all the public ferment and that the colored were generally content because the way things were was generally fair and correct. Accordingly, they blamed the discontent and restiveness of their Black neighbors on "outside agitators." And some of them were just then beginning to learn, to their chagrin, how terribly wrong they had been—about everything.

I had to think about how, in my native Mississippi, the social order imposed by Jim Crow created an expectation that Black and white people should be cordial and friendly with each other, but it was understood by everyone that being cordial and friendly is not at all the same as being friends. Friendship can only exist between equals. And in the Mississippi of my youth, every detail of public life had been carefully organized to preclude even the slightest glimmer of equality between Blacks and whites.

So, quite naturally, the centuries of enforced proximity created by slavery never produced true intimacy. It was a system in which intimacy was strictly a one-way street. To get by, Black families needed to know everything about the white families they served, but those white families didn't need to know anything at all about their "servants." There was lots of sex going on, but only as a tool of domination and control. The rape and sexual abuse of Black women during the centuries of slavery was so common that the genome of the average Black American is one-quarter European.[1]

For generations, white infants were suckled at the breasts of Black wet nurses ("mammies"), and these women played a major role in the raising of these young masters and mistresses. Despite how elements of all this may have looked like intimacy on the surface—at least some of the time—it remains shocking to think how little the white people around us understood us at all.

During the height of the movement for civil rights, I recall interviews with whites in the press that echoed each other with the same specific concern: "These outside agitators coming down here all the time, just stirring up trouble ... they've upset things so much that now, when I go on my errands downtown, I never hear the colored sing anymore like they used to.

It used to be so lovely. You'd just hear their singing everywhere. You'd hear 'em sing from a ways off, and then, when they saw you, they'd smile and give a little wave. But no more. The colored just seem so silent and sullen now. It ain't right."

Well ... to paraphrase the great Toni Morrison, "These people didn't understand the slightest thing about us. Our people didn't sing all day because they were happy. They sang to *make* themselves happy. And that's a whole other thing."

Our mistake in helping the women who came and asked for our assistance with creating this social experiment was to lose sight of how powerful the fault lines of race, class, and caste really are in this country. The mere fact that they were all women, who on a daily basis needed to navigate a profoundly sexist society, provided nowhere near enough common ground on which to build friendships. The white women and the Northside residents they had just met lived only a few miles away as the crow flies, but they were light-years away in terms of every major aspect of their lived experience in the world, from the level of comfort and privilege they'd always been able to take for granted to education, to work, to family wealth, to access to quality health care, and to much more.

Had we focused on making sure the women chosen had been much closer to each other in terms of social class, there might have been a greater likelihood of success, but even then, the remaining barriers erected by race and caste would have required time and patience to break down. We didn't help them begin from a clear-eyed assessment of where things stood at the very beginning of their interactions: an understanding that they were women who'd been living in separate worlds, and there hadn't yet been enough uncontrived opportunities to bring them together for the kinds of shared experiences on which authentic relationships are built.

One small, intimate example of how running up against this divide continued to frustrate them occurred after the formal part of the experiment fell apart. The women did exchange contact information at that first meeting, and one of the white women had continued to stay in touch with one of the Black women, a single mother with several children.

The white woman was feeling guilty about the privilege into which she'd been born and also a great deal of empathy for the Black mother and her children. This led her to begin buying clothing and food for the family. But frustrations soon set in because it seemed as though the only time the Black woman wanted to see the white woman was when she was buying things for her family.

I could see that the relationship had become unhealthy and unhappy, so I had a discussion with both women separately about what had happened between them and apologized for putting them in that situation. There was a sense of relief from the Black woman involved because, although she felt grateful for the assistance she'd received, she didn't see any other basis for a relationship. The white woman had hoped for a friendlier outcome and wanted to be able to say she had a Black friend in the same way she has white friends.

Looking back, I'm not sure what I expected to achieve from this experiment, and I've sometimes questioned why I did it. Perhaps I stayed with it longer than I should have, but I didn't want to have to look back and feel there was something more I could have done to help this effort succeed.

Despite the failure of the group to build lasting relationships, a few individual members from the white group wound up redirecting their genuine goodwill and good intentions into long-term work as volunteers with several local community organizations. People who have empathy, and who possess a genuine desire to make a difference in the world, will find that if they take the time to educate themselves about the issues that have inspired them to action, and if they exercise the patience required to learn where and how their skills can best be put to use, they have the potential to become powerful servant leaders and agents for change.

14

THE AMERICAN
LUTHERAN CHURCH

Like most of the Mississippians I know, I was raised in the church—the Black Baptist Church, to be precise. Even Black churches were often targeted for attack, though during times of extreme racial strife church was usually the place one could go and feel safe and protected. It was the place where people who knew and cared about you and your family would pray for you and take up an offering to help get you through hard times. The Black church is a homegrown institution that has always been a powerful mediating force in the lives of Black people in this country. In many ways, the church has been the premier molder of our cultural identity. On a philosophical and spiritual level, the church has prepared believers for soft landings, both in the here and now and in the hereafter.

Throughout my childhood and early adult life, the Black church was my rock and my refuge—the one place other than home where I got the "home training" that nurtured me, molded me, and made me who I am. After getting married and starting my own family, I switched religious affiliations and became a Lutheran. Since I've lived in Minnesota, my denominational affiliation has been with the American Lutheran Church (ALC), which later became part of a merger creating the Evangelical Lutheran Church in America (ELCA).

Following the death of Dr. King, I was inundated with invitations to speak both locally and out of town to a variety of mostly white groups and organizations about issues of race and poverty. Many of the invitations came from suburban Lutheran churches throughout the metropolitan Twin Cities—and even a few Lutheran churches outside the Twin Cities— in response to a campaign of the ALC. In 1968, the ALC launched Project Summer Hope, whose stated goal was to "wipe out white racism" in a single summer. This project was developed exclusively by the all-white staff at the ALC headquarters, a group that had not consulted with any of its handful of Black members or its even tinier handful of Black ALC clergy. A couple of us who were members of Prince of Glory, a North Minneapolis ALC congregation, visited with the ALC bishop and members of his staff to express our concern about the project. They were preparing unusually large packets of printed materials about race and racism in the church and society and mailing them to each ALC congregation, with the expectation that pastors would use this material throughout the summer to help them prepare sermons for their mostly white congregations.

There was *no other preparation* planned for these pastors beyond sending them all of this material. We told the project leaders we thought it was commendable that the ALC wanted to do something to address the problem of racism but believed what they were proposing to do was simplistic and naive—and therefore, not likely to be particularly effective. Following this discussion, the bishop asked if I would agree to have my name placed on a list of people from which churches could invite speakers to address their congregations on issues of race and poverty.

That's how I ended up in Auburn, Nebraska, an all-white town about twenty miles outside of Lincoln, spending the weekend with a young white family of four who hosted my stay.

When I arrived at their church that Sunday morning, I learned that the congregation had been embroiled in conflict. The church was formerly a member of a German Lutheran synod that had merged with the American Lutheran Church. Earlier in the year, the congregation had discontinued the one Sunday service that was still conducted in German. Now all services were being conducted in English, and this displeased some of the members, particularly the older members who still spoke German at home as their primary language and who missed the comfort and the cultural anchor of a weekly service in their native tongue. I also knew that the audience understood poverty, because there were significant numbers of people in poverty among them.

This knowledge was invaluable. I knew not to pull out my fourteen pages of prepared speech. Instead, I conducted a conversation about issues of race and poverty. During our discussion, I learned some things about them, and they learned some things about me. For example, they were fascinated by the story of my great-grandfather escaping his enslavers during the Civil War and joining the Union Army, then fighting against the Confederates at the Battle of Vicksburg. My story was a sobering reminder for many that the current national crisis echoed aspects of the Civil War, and that the Civil War *was really not so long ago.*

I was able to reach the group at a feeling level, but I probably didn't change anyone who had walked into that room with a heart and mind full of racial prejudice. As was often the case in settings like this, some of the people in that congregation were having their first-ever close encounter with a Black person. I did feel I almost certainly made those who might have been generally frightened of Black people a little less afraid. If that was indeed the case, then mission accomplished.

Despite the expectation set up by Project Summer Hope, after further planning, the ALC was able to offer a generally helpful, real-world response to the street violence of the late sixties. In 1968, the Fourth General Convention of the ALC established the Coordinating Committee on National Crises (CCNC) in response to pressure from the leadership in a small number of its inner-city congregations, like Prince of Glory in Minneapolis and Holy Angels in Chicago.

Both of these congregations were located in cities that had experienced street violence. By 1970, the CCNC, which was designed to support church communities responding to the urban crisis, had over a million dollars available to bolster projects not run by the church, and at the 1970 Fifth

General Convention in San Antonio, Texas, the ALC allocated additional funds to support CCNC, including $150,000 for minority scholarships and grants. Assistance for establishing the scholarship came from those same inner-city congregations that had helped create the CCNC. Those same leaders lobbied at the San Antonio General Assembly for the scholarship and grants fund to have its own leadership and identity—and to control the allocation of its resources. The assembly responded by creating the National Scholarships and Grants Program for Minority Students.

I was eventually appointed to chair the committee responsible for awarding scholarships and grants to minority students attending ALC colleges and universities. I held that position from 1970 to 1987, until the ALC merged with two other Lutheran synods to become the Evangelical Lutheran Church in America. During the life of that committee, over $3 million in scholarships and grants were awarded to students of color attending eleven ALC colleges and universities, including Augsburg University in Minneapolis, Capitol University in Columbus, Ohio, and Gustavus Adolphus College in St. Peter, Minnesota, among others. The committee worked closely with all of the schools to enroll students of color (especially Black students) and to assist in addressing the needs of these students— and in better understanding and respecting their cultures.

Prince of Glory Lutheran Church played a critical role, not only at the San Antonio General Assembly but also in North Minneapolis and throughout the ALC during the sixties and seventies. My family had joined Prince of Glory when we first moved to Minneapolis in 1965 because we felt valued and because we had seen that the congregation was willing to challenge the orthodoxy of the ALC. The congregation had a place-based ministry, with much of its outreach dedicated to the Glenwood Lyndale low-income housing project, even though many of its members did not live in the low-income neighborhood where the church was located.

Following the 1966–67 Plymouth Avenue street violence, Prince of Glory had attracted several transfer memberships from suburban white congregations. These were people who expressed an interest in helping the church become a center of activity in terms of problem-solving on issues related to race and poverty. Prince of Glory was also an attractive place of worship for Augsburg College students.

The church's leadership, both lay and clergy, had a significant impact on the Northside community throughout the sixties and seventies. One of its members, Reverend Ewald (Joe) Bash, was able to establish crisis colony housing for Augsburg College students in 1968 at Glenwood Lyndale and on Plymouth Avenue. These students, mostly white, lived and studied in the community. The idea behind this long-term project was to take volunteering to the next level by giving students an opportunity to live among the people served by the volunteer activity for months at a time. The hope was that this "experiment in living" would foster empathy and a deeper understanding among them about the social conditions and realities faced by urban Black populations.

Reverend Bash also played a critical role in establishing KMOJ radio, a nonprofit that became the only culturally Black station in the Twin Cities' unique, new network of low-powered community radio stations. KMOJ took shape after he was able to secure a $150,000 grant from the ALC to support the Center for Communications and Development (CCD), a grassroots initiative organized in 1976 to provide advocacy for low-income public housing residents on various issues. In 1977 the Federal Communications Commission awarded CCD a license to operate a broadcast radio station. The station's call letters, KMOJ, were inspired by the Swahili word for unity, "umoja." During its early days the radio station was operated by public housing residents. Despite the low initial power of its broadcast signal, KMOJ quickly gained a large and loyal audience, appreciated by the community for its mix of entertainment and public affairs programming. KMOJ is still broadcasting, but now it has considerably more signal power and much wider geographic reach.

Prince of Glory Lutheran Church continued to be a place of refuge for our family. Its members also demonstrated that the community itself is best at providing a place where people can work together, solving real problems.

15

INCREASING PHYLLIS WHEATLEY'S COMMUNITY VISIBILITY AND VIABILITY

The urban street violence that marked the summers of the mid- through late sixties heightened both local and national interest in creating and funding programs designed to aggressively tackle racial disparities and poverty. Local agencies received increased funding from a number of different federal agencies, the most notable of which was the Office of Economic Opportunity (OEO), established by President Lyndon Johnson in 1964 as a part of his War on Poverty initiative. Many local nonprofits benefited from OEO funding delivered through the local Community Action Program (CAP) agency.

In Minneapolis, throughout the sixties and seventies, the local CAP agency was an independent agency of Hennepin County. By statute, the OEO could only fund government agencies, but each program funded by the OEO was required to have its own independent board of directors, responsible for governance and accountable to the local CAP agency. Each of these boards needed to be representative of the community it served and to reflect the OEO's guiding motto: "maximum feasible resident participation." This meant that all local CAP agencies had to have board members who benefited from the services provided by the agency.

Phyllis Wheatley was among many existing and newcomer nonprofits seeking to benefit from the new resources available through the OEO. This, at times, made for conflicts among the old and new nonprofits. The older nonprofits, which had been around for many years serving the community, felt they deserved to benefit from these new sources of funding. These "old guard" agencies believed they had been underfunded for many years. The newer nonprofits, such as the Citizens Community Centers and The Way, believed the urban crises could in part be attributed to the failures of the established nonprofits, which included United Way member agencies such as Phyllis Wheatley and the other settlement houses, the YMCA, and the Boy Scouts of America.

These were challenging times for Phyllis Wheatley, because we were being pressured by the United Way and the Health and Welfare Council to merge with Unity Settlement and Wells Memorial to form Northside Settlement Services.

At times, the United Way, the Health and Welfare Council, and the Minneapolis City Planning Agency saw me as an impediment to "progress" because I thought Phyllis Wheatley shouldn't enter into a merger if it was perceived to be the weakest of the three organizations. I believed that if Phyllis Wheatley was not seen as equal or superior to the other two organizations, a merger would not be in the best interest of the community it served. I wanted to demonstrate to the community and to local decision-makers that Phyllis Wheatley was an essential community resource holding a unique and indispensable place in the ecosystem of agencies on the Northside. It was an institution with credibility and deep connections, both in the halls of political and economic power *and* with our Northside neighbors; an organization well positioned to provide a bridge across the racial and economic divide that existed at the time; an institution that remained the one place in the community where people with diverse points of view could safely discuss how the community should solve problems or navigate through a crisis. Phyllis Wheatley uniquely could mediate these discussions without being perceived as being *for* or *against* any one particular point of view.

Enter Control Data Corporation

In the sixties, Control Data Corporation was one of the largest supercomputer makers in the world. Seeking to have a positive impact, the company looked at its own expansion plans. Instead of continuing to expand their campus in the suburbs, why not build in an inner-city location and create some well-paid jobs in an area where those jobs were badly needed? Why not find a location that might actually serve to attract other business development too? In 1967 the company began planning to establish a plant on the Northside and to hire workers from Northside neighborhoods.

With this goal in mind, Control Data executives began holding meetings at Phyllis Wheatley. Control Data's position—as often expressed by Norb Berg, a Control Data senior official—was that the company would not go into communities where they weren't invited. Control Data saw Phyllis Wheatley as the logical partner in building community communication and trust because they believed the agency could provide the most comprehensive point of entry into North Minneapolis—an opportunity to be introduced to the community and get to know the place and its people.

So when Roger Wheeler, the Control Data executive assigned to lead this effort, visited with me at Phyllis Wheatley, I offered him an opportunity to become directly involved with neighborhood youth. His company was interested in opening a plant on the Northside that would create scores of good-paying jobs. And he was well aware that the street violence that had occurred along Plymouth Avenue in 1967 had been sparked and driven by disaffected local youth whose primary complaint was that there was no work in the neighborhood that paid a living wage and no prospect for any such work anywhere on the horizon.

I felt particularly proud of the work we at Phyllis Wheatley had been doing with neighborhood youth, and I was confident that, if he got to meet and spend a little time around them, he'd be impressed with their energy and enthusiasm. I was right. After Wheeler took that opportunity to meet with our neighborhood youth and had come away highly impressed, he and several other Control Data volunteers decided they'd like to help PWCC youth participate in Junior Achievement (JA) programs. Junior Achievement offered a logical place to start as it was a program that was already very much in the wheelhouse of Control Data executives, and it gave them an opportunity to offer low-income Black youth some mentoring and hands-on experience with what it takes to think through and create a business from the ground up.

But first, interested youth would have to join JA, and they'd have to participate in its programs at the JA offices on Hennepin Avenue in downtown Minneapolis. I told Wheeler that while it was not practical for our youth to go to the JA offices, the program could be offered at PWCC, as space was available there, and the youth already had an established pattern of coming to the center for programs and other activities. They agreed, and soon Wheeler and other Control Data people began working with the Junior Achievement youth to organize a "company." As a part of this project, the youth selected a product, sold shares, and marketed their product. At the end of the school year the company was liquidated, because each year a new company would be formed. All of the investors in the company were paid a dividend.

Creating and running the JA program with neighborhood youth gave Control Data executives many natural opportunities to interact with the leadership of several community-based organizations. These included the Minneapolis Urban League, the Minneapolis Housing and Redevelopment Authority (MHRA), Wells Memorial, The Way, United Way and the Health and Welfare Council, Minneapolis Public Schools, and the Twin Cities Opportunities Industrialization Center (TCOIC).

As a result of discussions with representatives from these organizations and others, Control Data soon felt ready to make its proposal to establish a manufacturing plant in North Minneapolis. The community was excited, but skeptical. Would North Minneapolis residents really get a fair shot at jobs in the new plant? Community discussions that followed Control Data's announcement became learning experiences for both the community and Control Data.

In every discussion, the issue of trust emerged. Community leaders were wary of Control Data and full of questions. "What's in it for the community?" "Will we be better off with Control Data as an employer, or will they simply exploit the community and then leave?"

For their part, Control Data executives had to learn to be more patient, allow the community to ask questions, and not be disturbed when challenged. For many Control Data executives, these meetings gave them an unusual opportunity to understand some of the local dynamics of racial discrimination and disparities and to understand them within the context of national history.

They also, of course, needed to use these meetings to help think through whether the plant would be a financially profitable venture. In the end, these community discussions afforded Control Data and the community an opportunity to get to know one another better, which was important for future negotiations.

The path to building the permanent, 85,000-square-foot manufacturing facility they were now envisioning presented some real challenges. The site Control Data initially wanted was along Seventh Street at Twelfth Avenue North, but the neighborhood wanted that site for housing. When Control Data attempted to play hard ball—threatening to pull out if they couldn't get the site they wanted—the discussions stopped until I offered to host a meeting at PWCC, with all of the key stakeholders present, to discuss an alternative site that could meet all Control Data's specifications and satisfy any neighborhood concerns.

Present at the PWCC meeting were Norb Berg and Roger Wheeler from Control Data, plus representatives from the Office of Economic Opportunity, the Urban League, Minneapolis Public Schools, the mayor's office, the Northside Youth Opportunity Center, the Twin Cities Opportunity Industrialization Center, and several others.

During that meeting, community representatives asked Norb Berg what Control Data needed in a site. He said Control Data was building a training center at 1001 Washington Avenue North, and that it was important for the factory to be close to the training center. "Would next door be close enough?" I asked. Minneapolis Public Schools had decided to close the Blaine Elementary School, located at 277 Twelfth Avenue North, which was right behind the 1001 Washington Avenue site. Control Data didn't own the land, but Minneapolis Public Schools planned to offer the site for sale.

When Marv Tenhoff from Minneapolis Public Schools was asked what it would take to acquire that property, he said a request would need to be presented to the Minneapolis School Board at its next meeting, which was already on the schedule a mere week away. Minneapolis Housing and Redevelopment Authority would need to present an offer to buy the property. In turn, MHRA would purchase the property from Minneapolis Public Schools and negotiate a sale to Control Data. This was acceptable to Berg, who offered Control Data's services to help expedite any and all of the legal work necessary to complete the sale. And that's how the Minneapolis School Board authorized the sale of the Blaine School property to MHRA for $100,500 at its May 28, 1968, meeting. Within two weeks, Minneapolis Public Schools sold the property to MHRA, which in turn sold it to Control Data, which began construction on the North Minneapolis plant during the summer of 1968. Upon completion, the plant at its peak employed some three hundred people, many of whom lived in North Minneapolis and could walk to work. In 1988, after much financial loss, Control Data Corporation began withdrawing from making computers and closed the plant.[1]

Standing Tall as a Community Forum

Following the 1966–67 riots and throughout 1968 and 1969, Phyllis Wheatley frequently hosted meetings at which issues of race and poverty were in some way at the center of the discussion. Some of these meetings got to be quite heated, but we never shied away from them because I believed PWCC should continue to play an essential role in helping to define the critical problems facing the community and to be a trusted partner in helping find solutions. In order to credibly play such a key role, Phyllis Wheatley had to be seen as a mediating force in the community. My plan was to find ways to attract people who could offer a variety of strategies—radical, moderate, or conservative—for developing solutions to our urban crises. There was no other public place in the city where gatherings of residents with truly diverse views could air them freely in the hopes of finding common ground. Certainly, if a forum or meeting were held at The Way, the audience most likely to attend would have a strong bias toward the views of The Way, an organization which was perceived as radical. Any community member with a contrary point of view might feel intimidated and would be less likely to attend and/or participate, which would surely diminish the likelihood of finding common ground.

I decided to test my plan. Shortly after my appointment as Phyllis Wheatley executive director, I had learned that the annual meeting was a special occasion. Held every April in the settlement house gymnasium, it was an elaborate, labor-intensive fried chicken dinner, prepared and served on-site for two hundred or more attendees. Extra help was brought in to prepare the meals, and our youth were trained as servers. Guests included leaders from business, government, church, and other nonprofits, along with longtime friends and supporters who were of every possible political and social background. The 1967 annual dinner would, indeed, be a great test audience.

I liked the idea of inviting people to speak at Phyllis Wheatley who might not otherwise get an opportunity to be heard in Minneapolis. Instead of inviting one person with a single point of view, I thought it might be interesting to have two people whose views on the same issues may show some sharp contrasts. I invited Reverend William (Bill) Youngdahl and Ernie Chambers, who had both been featured in the 1966 NBC documentary *A Time for Burning*.

This documentary film examined the struggles between two Lutheran Church–Missouri Synod congregations—one Black and the other white—over the desires of the two pastors to set up a visitation program between their congregations. The documentary filmed the dynamics of the back-and-forth discussions at both churches, which highlighted racial tensions, especially among members of the white congregation. Ernie Chambers, a barber, was a young Black activist who'd made a name for himself by questioning the behavior of people who considered themselves Christians and calling them out for their hypocrisy. Chambers came across in the film as eloquent, outspoken, and angry at times. The film received national acclaim and was frequently used in interracial training sessions around issues of race and poverty. I was familiar with many of the issues involved in that struggle between the two churches, because I had recently recruited and hired Vivian Jenkins, the daughter of Reverend R. F. Jenkins, the Black pastor featured in the film, to come to Minneapolis and work as an arts and culture program worker at Phyllis Wheatley.

I invited Bill and Ernie because they had done this before in other settings, and I knew they worked well together. I thought Bill would probably be more acceptable to the Phyllis Wheatley and Minneapolis audience than Ernie, especially since Bill was a white Lutheran pastor from the Youngdahl family, which was well known and highly respected in Minnesota. Ernie wore a beard and thought of himself as an agnostic, and sometimes as an atheist—a man who saw a lot of hypocrisy when it came to religion and often called it out.

My plan was to put Bill and Ernie onstage facing one another and ask each of them to speak to the issues that were so dominant in our ongoing urban crises. Ernie did come to Minneapolis with Bill, but he declined to participate in the presentation as I had planned it. He thought his presence on the stage would detract from the real message—the need for white people to change their behavior—and he believed the media would be determined to generate conflict between him and Bill where there was none. He did, however, agree to play a different role while in town, offering to lead discussions about race and racism with small groups.

One of the events we arranged with Ernie was a breakfast meeting attended by a group of Lutheran pastors in Edina. Ernie's presentation there created quite an uproar, which made it into the *Minneapolis Tribune* on March 30, 1967, with the headline, "Omaha Negro Calls Ministers 'Hypocrites,' Christ a Pimp." Chambers had told the preachers, "You ... try to get a respect you're not entitled to ... people come to your church so you can make them feel comfortable, and you're not about to let them feel uncomfortable. Ministers talk of brotherly love, but they don't practice what they preach." Chambers reminded the preachers that Jesus spent much of his life hanging around with poor people, including women many would call prostitutes. He went on to say that where he came from, men who hang out around prostitutes are referred to as pimps. He further challenged the preachers when one of them asked for practical ways in which they could express their concern. He said, "You've got realtors who are responsible for segregation in your congregation. Why don't you expose them, stand in opposition to the practices of realtor boards? *Jesus called names when he preached.* Every Sunday you could have a Realtor of the Week."

For his part, Youngdahl's presentation at the dinner meeting strongly embraced many of Chambers's views. He acknowledged the hypocrisy within the church and said the church could and should be contributing more to bring about stability and justice in communities across the country.

By the time they left town, both men's appearances as Phyllis Wheatley's guests had helped to raise the agency's profile as an important community-based organization where the critical issues of the day could be discussed in ways that were distinctly different from any other organization's programming. We made our case that we could and should be playing a lead role in helping our community plot out whatever pathways toward racial justice and unity might serve us best.

All the Difference in the World

I remained involved with the Urban Coalition after leaving the staff, and I continued to raise the question about minority participation in both public and private sector ventures. Few people of color served on any of the city, county, or state regulatory or advisory boards. Most people didn't know what those boards and commissions were, or how they operated, or how one went about getting selected to serve on them.

I learned as much about all of this as I could. My people had suffered so much just to hang on to what should always have been their birthright as citizens—the right to vote. I wanted Phyllis Wheatley's core constituency to understand that the full exercise of their franchise as citizens meant not only voting every election year in all the many, less-talked-about down-ballot races but also educating themselves about the power wielded by members of the various commissions, committees, and boards of the City of Minneapolis and of Hennepin County who were not elected by the public but appointed by elected politicians.

I encouraged the Urban Coalition to take on the issue of the need for diversity on public boards and commissions, because the decisions they make affect everyone. This reality is a big part of what the political pundits mean when they say, "All politics is local." As coalition members and I surveyed the status of our own local civil governance, we could see that few people knew anything about the individuals selected, and their backgrounds and experience were seldom shared with the public.

I observed the selections governors made to serve as department heads (or commissioners) in their administrations, as well as how many people of color were selected and for what positions. I began this process in 1968 with Governor Harold LeVander, who named one Black person as a commissioner in his administration——Frank Kent, who served as commissioner of human rights.

After the selection, I wrote to Governor LeVander, congratulating him on Kent's appointment and telling him that Black candidates should be considered for positions besides that of commissioner of human rights and pointed out that when public officials named Black people to key positions in government, their appointments were invariably limited to human and civil rights roles. I heard back from the governor, and also from Commissioner Kent, who thanked me for my letter and my interest but insisted there was nothing discriminatory in the governor's actions.

My agitation about the need for diversity on all public boards and commissions also got me an invitation to serve on the Minneapolis Capital Long-Range Improvement Committee (CLIC). Few people knew what CLIC did, and certainly few in my community. It was one of those bodies that operated under the radar but with enough authority to significantly influence the city capital-improvement program. Infrastructure is critical to capital improvements, and CLIC made annual recommendations to the city council that affected which capital projects—street pavement, sewer and power, street lighting—should be undertaken over time. Historically, the people who had served on CLIC were all white and predominantly male, mostly from Southwest and Southeast Minneapolis. North and Northeast Minneapolis had been chronically underrepresented.

When I agreed to serve on CLIC and other boards as the lone Black person, I was frequently asked by my Black friends and colleagues what difference I thought one Black person could make among all those white people. My reply was always, "All the difference in the world. Never under-estimate the power of one in such circumstances." I'd often add, "Intro-duce a person with a noticeable difference such as race, gender, or age into a group for the first time, and their presence will *always* affect the nature of the discussion. This dynamic often happens even if that newly selected member seldom speaks up. Their mere presence in a mixed race and gen-der group will usually affect how issues of gender and race are discussed." Whenever I was involved with such groups I felt obliged to raise people's consciousness by asking certain questions, particularly about how a given decision might affect a poor person or a person of color.

I was never satisfied being the only person of color on boards or com-mittees, always encouraging them to look for other people of color to serve. I knew it would be a win-win for everyone, not just for me, if the political power brokers expanded the circle of people who were always asked to serve again and again beyond the handful of us whose qualifications made us "exceptional" in their eyes.

My first experience of this "first Black person/only Black person" syn-drome happened when I moved to Minneapolis and my boss at Unity House suggested I become a member of the North Minneapolis Kiwanis Club. She believed my membership could benefit both me and Unity House. So I was welcomed as the first and only Black member of that Kiwanis Club. In my fourth year, still the only Black member, I was elected as club president. And while the members of the club were wonderful people, I didn't want to be the lone Black person in the club forever. I also knew the only way another Black person was likely to become a member would be if I invited him, because I was the only member who had many other Black people as friends or professional or business associates. So I made sure I had invited enough Black men as my luncheon meeting guests to comfortably recom-mend one or more for membership. When I left the North Minneapolis Ki-wanis after approximately ten years, there were three other Black members, all of whom were people I had recommended.

As another example, I recall that after the street violence of the sixties had passed, I was invited to replace John Warder, the lone Black person on the Minneapolis Foundation board of directors. James Shannon, the

Minneapolis Foundation's executive director, visited with me and told me that Warder was leaving and he would like to recommend me to the board as a replacement.

I was pleased to be asked to serve on such a prestigious board, but once again, I had that sinking feeling in the pit of my stomach, knowing I'd be the lone Black person serving on this board of mostly high-powered white men. While I was on the board, a woman, Mary Lee Dayton, was named for the first time to chair the foundation's contributions and allocations committee, which reviewed and passed on all grant applications. She later became the first woman to chair the foundation's board of directors.

Near the end of my tenure on the board, I was invited to join the nominations committee to help select nominees for the board. I realized right away that I was in very familiar territory, because essentially I was being invited to help identify my Black successor. As I participated in the discussions about potential board members, I noticed that the name of only one Black person emerged as a potential replacement for my position. No other person of color was mentioned until I asked whether there was anything in the foundation's bylaws that said only one person of color at a time could serve on the board. This brought a quick negative response, which resulted in the nominating committee selecting, for the first time, three people of color to be recommended for positions on the board. Two African Americans and one Native American were seated on the Minneapolis Foundation's board of directors, changing forever the diversity composition of the board. My crusade for increased diversity in our public, private, and nonprofit sector institutions continues to this day.

Community Organizing

By the time I came to Phyllis Wheatley, the center had lost some of its luster. Members of the younger generation did not hold it in as high esteem as their predecessors did when Phyllis Wheatley was the only agency whose resources were specifically dedicated to the well-being of Black people. By 1965, Black people had a few more options for cultural and recreational outlets than they'd had in 1945. My goal was to reestablish Phyllis Wheatley as a dominant force in the Black community while simultaneously raising the center's profile in the community at large. I believed strongly that the good Phyllis Wheatley had been able to do in the past on behalf of the Black Northside could be done for the entire Northside, especially since Phyllis Wheatley's building was located in the heart of Sumner Field, a low-income public housing project that was about 50 percent white in 1965. The two high-rise apartment buildings for senior citizens, located in the same neighborhood, were over 60 percent white.

Minneapolis was also beginning to receive federal funding through the OEO for a wide range of economic, education, and health and human services programs. Funding for these programs would be channeled, for the most part, through existing local nonprofit and public institutions. At the time, most nonprofits—and virtually all of the public agencies—had no history of involving residents in program planning or development. The thinking had always been that residents in the poorer neighborhoods were incapable of participating in program planning and development. But in order to receive OEO funding, the funded program had to show that community residents played a significant role in its planning, development, and implementation. Eventually, these agencies began to develop strategies for engaging the residents, but they were slow to fully embrace the concept of resident participation.

As a result, new agencies began to emerge to fill the gaps. For example, when Minneapolis Public Schools did not show enough flexibility and creativity to be selected as the agency to run the federally funded Head Start programs, an independent nonprofit, Parents In Community Action (PICA), was established to take the reins. Grassroots leadership at PICA had a powerful, demonstrable commitment to both community engagement and the empowerment of parents that made the organization a perfect fit.

Efforts were also made to establish alternative agencies to Minneapolis's settlement houses, because a few people were condemning them for being irrelevant and not on top of critical issues and needs when the riots occurred. In particular, they talked about how these organizations were not meeting the needs of Black and poor inner-city youth.

One group of community residents, some of whom had participated in the 1966–67 street violence, was able to convince the local OEO agency,

Mobilization of Economic Resources, to support the creation of four neighborhood centers that would essentially be run by residents. These Citizens' Community Centers would be located in South, North, Northeast, and Southeast Minneapolis, and they would organize and engage the community in efforts to improve the social and economic conditions of their neighborhoods. The centers were funded for a year with federal funds and managed by an executive director, John Sims, who took a leave from his supervisor position with Hennepin County Welfare Department. Each center also had its own local director and staff, most of whom were neighborhood residents.

It didn't take long for these centers to spin off into relative chaos. Each went off in its own direction, as if they hadn't started life with one common mission, making it very difficult for the executive director to manage these four increasingly separate organizations.

The beginning of the end came when Matt Eubanks, a community organizer for the Eastside office, led a group of residents into an Urban Coalition meeting and literally shut it down. His agenda had been to seek support from the coalition for the Poor People's March on Washington, DC, which was being organized in the spring of 1968. His anger grew hotter and hotter as it became apparent the coalition was going to decline to support his demands. Before storming out of the meeting, he rose to verbally attack the board, telling them to, "Take your money and shove it." Before long, federal funding for the Citizens' Community Centers was in jeopardy because Eubanks's behavior was seen as political, and the federal government did not fund political action.[2]

Institutions as Tools

The Urban Coalition did, indeed, care deeply about the national developments, but our primary focus was on the urgent needs right here at home. Northside residents were concerned about the availability of health care and social services in the community. North Minneapolis had been underserved in these two critical areas of need for some time because all of Hennepin County's health and human services were centralized, which meant residents in need of health or social services had to go downtown to open a case file and begin the process of receiving assistance. The county commissioners and executive staff had strongly resisted establishing decentralized neighborhood or community facilities.

But all the effort that had gone into the creation of the Urban Coalition had awakened a sleeping giant. Northside residents had begun to see that when everyday people organize, they can make things happen. It wasn't long before North Minneapolis residents effectively used the local OEO as a tool to secure a federal grant to help establish the Pilot City Regional Center in a vacant synagogue. The residents had been instrumental in getting Hennepin County to be the grant recipient (fiscal agent), and they also steered the process that established a governing board of community residents charged with overseeing the operation of the facility.

The board, known as TACTICS (Technical Assistance To Improve Community Services), had an elected membership, which was responsible for hiring staff. Phyllis Wheatley was one of the Northside agencies that served as a signatory on the initial grant application, and a longtime PWCC employee, Cozelle Breedlove, chaired the TACTICS board for many years.

For quite some time, the relationship between Hennepin County government and Pilot City was strained. The leadership at Hennepin County Human Services seemed to strongly prefer that health and human services remain centralized. More than once, Hennepin County Human Services threatened to fully take over the management of the facility.

But the attitude and behavior of Hennepin County changed. Pilot City has morphed into North Point Health and Wellness Center, and a new facility was built next to the former synagogue to house the health services. In 2016, the Hennepin County Board of Commissioners approved an expansion to North Point Health and Wellness Center of over $60 million. Questions about the viability of regional and community-based health and human services seem to have disappeared, as major service centers have popped up all over the county. Today, what was unthinkable in the sixties and seventies is the norm. These changes emerged out of street violence, and PWCC played a role in helping to shift the human services landscape.

Another Way to Engage

The Minneapolis Housing and Redevelopment Authority took a different approach to addressing its lack of resident participation for the funding it was receiving to support its residents' programs. In 1967, Minneapolis had three distinct low-income family public housing projects, two in North Minneapolis and one in Southeast Minneapolis. Two of the projects had well-organized and functioning resident councils that advised local management, but the Sumner Olson Public Housing Project did not. The MHRA provided Phyllis Wheatley with a grant to help the Housing Authority organize one.

In October of 1968 we created an internship for a University of Minnesota School of Social Work graduate student who was assigned to work with Phyllis Wheatley staff and public housing residents on organizing and helping coordinate a residents' council. During the organizing process, the public housing residents decided they wanted the council to be more inclusive of the wider community. A group working together on a community project will often expand its original vision, because the sense of empowerment that is a natural part of the process encourages residents to see other issues that should also be addressed. In this case, residents simply realized that the wider community beyond Sumner Olson shared the same concerns around neighborhood safety, greater economic opportunity, and the need for more affordable housing. Residents were fully engaged and optimistic about the outcome. By April 1969, the organizing work was completed and the Northside Residents Redevelopment Council (NRRC) was formed. The initial Residents Council boundaries were Lyndale Avenue on the east, Penn Avenue on the west, Olson Memorial Highway on the south, and Plymouth Avenue on the north.

The NRRC proved to be effective in helping generate the resident participation critical to federal funding coming into the entire Minneapolis Northside. Thus, the organization that had begun as a voice just for Sumner Olson became a voice for the entire neighborhood. Soon after, it became a Community Development Corporation with an emphasis on affordable housing for all of North Minneapolis.

16

HIRING PRACTICES, JOB OPPORTUNITIES

In the 1970s, the corporate members of the Urban Coalition were un-der constant pressure to improve their minority recruitment and hiring practices. Many of the newer corporations, like Control Data, had made remarkable progress, because setting goals for minority recruitment and hiring was part of their corporate culture when they were founded. But for older corporations like Honeywell and General Mills, Inc., much work still needed to be done.

The Urban Coalition had asked General Mills to show greater prog-ress in hiring minorities in managerial positions. In 1972, the coalition, led by its members of color, called for a boycott of General Mills be-cause members didn't believe the company had taken demands for im-proved minority hiring seriously. It was important for the coalition that all its corporate members should show they were *walking the talk* when it came to the hiring and retention of people of color.

In 1968, there may have been two or three smaller corporations with African American senior-level executives, but none of the founding mem-bers of the Urban Coalition had any African American staff members at senior levels. The call for a General Mills boycott was particularly thorny: the president of the Urban Coalition's board of directors, James Summers, was also president and chief operating officer of General Mills. To no one's surprise, Summers opposed the Urban Coalition's action, and he consequently resigned as board president. In his letter of resignation, he stated that although he disagreed with the action proposed by the board, he and his corporation would continue to support the work of the Urban Coalition.

At the time of Summers's resignation, General Mills announced it would be creating a new corporate executive position at the vice president level and would recruit an African American to fill the position. Summers indicated that General Mills was not creating this position to stop any Urban Coalition boycott proposal. He stressed that General Mills was taking this action because the company believed it was the right thing to do, for both the corporation and the community.

Because General Mills didn't have any African American employees at a senior enough level to be promoted to vice president, the company would have to recruit someone from outside. They focused their recruitment efforts primarily on local African American candidates. In October 1972, I received a call from William Humphrey, a General Mills vice president, who invited me to interview for the position. In April of 1972, Governor Wendell Anderson had appointed me Minnesota's (and the nation's) first ombudsman for corrections (discussed below), so I reminded Humphrey that I had just begun my current position in July. I had cared deeply about criminal justice system reform for a long time, and the opportunity presented by this new program meant everything to me. I made this clear to him, but he insisted I come for the interview because he believed I could be helpful as they went through their process. I agreed to go for an interview.

I showed up for my interview at corporate headquarters knowing from the beginning that I probably wouldn't accept a job offer, but I really wanted to know more about General Mills' thinking about the position. What were their expectations? How would this vice president's portfolio differ from those of the corporation's other vice presidents? To whom would this position report, and would there be anyone reporting *to* them? I arrived for my interview at 8:30 in the morning. By the time I finished at three in the afternoon, I had spent some time with at least six senior General Mills executives, including the CEO. I finished my day with James Summers, president and chief operating officer. By then, *I* was the one with the most questions, and to be honest, for the most part I felt that General Mills had few good answers for them. So I told Summers that while I admired what General Mills was doing in hiring an African American at such a senior level, I wasn't convinced, for several reasons, that they really expected this new hire to be an integral part of the corporate decision-making structure.

First, I didn't like the job title: vice president for social action. What, exactly, would this title mean in terms of specific job duties? Would this new vice president preside over a department of social action, or would he or she basically serve as adviser to the president and CEO and the other vice presidents on social issues? Second, I didn't trust the company's interest in hiring someone with my background to fill the position. I was from the world of nonprofit human services management, not business management—an outsider in their world. And from the sound of it, their intention was to limit this new vice president to involvement in whatever the corporation might choose to do in the arena of social action. To me, this sounded like an invitation to stay perched there as a permanent outsider.

Finally, I wondered what their plan would be for the person in this position when it was eliminated—and it was sure to be eliminated when he no longer held his position. I felt that unless they carefully rethought this vice president's portfolio, there would always be lingering questions that could sabotage the position in the absence of some clear answers as to what the new position was contributing to the corporation's bottom line.

I told Summers, "I'm not the person for the position. I don't have any corporate experience. My background is in social work. I don't look like a corporate executive. I don't own a pair of wingtip shoes." But, I told Summers, I did have an ideal candidate to recommend for the position: Cyrus Johnson, my college roommate from the University of Illinois. He was working as a manager for Illinois Bell Telephone Company in Chicago. General Mills followed up immediately, contacted Cyrus, and invited him for several interviews. Ultimately he was their choice to serve as the corporation's first African American vice president.

Around the same time General Mills was creating this position, the company purchased Stevens Square housing properties, and the management of this property was added to the vice president for social action's portfolio. Cyrus Johnson assumed his position at General Mills in early 1973 and retired from General Mills as a senior vice president in 1991. As I had predicted, a change in leadership at General Mills led to the elimination of the title of vice president for social action, but it did not lead to Cyrus's departure from the corporation. He moved from that position to vice president for corporate personnel and, later, to vice president for corporate properties and security, the position he held when he retired. Cyrus Johnson may have been General Mills' first African American vice president, but he certainly hasn't been the last. General Mills has had, at one time since then, as many as six African Americans among its most senior corporate officers.

Cyrus E. Johnson (left), General Mills' first African American vice president, at his retirement party in 1991.

17

My Bush Fellowship Experience

Shortly before I became Phyllis Wheatley's executive director in 1965, I had been exploring the possibility of applying for a Bush Foundation Leadership Fellows grant to continue my graduate education. My original plan when I moved my family to Minneapolis was to stay for only two years. That plan, of course, was interrupted when I was named executive director at Phyllis Wheatley.

It was now five years later, and I was still interested in the Bush Foundation Leadership Fellows program, but not as an opportunity to earn another degree and get out of Minnesota. I was now interested in using fellowship time and resources to study how our social and economic policies were being developed and implemented at the local level. I was especially interested in how people of color were represented on the decision-making bodies of our public and nonprofit institutions. My broader plan in seeking a Bush Foundation fellowship was to expand my knowledge and experience in economics and political science.

I applied for and was successful in receiving a Bush Leadership Fellows award in 1970—one of the four short, four-month fellowships. During the time of my award, Donald Peddie was in charge of the program. Peddie was a Harvard graduate, and he encouraged the fellows to consider Harvard for the academic part of their program. He especially urged me to consider the Program for Management Development at the Harvard Business School. But Harvard was not in my plans. Mary Lou and I were expecting our third child, Laurie, who arrived in May of 1971. I postponed using my fellowship until summer of 1971 so that I could be home when she was born.

When I was ready to work on the fellowship, I convinced Peddie that Harvard was not the place for me and that I could develop a program that fit my needs at Northwestern University in Evanston, Illinois. This would make it practical for me to bring my wife and children, including our five-week-old daughter, Laurie. We would live in a duplex apartment building near campus in north Evanston, our first and only experience with suburban living.

The Phyllis Wheatley board of directors granted me a four-month leave of absence, which enabled me to begin in mid-June of 1971. The program I had designed was built around taking courses in economics, political science, and independent studies in city governance. In addition, I had an internship assignment with the Northwestern University Center for Urban Affairs. I was truly elated with my internship, because it gave me an opportunity to meet and work with two outstanding staff members at the center and also with Northwestern faculty members John (Jody) Kretzman and John McKnight.[1]

Educating Family and Neighbors

My summer at Northwestern University enabled me to further pursue my interest in the impact of race and diversity on city governance. It also provided my family with an opportunity to experience being the only Black family in our suburban neighborhood. We lived in an area of north Evanston near Northwestern University's campus—a pleasant neighborhood of tree-lined streets, single-family homes, and duplex apartments.

Mary Lou and me with Chris (in back), Jeff, and Laurie, visiting Mary Lou's family in 1974, a few years after our stay at Northwestern.

Our boys, ages four and eight, played frequently in the backyard of the family next door, which had boys of similar ages, along with the boys who lived upstairs in our building. One day, one of the boys from upstairs came knocking on our door, anxious and excited, and told my wife that one of the boys next door had called my eight-year-old son, Chris, a Nigger. When he told Mary Lou what had happened, he seemed surprised and a little confused at Chris's nonchalant reaction to the slur.

We knew then that it was time for us to have our first real talk with our children about race and racism. We also knew that it was important for us to speak to the parents of the boys next door.

We visited with the boy's mother and shared with her what had happened. She, of course, was horrified that her son would use such a word, and she swore that they never used that word in their home. She thought he must have picked it up at school or from the streets. We encouraged her to talk with her sons about race and explain that the "N-word" is used to hurt and diminish Black people in order to assert white superiority and supremacy. Kids need to understand that it's a highly provocative word with an old and ugly history, and it can often lead to physical confrontation. If her son had called a Black kid at school or in the park a Nigger, a fight may have ensued, and her son might not have understood why.

Again, she was very apologetic and reassured us that she and her husband would have that talk with their sons. She also said she hoped our kids would continue playing together. We assured her we had no problem with that, but we would certainly let her know if it happened again. The boys continued to play together throughout the summer and, to my knowledge, the word was never used again.

Meanwhile, we were very curious about Chris's reaction to being called a Nigger and asked him to share with us the circumstances leading up to the incident. Chris wasn't at all sure about what had happened. They were playing and he heard the kid use the word, but he didn't know that it was aimed at him. We asked him if he had ever heard the word before. He said he probably had but wasn't sure. We asked if he knew the word's meaning. He didn't. So, we used the moment to give him a brief, kid-appropriate lesson in Black and white race relations. We told him that when a white person calls a Black person a Nigger, it is meant to hurt, and he should let them know he doesn't like what they said. We said he should also let *us* know, and if it happened at school, he should tell his teacher. We lived in an integrated neighborhood in Minneapolis. He attended an integrated school, had white friends, and played with white kids at school and in the neighborhood. We counted our blessings that we had never heard about any incidents of racial conflict before this first one in Evanston.

Learning for Future Use

In 1967, Carl Stokes was elected mayor of Cleveland, Ohio, the first Black person to be elected mayor of a major US city. The following year, Richard Hatcher was elected mayor of Gary, Indiana, and in 1970, Charles Williams became the first Black mayor of East St. Louis, Illinois. This was the beginning of a period during which Black people ascended to power in major US cities across the nation—significantly, at a time when many of the cities where they gained political power were in economic decline.

On the one hand, there was optimism about the widespread rise of Black political power at the municipal level. But that optimism was tempered by the growing realization that political power and economic power are not at all the same thing. These newly elected Black mayors were all in the early stages of working out how best to take this reality into account and still find ways to make progress for all their citizens but also, very specifically, for the Black constituencies whose support had ensured their ascent to power.

The growth of a globalized economy meant that US–based companies were beginning to move manufacturing activity to other countries where labor was much cheaper. This meant the well-paid, largely union jobs that since the end of World War II had enabled millions of people of color to climb up from poverty into the working class or middle class were no longer going to be there to provide that opportunity.

President Richard Nixon's policies of "benign neglect," coupled with the "war on drugs," had most of urban Black America feeling as if, instead of being on a slow-moving train headed toward socioeconomic progress, the train had been stopped and slipped suddenly into reverse. To say that these newly elected Black mayors had taken the reins of power during challenging times would be an understatement.[2]

Gary, Cleveland, and East St. Louis were all on the list of cities I planned to visit in order to study changes in the composition of their governance structures following the elections of their Black mayors. I was unable to visit Cleveland, but, because of its proximity to Northwestern University, I spent a week visiting Gary. I also went to East St. Louis for two days.

My visit to East St. Louis was unremarkable, but my stay in Gary was most rewarding. Everything I needed fell into place to enable me to study exactly what I had hoped to learn about: whether a discernible difference existed between Mayor Hatcher's fundamental approach to governance and that of his white predecessor. I had set up this project to be an empirical research study, and accordingly I had developed a number of questions—for people within the Hatcher administration as well as key informants outside the administration—about differences between the current and prior administrations. I was especially interested in the newly elected mayor's hiring and appointment practices. Fortunately, the mayor's office gave me great access to people and resources. I was able to interview Mayor Hatcher himself, his human rights director, one member each of the library board, the school board, and the city council, plus the editor of Gary's major daily newspaper, the *Post Tribune*, and the executive secretary of the Gary Chamber of Commerce.

I also made it my business to take the pulse of community awareness and attitudes about the difference between the current administration and those of times past by getting out into Gary's streets. I spent some time in a couple of local bars, where I sparked random conversations on this topic with at least a dozen different people, most of them Black.

In some ways, the views of Black interviewees and white interviewees diverged even more sharply than I'd expected. White interviewees believed he was doing poorly, and the Black interviewees believed he was doing exceptionally well under the circumstances.

I asked those who believed he was doing poorly to give me specific examples of what they meant. One primary complaint was that they believed he was favoring Black citizens over whites. As one specific example, the editor of the *Post Tribune* cited reports that Hatcher had reduced trash collection in white neighborhoods. When I spoke to Mayor Hatcher about this, he said that yes, he had reduced trash collection from twice weekly in *some* neighborhoods so that he could provide once weekly collections in *all* neighborhoods. Hatcher claimed that when he took office, he had learned that some neighborhoods, mostly Black, were lucky to receive regular trash collection once a month. The more affluent citizens of Gary—including the editor of their town's daily newspaper—were apparently unaware of this fact.

I also had to wonder what the Black interviewees meant by saying they thought he was doing a good job "under the circumstances." Hatcher reminded me that he was elected mayor in spite of opposition from his own political party. In fact, the leadership of the Democratic Party in Lake County and Calumet Township where Gary is located did not support his candidacy in 1968, and it was currently working against his reelection. He had won the election by a narrow margin, forcing him to fundraise outside of the city and state for his *reelection*, because the party wouldn't provide any financial support.

This lack of support from the county and township party apparatus had made governing in Gary even more challenging. During the days after my conversation with Mayor Hatcher, as I interviewed others and got to know the town a little, it became increasingly clear to me how difficult— nearly impossible—the situation was. For starters, Gary is not a city of the first class in Indiana, which means that the city budget must pass through a process of state approval before the city can levy any taxes. And as if having to go to the state for budget approval wasn't challenging enough, Hatcher also had to get both Calumet Township and Lake County to approve the city budget.

At the time of my visit to Gary in late July 1971, the city was still waiting for approval of its 1970 budget by the county and the township before it could be submitted to the state for final approval. If Mayor Hatcher hadn't become very adept at writing proposals for federal grants, the city coffers would have run dry. At that critical moment, like walking a tightrope without a net, Mayor Hatcher was keeping the city afloat by juggling funds he had secured from multiple federal agencies, especially the Office of Economic Opportunity and the Department of Labor—funds which allowed for some flexibility in terms of how they were expended. But the city's good fortune would be short-lived, because Richard M. Nixon was elected president in November 1968. When he took office in 1969, his administration began to move the federal government several giant steps away from the social activism of the Johnson years. Hatcher had been well connected with the

Johnson administration, but those connections counted for nearly nothing now. The political pendulum had swung hard to the right, and it was anyone's guess how long it might take for left and right to find common ground and again move the country toward the elimination of racial barriers and disparities.

How well was Mayor Hatcher doing "under the circumstances"? He used the powers available to him by city charter very intentionally to begin diversifying the makeup of the sixteen boards and commissions for which he had appointing authority. During the three years he had been in office, Hatcher had appointed fifty-seven people to such boards and commissions. This initiative was deeply meaningful and impactful because, in the aggregate, these boards and commissions controlled or held sway over nearly every aspect of Gary's civic life, from zoning and licensing to public safety, to the funding of public projects, to public health, to fairness in employment and housing policy. Mayor Hatcher used his ability to appoint to these boards and commissions as a means of getting around some of the political impediments and barriers that opponents had placed in his way. It was a powerful tool for making local government a more effective instrument for Gary's residents—all Gary's residents, regardless of race. Thirty-one of his appointees were Black, twenty-one were white, and five were Latino. At that time, there was a total of six Latinos on all of Gary's boards and commissions.

Hatcher had used his power to appoint to these boards and commissions intentionally to correct some of the diversity imbalance on the city's commissions and boards, but it would probably take a second term in office for full balance to be achieved.

The Fight for Inclusion at Home

My work in Gary would lead me to undertake a similar challenge upon my return to Minneapolis at the end of my Bush Fellowship in September 1971. I was eager to look at the demographic composition of some of the Minneapolis boards and commissions and to examine their levels of diversity, qualifications for service, and selection process. By now, I had come to see participation on these metropolitan boards as a potentially powerful way for low-income people of color both to participate more fully in democracy and to protect some of the gains made during the struggle for civil rights that might otherwise be undermined or lost during this period of government retrenchment we had now entered.

I was especially interested to learn if any Minneapolis bodies required qualifications like two of Gary's most restrictive ones: to be a redevelopment trustee, one had to be at least thirty-five years old and a resident of the city for at least five years; to qualify for appointment to the Redevelopment Commission, one had to be at least thirty-five years of age, a city resident, and a property owner. The redevelopment trustees, who had sole authority to select Redevelopment Commission members, were named by three different appointing authorities—the mayor, the city council, and the circuit court.

My review revealed no similar requirements. None of Minneapolis's fourteen different commissions and boards required specific qualifications for members. The charter or ordinance creating these bodies merely stated the purpose, size, appointing authority, and term of appointment. I didn't research the qualifications for membership on county or state commissions or boards, and I didn't have the opportunity to carry out a certifiable count, but anecdotally it appeared to me that the total number of people of color serving on Hennepin County and the State of Minnesota commissions and boards was in the single digits.

Prior to 1970, the public had limited knowledge and information about the various state and local boards and commissions, not to mention their various qualifications for membership. I followed the appointments of people to major commissions and boards at the state and local levels of government to track the racial diversity composition of those bodies. Shortly after returning from Northwestern University, I wrote an op-ed for the *Minneapolis Star* about minority representation in government. The article, published on March 28, 1972, under the headline "Minority Decision-makers," was based on research I had conducted both at Northwestern and upon my return to Minneapolis on the demographic composition of twenty commissions and boards in Minneapolis, in Hennepin County, and for the State of Minnesota. Most of these were comprised of volunteer citizens named by a number of different appointing authorities including mayors, city councils, and county commissioners. At the state level, the governor was the principal appointing authority. The final paragraph of this article read: "Blacks, Indians and other minorities can bring to the governmental process a kind of difference that is needed and has been missing. This difference is high on human values and comes from a different lifestyle. If our form of government is to survive, then it will be because difference has made the difference."

I believed these words then, and I still believe them now. During our present political moment, we are seeing a fierce backlash against the idea that diversity is a value worth fighting for. Corporations large and small have cut back on their diversity, equity, and inclusion (DEI) efforts or eliminated them altogether, evidently believing that all the recent years of diversity-related training have failed to prove that diversity is a valuable asset.

In 1970, the same year I won the Bush Leadership Fellows award, Minnesota elected a new governor, Wendell Anderson, who was a state senator and attorney. I was curious about how he would assemble his staff, and I would be counting the number of people of color named to his cabinet. Would he have a more diverse administration than his predecessors?

It certainly wouldn't take much to exceed their records. Governor Harold LeVander had not followed my suggestion—contained in a letter I had sent to him—to increase the number of Black people serving in his administration. I had reminded him that Black people could head other government agencies in addition to human rights. I wrote a similar letter to Governor Anderson before I left for Northwestern University in June 1971, reminding him also to recognize that there were Black people capable of managing more than just the Human Rights Department, typically the only place one could find a Black person in government during the sixties and early seventies.

By the time I began serving my fellowship, Anderson had already exceeded his predecessors. In addition to making the predictable and safe appointment of a Black person, Samuel Richardson, to head the Human Rights Department, he broke with tradition and named another Black person, Elmer Childress, to serve as commissioner of Veterans Affairs, thus becoming the first governor to name a Black person to head some other state agency. In addition, Anderson named a Black woman, Wenda Moore, as a top aide in his office, tasked with focusing on education issues. It was through the work of the governor's office under Moore's leadership that the legislature selected the first Black person, Josie Johnson, to serve on the University of Minnesota's Board of Regents (1971). Moore would later succeed Johnson on the board of regents when she left the state.

I never received a reply from either Governors LeVander or Anderson. But since Wendell Anderson's administration, all Minnesota governors have made appointments reflecting the state's increasingly diverse population—surely not as many as they should or could have, but momentum toward more diversity began with Anderson. And in 1978 the state legislature mandated that all vacancies on state boards and commissions must be published in the State Registry—a significant move toward transparency in the time before the internet.

The journey from no Black appointees to one, then to a succession of appointees at that one particular portfolio and only that one, and from there to an administration that featured more than one Black appointee at the same time may well seem to contemporary eyes like too paltry a victory to note or to celebrate. But in the world I had known as a youth in Mississippi, even though there were many precincts in which Black folk were an overwhelming majority, there was no Black representation at the municipal, county, state, or federal level whatsoever. The slightest whisper that someone from my community might be planning to register to vote could easily get that person killed.

Children in a democracy need to grow up knowing for a certainty that one person can make a real difference in this world and that when citizens join forces to make whatever change they deem necessary, real and lasting change is possible. Talented people with empathy, creativity, and a heart that urges them toward community service need to see serving in *government* as a career option—whether as elected officials, appointees to key commissions, or employees of government departments.

In order to build and maintain a vibrant democracy that works for everyone, as well as to attract the brightest and the best to serve, all citizens need a broad understanding of how the various institutions of government work. For me, there is no doubt that the public discussions we sparked during the early seventies about the importance of appointments and appointees have had an important and lasting impact on the strength of Minnesota's level of civic engagement. Voter turnout here is consistently high, and African American participation in every level of government is strong and getting stronger.

18

MINNESOTA GETS
AN OMBUDSMAN FOR
CORRECTIONS

It was 1971 and I had returned from my leave of absence to resume my position at Phyllis Wheatley. Although I had been away from my job for the entire summer, I had remained connected to PWCC and Minneapolis. My employees, my board, my neighbors, and my church family had kept me fully in the loop so that I could hit the ground running. I had been in Minneapolis for over six and a half years—at Phyllis Wheatley for a full six years—which meant I had been in Minneapolis four years longer than I had ever planned. Minneapolis felt like home now. I had fully committed myself to doing whatever I could to make things better for the people who needed help the most.

The street rebellions across the country had ended by 1971, but not the unrest. The Urban Coalition and many of our other community institutions continued to be challenged. There were concerns about unemployment, housing, and underrepresentation of minorities in both industry and government. The Urban Coalition had played a major role in creating the

Hennepin County pretrial diversion program (Operation de Novo), which was designed to both provide employment to ex-offenders and to divert them from the criminal justice system. Just as this program was being established, a major prison riot occurred at Attica prison in upstate New York, on September 9, 1971. Forty-three people were killed, ten of whom were prison staff. This bloody incident sent shock waves around the world.

The impact of Attica reverberated in Minnesota, which had its own problems. Just two years earlier, the state commissioner of human rights had sued the administration at the Minnesota State Prison at Stillwater for using tear gas on a group of Black and Native American prisoners held in solitary confinement; a court ruled that he did not have power to monitor rights within the prison. When the Attica riot occurred, Governor Wendell Anderson was less than nine months into his first term in office. He had appointed a fairly controversial commissioner of corrections, David Fogel, who came from California. The Fogel appointment was not popular with some members of the legislature who thought his policy record was much too left-wing.[1]

Fogel believed the United States sent far too many people to prison and that even a state like Minnesota probably had more people in its prisons than it should. Further, he believed riots tended to occur at prisons and jails that were overcrowded and where the more mundane grievances of the incarcerated were consistently ignored. Consequently, Fogel teamed with a colleague at the University of Minnesota Law School, Richard Clendennen, to draft a proposal for a corrections ombudsman modeled after the ombudsmen in Scandinavian countries. "Ombudsman" is a Swedish, Norwegian, and Danish term meaning *representative* or *proxy*; in this context, an ombudsman is a government appointee who investigates complaints and tries to resolve them by recommendations or mediation. Fogel presented his proposal to Governor Anderson and encouraged him to use his executive powers to create the position of Minnesota ombudsman for corrections.[2]

Fogel and his colleagues had secured a grant from the federal Office of Law Enforcement Assistance Programs to support an Ombudsman Project Initiative before an executive order was even issued. The program initially was seen as a demonstration project, funded for eighteen months; the hope was to secure public support for its continuation. Commissioner Fogel succeeded in getting Governor Anderson to issue "Executive Order No. 14 ... in regard to the establishment of an Ombudsman Commission for the purpose of establishing an office of Ombudsman for the Department of Corrections." The office was established as an independent state agency with the authority to investigate complaints from any source concerning an action of any division, official, or employee of the Minnesota Department of Corrections, the Minnesota Corrections Authority, as well as the board of pardons and all regional corrections or detention facilities. The office was funded for eighteen months by a grant from the Law Enforcement Assistance Administration, although the funds allocated were actually sufficient for only twelve months of operation.[3]

During Commissioner Fogel's community appearance at The Way, the issue of the ombudsman was an eagerly anticipated topic for discussion, centered on creating an ombudsman position that would report directly to the governor versus the Department of Corrections. No one really knew how this initiative would work, and there were also questions about how the person to fill this position should be selected. Fogel indicated that the executive order created the Ombudsman Commission, which would conduct the search and submit a name or names to the governor for his consideration. The commission was chaired by Control Data executive Norb Berg, and among its members were Minnesota Attorney General Warren Spannaus and Commissioner of Human Rights Sam Richardson.

Not many people in the meeting showed much interest in the ombudsman or really knew or understood much about the concept. I was familiar with the ombudsman concept, but my only reference point for how the position might operate was what little I knew about the experience of the Scandinavian countries, where the idea had originated. Hawaii had established an ombudsman office in 1967, but it was not well known. Given my long-term interest in corrections, I was highly intrigued and decided I would seek more information about the project and its potential.

The next day, I called Sam Richardson. He didn't know any more about the program than what had appeared in the newspaper. But since he was a member of the commission, he encouraged me to submit a letter of application with my resume to the governor's office.

I was uncertain about applying for the position because, in that same article about the creation of the ombudsman program, a University of Minnesota professor, Tom Murton, indicated he was going to apply for the position. Murton had gained recognition as a prison warden at an Arkansas state prison where a number of unmarked graves of prisoners had been unearthed. The governor, raising questions about how and why the prisoners were buried on prison grounds, relieved Murton from his position. Murton subsequently took a faculty position in the Sociology Department at the University of Minnesota. Despite the problems he'd left behind in Arkansas, I still thought his experience might give him an edge. When I discussed it with Mary Lou, she suggested that if I were interested, I should go for it. The other part of my uncertainty was that I wasn't sure I wanted to leave PWCC. Phyllis Wheatley had regained its prominence in the community, and I enjoyed my work there. And then I realized that Phyllis Wheatley and I had become almost synonymous. It was hard to think of one without the other, and that was not in the best interest of either me or the organization. A separation sometime in the future was inevitable, and we each could and would survive without the other.

I submitted my letter of application to the governor and continued about my business at Phyllis Wheatley. It must have been two or three weeks later that I received a telephone call from Sam Richardson asking me what had happened to my application. The commission was reviewing materials and had begun to schedule interviews. I told Sam I had submitted an application and when and where I had sent it. He promised to follow up and that he wouldn't let them proceed without reviewing it.

A few days after my conversation with Sam, the governor's office called to schedule an interview. I was offered a 2 p.m. interview time on the same day that I was scheduled to leave for a conference at Fisk University in Nashville, Tennessee, where I was set to make a presentation. Fortunately, I was able to change my scheduled flight to another that departed at seven the following morning.

I arrived about fifteen minutes early for the interview, but they were running a little behind and someone else was being interviewed at that moment. Paul Jones, state public defender, was in the waiting area. I asked if he, too, was there to interview for the position. He wasn't. He revealed that he was a member of the commission and that he had recused himself from participating in an interview of one of his staff but would rejoin the commission meeting for mine.

A million thoughts ran through my mind as I wondered what kind of questions they would ask. What kind of qualifications were they looking for in a candidate? Whatever the requirements, I was confident I was qualified. Besides, it didn't matter that much to me, because I didn't believe I would be offered the job and, if offered, I was uncertain I would accept it. Before too much longer, I was called in and introduced to the commission members. It was a good feeling to look around and realize how many of them I knew: Sam Richardson, human rights commissioner; Paul Jones, public defender; Dave Fogel, corrections commissioner; Warren Spannaus, attorney general; and Norbert Berg, senior vice president at Control Data. I had met Norb Berg when he took the lead in bringing the Control Data manufacturing plant to North Minneapolis in 1967.

As the interview began, I tried my best to read the room. I wondered how many commission members had already made up their minds and were simply extending me a courtesy interview. Regardless, it felt right to be there, and I was glad I was.

After the first few questions, I relaxed and began to feel comfortable and in control of where the questioning was headed. I focused on my greatest strengths, and I could feel their appreciation of what I could bring to the position growing. Some commission members were concerned about my limited experience in the field of corrections. Would that be a handicap? My response was that it could be more of an asset than a liability. I felt they were largely with me when I stressed my belief that the effectiveness of the ombudsman need not rest upon their specific experience in the field of corrections but upon their ability to understand and relate to people whose interests are frequently antagonistic. The effectiveness of the ombudsman would depend upon their ability to quickly develop credibility with both the incarcerated and corrections staff. I told them any experience I may have had in corrections was not nearly as valuable to me as the experience I had gained in working with hostile people in the welfare department, in the community center, or in executive suites. I believed my ability to form meaningful relationships with diverse groups of people whose points of view were often oppositional was key, and I suggested that being Black and having suffered the slings and arrows directed toward me in Mississippi, Maine, and the South Side of Chicago might hold some experiential value as well. In addition, I brought up my graduate social work degree from the University of Pennsylvania, providing a body of knowledge that enabled me to work effectively with people who needed to navigate through a considerable amount of trouble.

The interview was near an end, and I had talked mostly about myself. Not much time had been devoted to the specifics of the ombudsman program. I really couldn't say much about it, because I had not had an opportunity to read the proposal that established the program. There wasn't much I could say about the Department of Corrections either, because I didn't know much about its workings and I had no personal connections with its staff, nor with any of the currently incarcerated. Still, I left the room feeling very good about the interview, and I felt intuitively that I had probably done at least as well as anyone else the commission had interviewed. I was thanked, excused, and told that within a few days the commission would make its recommendation to the governor.

When I shared my interview experience with Mary Lou, she suggested that we discuss the job in greater detail when I returned from Nashville, because she had a feeling I was going to get an offer. At that point, I did begin to think very seriously about the job and how our lives might change if I accepted it—perhaps a bit too much. I didn't sleep well that night, which caused me to be late for my 7 a.m. flight. That was a *real* mistake, because now I suddenly had even more time to think about the ombudsman job as I made my way to Nashville.

What should have been a quick and routine trip turned into a nightmare I'll never forget. Instead of my nonstop flight to Nashville, I was placed on a jet flight to St. Louis with a prop-jet connection out of St. Louis to Nashville. But that flight between St. Louis and Nashville made four stops.

Each of those takeoffs and landings in our small plane wreaked havoc on my stomach, and I got sick several times before we arrived, *a full seven hours* after leaving Minneapolis. Fortunately, after getting something to eat and grabbing a few hours' rest, I felt much better and was able to make an effective presentation at the conference the next day.

When I returned from Nashville and discussed the interview with Mary Lou, I told her I was pleased with how I had done but thought it didn't mean much because this would be a political appointment, and I hadn't worked at all in the governor's campaign. I had been introduced to him shortly before the election, in the lounge of the Sheraton Hotel in downtown Minneapolis. Our meeting was perfunctory, memorable to me only because he later became governor. Still, Mary Lou felt better about my chances to be named to the position than I did and told me I should be prepared to be offered the job. I continued to go about my work at Phyllis Wheatley without much more thought about it. About a week after my Nashville trip, I received a phone call from Jim Pederson in Governor Anderson's office, informing me that I was one of two finalists for the position and that he wanted to schedule an interview with me. I was given an appointment for an interview with Pederson and Tom Kelm, the governor's chief of staff.

When I told Mary Lou about the call, she wanted to know what I planned to do when offered the position—she continued to be more confident than I was. We decided I would, indeed, take the job if the governor offered it to me.

The day of my interview, I showed up a few minutes early and told the receptionist I was there for a meeting with Jim Pederson. There were several other people waiting in the reception area, which was a poorly lit, somber-looking place, reminiscent of a funeral home. After a short wait, Pederson came out, introduced himself, and invited me to come with him to a large office, where I met Tom Kelm, the governor's chief of staff. Pederson was a tall, skinny man who chain-smoked. Kelm was a big, tall man with a booming voice that matched his size. Kelm had the reputation for being a no-nonsense person who ran a tight ship. They told me the commission had sent two names to the governor without recommendation. It was their job to interview the two finalists and *make* that final recommendation.

We talked for over an hour. We spent little time discussing the specifics of the job because, in truth, none of us knew what the job would entail. I had not yet read the proposal, but Pederson promised to give me a copy before I left the office. We talked more about my involvement at Phyllis Wheatley and the Urban Coalition and how those experiences had prepared me for the responsibilities of the ombudsman's office. I shared with them my understanding of how an ombudsman should function, regardless of the setting. I recognized that the ombudsman would not have the authority to force the Department of Corrections to accept and implement his recommendations. The role, as we then understood it, would be to investigate complaints, make recommendations to the appropriate officials, and encourage their adoption.

We eventually discussed whether my race would have any impact on my effectiveness in the office, and I told them I didn't think it was an issue that should concern anyone. It certainly didn't concern me. Although I knew some of the Black people incarcerated in the system might be at least slightly more inclined to give a Black ombudsman the benefit of the doubt, I felt confident that they would be much more concerned about whether or not I could be effective in helping them resolve their grievances. I didn't foresee any special problems with the corrections staff or administration. I recognized that they were almost all white, but I had worked with white people all my professional life and had been effective. I was beginning to look forward to being one more Black appointee to a major, highly visible position that wasn't titled commissioner of human rights. Our countrymen of every stripe, including our own people, need to see that we are as capable of wearing many hats and doing many things as anyone else.

Race is always a factor in the lives of Black people, and we've always had to do those things that feel crucial in the moment to our mental health and survival. So, I made it clear that I would not tolerate racial prejudice in any environment where I was expected to lead—directed neither toward me nor toward anyone else. This didn't mean I believed I was completely free of racial prejudice. I don't think anyone is. It did mean that I knew myself well enough to not allow my prejudices to get in the way of being fair and just in my interactions with other people.

The ombudsman needed to appoint a deputy and a secretary in order to start the program, and Kelm and Pederson wanted to know if I would have any problem considering a white person for the deputy position. I told them I wouldn't, provided the candidate was qualified, and I was not *limited* to considering whites only. I would give serious consideration to a non-Black person for the position *with the understanding that the final decision on such an appointment would be mine.*

I left the office feeling good about the interview. I knew I had made a good impression. I told Mary Lou when I got home that I thought I would be offered the job and that, if offered, I would accept it.

Up to this point, I had not shared with anyone outside my family that I was a finalist for this position. I was now beginning to think more seriously about what leaving Phyllis Wheatley would involve. I had truly enjoyed my work at the center, and I appreciated my good and loyal staff. I knew they would understand why I would take advantage of this opportunity, as I had always supported staff when any of them considered other employment opportunities. My philosophy was that I never hired people on the assumption that they'd hold the position for life. An employee should feel free to leave at any time, because their sojourn at Phyllis Wheatley should, ideally, be about preparing them for whatever comes next. My one request was that people leave in a responsible way that would enable me to provide a proper reference. I firmly believed an employee shouldn't stay in a position past the time that they were effective there—or beyond the time when the position was offering them opportunities for continued growth. I had begun to feel that my time at Phyllis Wheatley now matched this description on both counts. It was time to move on.

My interview with Kelm and Pederson was on a Thursday. The following Monday, I received a phone call from Pederson informing me that Governor Anderson wanted to appoint me to be Minnesota's first ombudsman for corrections. The governor wanted to announce the appointment as soon as possible, and he needed to know right away if I would accept. I indicated that I would gladly accept the position but asked for at least one day before it would be made public, because I needed to inform my board and staff at Phyllis Wheatley. He agreed to hold off until Tuesday evening to make the announcement. An article appeared in the Wednesday morning edition of the *Minneapolis Tribune* announcing my appointment.

Immediately after my discussion with Pederson, I informed Harry Davis, my board chair. I then met with staff and shared the news with them. This was the beginning of the next phase of my professional career in Minnesota.

My appointment received a great deal of local and national attention. Articles were written about the appointment and about me in the local newspapers as well as the *New York Times*. The headline in the *Minneapolis Tribune* for April 19, 1972, was, "State Convicts Get an Ombudsman." The article provided background information about me and a brief description of the position. It also said that the governor chose me from two names submitted by a ten-member commission, and that there had been eighteen applicants. I subsequently learned that Assistant State Public Defender Rosalie Wahl (later the first woman to serve on the Minnesota State Supreme Court) was one of the applicants the commission interviewed. I never learned the other name that had been submitted to the governor.

When the ombudsman appointment was announced, *Minneapolis Star* photographer Charles Bjorgen came to the PWCC office and took some publicity shots. The article ran on May 12, 1972, with the headline: "Ombudsman's Job Fits Him to a 'T.'" *Minnesota Historical Society*

I spoke with Catherine Young and Carrie H. Wallace.

19

ESTABLISHING THE OMBUDSMAN'S OFFICE

Wow, I thought. *I now have a job I know nothing about, and there really isn't anyone I know who can tell me what to do or how to do it.* In addition, I was leaving Phyllis Wheatley, where I knew every nuance of my work like the back of my hand, and where I enjoyed a connection to the community in which I worked and lived that was both profound and intimate. I would be giving all that up to take a position with an uncertain future, where political appointees tended to last only as long as the person who appointed them—if *that* long.

In fact, it made me nervous that people around me kept referring to the ombudsman's office as a project. To me, that word sounded perilously close to the word *experiment.* And as a family man, it made me a little queasy to think how I had given up a secure position to helm a project that might easily turn out to be unsustainable.

I would also be working in a setting where crises seemed to be the rule instead of the exception. April 12, 1972, was the date of my appointment, and I was able to negotiate July 10, 1972, as my starting date. Between those dates, I had to learn as much as possible about the project and what kind of outcomes those who established it were expecting. What resources were available for startup? What resources might be available, now and in the future, to help sustain it?

I began my preparation for the job by meeting with Fogel and Clendennen, the authors of the project proposal. They provided me with a copy of it, which essentially was a model ombudsman bill. It discussed and described the position's purpose and function, but how to implement these would be my responsibility. And I would have to figure it all out in a hurry.

I soon discovered that I had considerably less funding to work with than I'd been told to expect. Initial staffing for the program covered a full-time ombudsman with a salary of $23,000 per year, a deputy ombudsman at $17,000, and a half-time secretary at $6,000. The grant amount was about $75,000. Simple math told me it would take a miracle to get eighteen months' worth of service out of it. For example, we needed office space and equipment, but there was nothing in the budget for even these basic costs. While receiving this kind of information about the resources to support the project gave me yet another reason to reflect on my decision, I decided the opportunity and the cause were too great to worry about the budget. I believed we could overcome those obstacles. I'd have to adopt a management strategy that was as creative as it was frugal.

I had set up offices at Phyllis Wheatley when we moved to the new center, but in that instance, I had the advantage of resources I could control. Now I was in uncharted waters: I had no idea how to set up a government office, and I was at the mercy of the person assigned to work with me from the Department of Administration.

As it turned out, I needn't have worried. The ombudsman's office was treated, in many ways, like an extension of the governor's office. All the foundational administrative work was managed by the governor's staff. The people working to help me find space and equipment had to report their efforts to the governor's office, and I knew for certain that his commitment to the establishment of the ombudsman's office was ironclad. We were able to secure office space and sufficient supplies and equipment to set up shop at 136 Thirteenth Street in St. Paul. This was a historic building, the Dahl House, about a block from St. Paul–Ramsey (later Regions) Hospital.

The only thing left on my agenda now was to hire a deputy. I identified my top three candidates and interviewed each of them twice. My three finalists included a human resources manager from Honeywell who had served as a military policeman in the US Army, an attorney and recent graduate of the University of Minnesota Law School, and an individual who had worked for me at Phyllis Wheatley as a community organizer. The last was my choice to fill the position. The Honeywell employee and the community organizer were African American; the attorney was white. I knew that Kelm and Pederson would probably expect me to name the attorney as my deputy, in part because his professional training lent some gravitas and credibility to the position, but also because he was white and they had already expressed discomfort with the possibility of having two Black people in the top positions. Such a move wouldn't raise many eyebrows today, but in 1972, having two Black managers at the top of an office whose very creation had already been controversial would have created yet more controversy and political risk for its proponents. I had to be sure I could defend my choice, so I took my time and kept my own counsel about it for a while.

First, I needed someone who was intelligent, resourceful, and able to work well with people from diverse backgrounds. I was satisfied that all three candidates could fulfill those requirements. Second, I needed someone who had worked with people from communities and backgrounds and experiences that were similar to the people in our prisons and jails. All three candidates offered some of those qualifications, but the community organizer offered the most. A third consideration was the need for this person to have good communication skills and be comfortable interacting both with the incarcerated and with corrections staff. All three candidates could do that, especially the attorney. A fourth consideration was that the candidate needed to understand and be comfortable with the fact that the ombudsman did not have the authority to *require* corrections officials to accept any of their recommendations. Our effectiveness would depend upon the thoroughness of the investigation and the persuasiveness of our arguments. The attorney may have understood this point best, but my bias about attorneys was that they have a strong tendency to look *first* for legal solutions to problems. The final considerations were 1) that the person selected to this position would harbor no ambition to *be* ombudsman, 2) that they understood the enabling funding covered only twelve months, and 3) that they would be loyal to the ombudsman and the program. After my internal review, I was pleased with my choice of Melvyn Brown to be deputy ombudsman for corrections for the State of Minnesota. I was ready to defend my choice.

I knew Brown would be loyal and would not undercut me in the position. He had no interest himself in becoming ombudsman. But I believed strongly that the attorney did. I had recruited Brown from Sisseton, South Dakota, to come and work for Phyllis Wheatley—he had been working as an organizer on the Lake Traverse Reservation, home of the Sisseton-Wahpeton Dakota people. Before that, he had worked for the YMCA in both Dallas and Kansas City. At Phyllis Wheatley, Brown worked to help organize low-income public housing residents. He was very good, and I trusted him implicitly, which was important to me as I ventured into brand-new territory.

I submitted the three folders to the governor's office for Kelm and Pederson to review before I made the appointment. A couple of days later I stopped by to pick them up, along with the papers I needed to process in order to complete the appointment.

Pederson met with me and said he thought the attorney would make a fine deputy. I told him the attorney was not my first choice. I liked the other two candidates better, both of whom were Black. He was furious. He thought I'd understood that the deputy *had to be white*. He believed I had made that commitment at an earlier interview prior to my appointment. I recalled that discussion with him and stated that the question was whether or not I would have any problem with naming a white deputy. My response had been that I would have no problem with that, as long as I was not limited to considering white candidates only. Under no circumstance would I have *promised* to name a white person as deputy. I knew how political systems and governmental organizations work: the perception would be that the Black person was placed in that position to make the governor look good while the white deputy would really be in charge.

Pederson believed the credibility of the program would be in question with two Black men in charge. I hardly thought so. I told Pederson that the incarcerated would be more concerned about whether we could help them resolve their complaints than the color of their helpers. I also didn't think the staff and administrators in the prisons would be overly concerned about the race of the ombudsman and his deputy. Furthermore, I had always believed trust isn't something that can be assumed or conferred. It is earned. Race would not be a negative factor in terms of our ability to earn credibility and trust. The only relevant factor would be our demonstrated ability to do the job well. I left Pederson's office with the issue unresolved. He suggested we meet again with Kelm, the governor's chief of staff.

I discussed the issue with Mary Lou when I got home. I told her they wanted me to name a white deputy and I was prepared to tell them they could have the job back if it came to that. She suggested I calm down and play it through to the end. "You're really in the driver's seat. They're not going to want this to appear as if the governor, who is making the appointment, is a racist."

A few days later I was back in the governor's office, this time to meet again with Kelm and Pederson. We rehashed the discussion I had earlier with Pederson. Kelm suggested that since the program was experimental, the legislature would have to pass a bill to approve it, and having two Black men in charge could make it difficult for them to support. I wondered if they were suggesting that the Minnesota legislature was a racist body. I was sure I had had a great deal more experience in working with white people in positions of power than white people had had in working with Black people in positions of power. I had learned over time not only how to survive, but how to thrive in the white man's world. I was confident I had the necessary skills and experience to do well in this position, Black deputy and all. I didn't believe that either the legislature or the Department of Corrections staff would be at all concerned about the race of the deputy. The deputy simply would not have that kind of visibility. If he did, he would quickly become a former deputy, or I would become a former ombudsman.

The discussion continued without much progress until, finally, I said this was one battle I had to win if I were going to be effective in this new position. After all, the ombudsman's authority was limited to investigating and recommending—the *acceptance* of his recommendations would depend for the most part on his powers of persuasion. I told them it seemed, at this point in time, that I was not being persuasive, and I added that I didn't like being put in a position of having to say what I would not do. That was how I was feeling about the deputy's job. Finally, I said, "What I *am* going to say, however, is that I will not give the matter any further consideration unless I am personally asked to do so by the governor." I told them they should arrange for me to meet with him and agreed that if he personally asked me to name a white person as deputy, I would have to think about it and ask myself, "How important is it for me to be the Minnesota ombudsman?"

It was a gamble, and a leap of faith—but I simply believed that once this "issue" was stated to the governor in plain English, and if he had *to listen to himself defend the need for a white deputy out loud*, he would quickly discover that the issue raised was much more important to his deputies than it really was to him. If I was wrong, I was ready to walk away. The person I wanted to name was simply a better fit, and I knew I could work with him. Furthermore, I couldn't afford the luxury of taking time to get to know my new deputy—we'd have to hit the ground running.

We had precisely twelve months to make this experiment work. In reality, we had less time than that, because we would have only six months to develop a track record and convince the legislature the program warranted further support. To their credit, after they heard me out and mulled all this over, Kelm and Pederson decided it would *not* be necessary for me to meet with the governor. I could go ahead and make my appointment. I had learned a valuable lesson about the importance of sticking to my guns and about how to craft an argument persuasive enough to win in a high-stakes situation like this. Settling this issue became a great trial run for the kind of persuasive clarity and intensity I would need in order to be successful as ombudsman. From that point forward, I had unqualified support from the governor's office.

Family Respite

My tenure at Phyllis Wheatley ended with a special recognition dinner at Skip's Barbeque, organized by Gleason Glover of the Minneapolis Urban League. It was his way of expressing thanks and appreciation for reaching out to him when he first came to Minneapolis as the Urban League's new executive director. At the time, Phyllis Wheatley and the Minneapolis Urban League had the only two Black executive directors of United Way–funded agencies. Glover and I often shared our frustrations and challenges over the lack of adequate financial support for the respective work of our organizations in the community. But my leaving Phyllis Wheatley did not end my commitment to Minneapolis, especially North Minneapolis. I maintained my relationship with the Urban Coalition and continued to support the work it was doing.

There was one more thing I wanted to do before assuming my new position, and that was to take my family on a long vacation. In this case, "long" referred more to the distance we traveled than to the amount of time we'd be able to spend together. We planned to drive from Minnesota to Mississippi for a wedding, but our first stop was a side trip to Denver, Colorado, where we participated in a meeting of the Conference on Inner-City Ministries (CICM) of the American Lutheran Church, an organization that I had played a role in helping to launch. The CICM was another organization that had grown out of the street violence of the sixties, brought about by a group of us in the American Lutheran Church who were disappointed that the church was failing to play a more prominent role in responding to the urban crises of those times.

I did a lot of thinking behind the wheel as we drove through Colorado, New Mexico, Texas, Arkansas, and then on into Mississippi about how to set up an ombudsman's office and what the work of an ombudsman could encompass. I even thought about it as I took pictures at my niece's wedding and on the drive back. We took a bit of a detour, because I wanted to show my children the University of Illinois Champaign–Urbana campus, where I had gone to college.

I graduated from the university in 1956. It was 1972 now, and much had changed since then. When I looked around for familiar landmarks,

I noticed new buildings everywhere, even on the south campus, which was mostly a cornfield when I was there. I must have looked extremely disoriented to the kids. During a rare pause in their general rowdiness, my nine-year-old son, Chris, asked, "Dad, are you sure you went to school here?" I resisted the temptation to throw him out of the car and kept driving.

I was disappointed that the detour I'd planned hadn't made much of an impression. But our little side trip provided one small bit of reinforcement for an assumption that had always been fundamental to our family culture: all our children would attend college and complete a degree. It was pleasing to me to see that they seemed to understand and accept this as a given.

Even with a car full of noisy kids, I found I was able to use my hours behind the wheel as quality thinking and planning time. As we continued to roll homeward on the final stretch of our journey, my thoughts about the challenge of the new position awaiting me grew more focused and intense. We got back to Minneapolis on July 7, 1972, and my first day as Minnesota ombudsman for corrections was July 10.

The New Adventure Begins

My deputy, Mel Brown, and I started our jobs on the same day, along with a part-time secretary (eventually replaced by Kathleen Coon, who remained on staff for as long as the ombudsman's office lasted). Before I could even begin to settle in, I received a call from a radio station in New York City. The interviewer wanted to interview me live on the air. He was fascinated that Minnesota would create such a position and would name someone with my background to fill it. He wanted to know all about the job. How would I be able to gain the trust of the incarcerated and the prison administrations, in order to be effective? I acknowledged that being an ombudsman was new and challenging, but I believed I would find ways to be effective.

After that first day in office, I realized I would have to add being interviewed to the multitasking mix in order to make this thing work. The creation of an ombudsman for corrections was a big thing, and the media was all over it, both locally and nationally. Dozens of articles were written about the Minnesota ombudsman during our first year of operation, even before I was on the job. Local papers covered it closely, and later that year the *New York Times*, the *Christian Science Monitor*, the *Boston Globe*, the *Buffalo Times*, the *Los Angeles Times*, and newspapers in Florida, Kansas, and God knows where else were writing about the Minnesota ombudsman. I worried a bit that all that media attention could get in the way of being effective in the job if I weren't careful.

When I finally got a copy of the program's budget, I learned that our situation was even worse than expected. We had funding for only nine months. If I couldn't quickly find additional financial support, we wouldn't last long enough for the legislature to fund us. A deputy, a part-time secretary, and I weren't going to be an adequate staff.

I was still trying to figure out how to manage the budget when a folder was sent over to my office with over a hundred letters sent by prisoners to the governor. While there had been considerable publicity about the ombudsman program, I couldn't assume the incarcerated had heard anything but rumors about it. So we had to develop a plan for informing everyone in all of Minnesota's state correctional facilities about the existence of the program, provide instructions on how to file a complaint, and establish procedures for receiving complaints.

The ombudsman's responsibilities covered eight state correctional facilities—six adult and two juvenile. Any plan we devised for communicating with the incarcerated needed to be simple. Many of them didn't have ready access to telephones, and their mail, both incoming and outgoing, was censored. We needed the Department of Corrections to give its assurance that communications with the ombudsman would always be an exception to this, that letters would not be opened or censored in any way.

The commissioner of corrections was on board because he had initiated the program, but this was not necessarily the case with every warden or superintendent. For example, the warden and superintendent at the Stillwater and St. Cloud correctional facilities were skeptical about the program, and about me. Neither one of them knew me before I took the position, and they both believed that because I didn't have a background in corrections, I would have a difficult time understanding the complexities of running a prison. I decided to focus on developing credibility with those two facilities, because as the largest in the system, they would more than likely generate the largest number of complaints.

With only a deputy and part-time secretary, it would be difficult for me to find the time needed to develop a trusting relationship with the leaders of those two institutions. It was becoming more and more apparent to me how crucial it was to find some additional resources just to keep our doors open.

Since 1967, I had been building a tremendous network within the corporate and nonprofit communities. My work with the Urban Coalition had exposed me to a cornucopia of corporate, human, and capital resources, and I had a similar network of resources to explore for possible assistance in the nonprofit world. I knew there were probably public resources available too, but I needed to quickly find and activate those that were readily available. I figured my status as a Bush Foundation Leadership Fellow could help me find them.

My corporate and nonprofit networks came through with flying colors. On the corporate side, my knight in shining armor was Control Data's Norbert Berg, chair of the Ombudsman Commission. My nonprofit champion was the Bush Foundation. As one would expect, there was a great deal of overlap between the management of these resources.

Berg wanted the program to succeed not only because he understood the political risk the governor had taken: establishing the office was not going to earn him any votes, because the incarcerated represented a considerable constituency who *couldn't* vote. The program also fed Berg's sense of *mission* in helping incarcerated citizens resolve their grievances within the construct of the prison community: it was simply the right and just thing to do. Also, Control Data had begun to cultivate relationships with Minnesota and other states to develop prison industries that would help the incarcerated learn vital computer technology.

Many Americans don't know that inmates in US correctional facilities create a wide variety of products for American industry—from license plates to military and sports team uniforms. These prison-based industries pay pennies on the dollar to what inmates would earn for similar work on the outside, but beyond that, the skills for most of those industries would pay them barely above minimum wage. Berg's intent was to create prison jobs that allow released inmates to find jobs that paid a living wage—jobs that would catapult workers into the middle class.

When one of the incarcerated at Stillwater shared with Berg the prisoners' concerns that the ombudsman needed more staff support to be able to handle the grievances coming out of Stillwater alone, Berg became open to helping me consider any practical staffing options that might be available at the time. Two recent developments made the exploration of staffing options timely for the ombudsman. First, in March 1972 Governor Anderson established the Governor's Loaned Executive Action Program (LEAP). Corporations could loan an executive to a state agency, at the corporation's expense, for a specified period of time, using their expertise to help that agency implement a program or strategy, or to complete a project. The length of time the loaned executive devoted to an agency varied, but it could be up to a year. In rare instances, an executive might opt to stay and become a state employee. Berg had recently promoted Richard Connor, one of his employees, to vice president, but Control Data needed approximately six months to set up his new office and further develop the scope of his new assignment. Control Data was willing to offer Conner to the Office of the Ombudsman for Corrections through LEAP. I had met Conner when Control Data was establishing its North Minneapolis manufacturing plant, and I believed he would be a great asset to our office.[1]

We agreed that Conner would focus on developing legislation that would establish the office as an independent state agency reporting directly to the governor. Enacting such legislation would make the ombudsman a member of the governor's cabinet. Conner engaged in other activities as well, such as investigating prisoner complaints. This assignment helped him develop a full sense of the overall operation and impact of the program, since we knew we would want to call on him to help us present our report to the legislature on the program's first year.

The second timely event was my decision to approach the Bush Foundation for a grant to help support the operation of the office for at least one year. Humphrey Doermann, Bush Foundation president at the time, was skeptical. Making a grant to a state agency was very much out of their norm. He was also concerned that the agency was temporary, established by executive order with no assurance that the state was prepared to make it permanent. He didn't want it to seem as if the foundation were attempting to influence the outcome of a political process. Finally, he would have to be able to convince his board that this was a proper investment of foundation resources.

Doermann eventually agreed to proceed with the application process and assigned Program Officer Emily Galusha to work with me. This was a unique grant application process because, for once, I wasn't competing against any other grantee applicants. This fund would be tailor-made for us, and approval would depend upon how convincingly I could tell my story, and the quality of assurance I could provide that it would ultimately be a good investment for the foundation.

I also needed to assure them that a grant would not be seen as an attempt to influence the legislature. Emily Galusha provided outstanding counsel throughout the application process, which resulted in approval of my request for $135,000. In addition, I had applied through the Governor's Commission on Crime for a continuation of the original federal grant through 1973.

The Bush Foundation grant was available for the calendar year 1973, which enabled me to hire two field investigators (also referred to as ombudsman's assistants) and a research analyst. The addition of a research analyst position enabled us to collect and analyze the data that would help us document the program's effectiveness. I was committed to staffing the ombudsman's office with individuals who could work well with both incarcerated people and corrections staff and who reflected the racial and ethnic diversity of the prison population. I also decided to develop the program's capacity to utilize the services of college and university interns. During my more than ten-year tenure as ombudsman, I was able to supplement the staff with interns from the University of Minnesota School of Social Work, the University of Minnesota Law School, the Atlanta University School of Social Work, and the Minnesota State Colleges and Universities system. My new hires included an American Indian man, a white woman, and a white man, as well as a Black man and a white woman who served as interns.

I felt free to hire the people I really wanted because all of the professional employees were considered "unclassified"—not covered by civil service rules. This gave me maximum flexibility in terms of recruiting the kind of people I believed would be the best fit for the work we would be doing. I wanted to avoid hiring people with strong preconceived opinions about prisoners or prison staff or who had established relationships with anyone in the corrections system, so I avoided recruiting anyone with prior correctional experience, especially anyone who had worked for the Minnesota Department of Corrections or at any of its facilities. And it was *especially* important to me that none of the staff, including me, had relationships with anyone within the corrections system that they believed needed to be protected. I needed staff members who could be unbiased in their approach to their work and who were good listeners—people who would base their decisions on the facts they learned from their investigations. These principles formed the bedrock of my overall strategy to staff the ombudsman's office with people who afforded the program its maximum opportunity for success.

The first six months of the program involved securing funding sources, recruiting staff, processing prisoners' complaints, and responding to the local, national, and international interest in the program. Nearly every day I would receive a phone call from a newspaper or magazine reporter. I always took time to answer questions, because I believed the external interest in the program was an asset that could be used in our relationship with the governor's office and the legislature. This was a time in our history when Minnesota was widely seen as a progressive state with creative approaches toward social justice issues.

A Make-or-Break Moment

The Minnesota State Prison at Stillwater had been in the news in July 1972 because of a prison break. Three prisoners had successfully escaped from the highest security area—in fact, they had managed to get over the prison walls and completely off facility grounds. Fortunately, they were quickly captured and returned to prison. But the capture of one man involved a gunfight, during which he wounded a deputy sheriff.

When these escapees were returned to the facility, they were not warmly welcomed back by the thoroughly embarrassed prison staff. Quite the contrary. They were immediately confined to the segregation unit with virtually no privileges. This was standard punishment for escape attempts.

I visited the men in the segregation unit upon their request. All three had complaints about how they had been treated since their return. Principal among their concerns was a lack of medical care for injuries sustained during their capture, as their request to see a doctor had been denied. They also complained about not having access to their public defender, a request which also had been denied. I promised the men that I would look into their complaints and get back to them. I knew my follow-up with them would be closely watched by everyone who was observing the ombudsman's office— and it would be critical to my relationship with these prisoners later. On my way out of the prison, I stopped and visited with the warden about the men. He was not at all sympathetic about their situation, saying they should count themselves lucky not to have sustained more severe injuries than they had. In fact, he put an exclamation point on that thought by adding that any injuries they had sustained were well deserved. But in the end, he did agree to allow a doctor to examine them in their cells.

A few weeks passed, and activities in the ombudsman's office continued to build on our early momentum. Much of our energy and focus now went into establishing our routine for visiting the different correctional facilities. We still had to overcome some staff resistance at Stillwater prison and St. Cloud State Reformatory. It was difficult for some of the staff at both institutions to accept that the ombudsman had the authority to enter their institutions at any time and review their records. But I didn't have a lot of time to think about what was happening in the corrections system and the ombudsman's role in it, because I found myself constantly reacting to what was going on around me. There was much to learn and much to understand. And I had to take it all in and process it as quickly as possible.

Perhaps the most startling example occurred on the morning of October 27, 1972. I was having breakfast when my phone rang and a frantic Bruce McManus, warden at the state prison at Stillwater, wanted to know how quickly I could get out there. "Why?" I asked. He told me the three infamous escapees who'd been confined to segregation were holding a correctional officer hostage. They were threatening to kill him and set the segregation unit on fire unless their unspecified demands were met. And he added that the prisoners had asked to see the ombudsman. I told him I would come right away, but it could take me up to forty-five minutes to get there from my house.

I made the twenty-six-mile trip in thirty minutes. On the way, I was continually asking myself, *What am I supposed to do when I get there?* This was not Hollywood. This was for real. And I had no plans to become a hero. I also knew that as ombudsman, I had no authority to force anyone to do anything, which meant the only role I could play would be that of a mediator, a good listener, and a go-between to help both sides think carefully about the consequences of their actions.

I pulled up to the facility, parked in a hurry, and rushed into the warden's office. There with the warden was the deputy commissioner of corrections. As we sorted out our next urgent steps, we decided that the warden wouldn't be part of the group that went back to talk with the prisoners. He was too volatile—his anger truly volcanic now—and his mere presence could escalate the situation. As we proceeded through the prison gates, I was startled by what I saw: dozens of corrections officers anxious to go into action, armed with double-action shotguns, tear gas canisters, and gas masks, not to mention full of adrenaline. The tension in the air was palpable and the place was ripe for disaster. *Attica,* I thought. *No, we can't have an Attica here in Minnesota. We're too civilized for that. We've got to find a way out of this mess.* I had to wonder if I was the sole representative of the state in the room who was actively clinging to this hope. As I quickly scanned the faces of the deputy and the men at his command, I felt reasonably certain I was. So, I took a leap of faith and convinced the deputy commissioner to let me take the lead. "Please don't challenge anything I say or do," I said. "I know enough not to put anyone at undue risk."

When we arrived in the segregation unit cellblock where the hostage was being held, I could see that he hadn't been harmed, and the unit looked remarkably good considering the circumstances. There were a couple broken chairs, smashed face bowls in a couple of the cells, and a moderate amount of water on the floor, but no fires had been set and the hostage was not restrained.

But the men holding the hostage were highly agitated, ranting and raving about what they would do if their demands weren't met, even though up to that moment no specific demands had been made. The three ranged in age from twenty to thirty-two years old. The youngest was by far the most volatile and the most challenging to deal with. The oldest was more levelheaded, more mature, and much easier to communicate with. I had to figure out how to strike an uneasy balance between directing my initial discussion toward the older prisoner without ignoring the younger, because he could easily cause the whole thing to blow up.

My first question to the men, keeping primary eye contact with oldest, was: "Are you ready to die?"

My question startled him. "What do you mean, 'am I ready to die?'"

"Just that," I said, "because there are a couple dozen officers standing ready to storm this place and take you out." I paused. "To me, some of them looked more than ready—happy even—to charge this place. They won't do it as long as we're in here talking and I tell them we're making progress. So it looks to me that you guys don't want to come to your death in this cellblock."

The youngest spoke up and let it be known he wasn't afraid to die, but he assured us that the hostage would die first. I commented that I was sure he wasn't afraid of dying, but it didn't make sense to do it here. I told them I was there to help them articulate their grievances and get the best results I could. I reminded them that when we first met, I'd been helpful in getting them medical attention. They acknowledged this, and suddenly, the atmosphere in the room lightened just a little.

We seized the moment and began to talk more specifically about what they wanted. They were extremely unhappy that their public defenders had not visited them after they had been charged with prison escape and assault. The outgoing mail they'd written had not been allowed to go out. They had been denied all visitors and essentially cut off from the outside world. And finally, they didn't trust the officers on their cellblock. They believed themselves to be living under the constant threat of harm by angry officers who felt embarrassed by the prison break.

I had arrived on their cellblock at approximately 8 a.m. Three hours later, our conversation was still going. Our discussions were wide-ranging, intense, and not always on topic, but that was fine with me. My goal was just to keep them talking until I could tangibly sense that some of their rage had dissipated.

When I felt reasonably confident that moment had arrived, I asked them for their bottom-line request to end the siege. They were reluctant to give me a bottom line, because they didn't trust the prison administration to stand behind *any* promises the officials might make. I assured them the department would deliver on any commitment made. My role was to witness commitments made by all parties involved in the discussion and to monitor the implementation of any and all commitments made by the Department of Corrections. They agreed that as long as I documented and witnessed their demands and oversaw the implementation, they would state their bottom line. I also reminded them that they couldn't make illegal requests. For example, their request couldn't include any promises not to be prosecuted for the prison escape for which they'd already been charged.

The men were ready to make their specific demands. First, they wanted assurances that the facility administration would not directly retaliate against them by charging them with prison rules infractions and placing them in isolation. In fact, all three believed they would be safer if they could be transferred to another prison. But the Department of Corrections said transfer to another facility was out of the question. The likelihood of finding another facility willing to take them on an immediate transfer was highly unlikely. No facility anywhere would be eager to accept prisoners who had taken an officer hostage. But since the concern was for their own immediate safety, the deputy commissioner offered the option of a temporary transfer to a nearby county jail, where I would have access to visit them and address any complaints they might have.

Their second and seemingly most important request was that they be able to have a visit from their court-assigned public defender. All of their prior efforts to secure such visits had been unsuccessful. Finally, they wanted to be able to contact their families, to let them know they were alright.

At approximately noon, we reached an agreement and the prisoners were immediately transferred. Two were sent to the Washington County jail in Stillwater and one was transferred to the Dakota County jail in Hastings. I visited the men the following day and met with the jail officials. They assured the men they would be safe and that they had the same privileges as any of the other people incarcerated there. I contacted the Washington County Public Defender's office and was assured that a public defender would visit the prisoners the following day.

Two weeks later, all three men were returned to the prison at Stillwater. They were subsequently tried on the prison escape charges, but not for the later hostage-taking incident. All three men were eventually transferred to prisons in other states. One of them, John Greshner, who had been twenty at the time, is still confined in a federal correctional facility in Phoenix, Arizona. His scheduled release date is June 29, 2055, at age 103.

A few days following the hostage incident, I received a letter of commendation from Governor Wendell Anderson. The letter gave high praise for the ombudsman's effectiveness during a time of crisis. A successful resolution of the hostage crisis earned the ombudsman's office high levels of credibility among both corrections staff and the incarcerated. Neither the corrections staff's nor the inmates' lives were put at risk. I wasn't expecting any thanks from anyone, but many diverse voices within the system said to me or members of my staff that they were thankful for the existence of the ombudsman's office and that people really felt in their bones that my presence that day helped prevent another Attica.

The ombudsman's office was still operating under an executive order, not yet one year from the date of issuance, so this success was important. We needed to have a strong presence, first and foremost, in the field, investigating and resolving prisoners' complaints, because the last thing we needed was an unsuccessfully resolved prison crisis; and second, at the legislature, understanding that not all legislators supported the governor or this program.

To move a successful bill through the legislature, we needed to document the positive impact the office was having on the Minnesota correctional system. The deputy ombudsman and I stayed on top of prisoner complaints at Stillwater and St. Cloud and worked with State Planning Agency staff to prepare a progress report on the first six months of the ombudsman's office. The six-month report included the outcome of the hostage incident at Stillwater and a racial disturbance at the Willow River Camp correctional facility.

Conner used this report in his advocacy work at the legislature. He worked with key legislators such as Senators George Conzemius and Dr. B. Robert Lewis, plus Representatives John Milton and Don Moe, to get a bill introduced.

The 1973 legislature passed a bill establishing the Office of the Ombudsman for Corrections with a sunset provision, specifying that the agency would be discontinued in 1977 unless reauthorized by the legislature. This meant that we would have four years to prove our office's worth. My approach was to continue to respond to prisoners' complaints and look for opportunities to address systemic issues that could be changed to benefit the majority of the incarcerated. I directed our focus toward systematically tracking prisoners' complaints so that we could identify patterns of grievances.

20

BUILDING AND
SUSTAINING CREDIBILITY

One defining, complicated feature of my life as ombudsman was that I had authority without power. Given this reality, my effectiveness in office depended heavily upon the credibility of the ombudsman's office and our reputation for doing good work. In the March 1976 edition of *Trial Magazine*, I wrote:

> *The ombudsman has the authority to investigate in response to complaints, or on his own initiative, any act of the Department of Corrections. He may prescribe the manner in which complaints may be made, reviewed, and acted upon. He may determine the scope and manner in which investigations are to be made. The ombudsman has the authority to request and be given any information within the possession of the Department of Corrections that he considers pertinent to his inquiry. The legislation creating the ombudsman is rather explicit in describing the ombudsman's authority. But, even so, it is obvious that the real authority is to investigate complaints and make recommendations to appropriate officials. The ombudsman can publish any investigation findings at an appropriate time. The authority to investigate is not taken lightly. It can be a very persuasive tool.*

During the early phases of the program, incarcerated people with complaints—and others, even members of the legislature—wondered how effective the ombudsman could be without having the authority to *force* the department to accept his recommendations. During the deliberations on the bill, at least one member of the legislature asked if we wanted to grant the ombudsman this power. My experience in the job thus far had actually brought me around to the belief that the lack of authority was not necessarily a liability. Consensus building, especially in a policy arena as full of ideological differences as corrections, absolutely depends on the ability to persuade.

Among the most frequent complaints of the incarcerated were some of the chronic, vexing issues of life in institutions like these: the denial of visits from loved ones; the denial of access to institutional programs; theft; the denial of access to adequate health care. This latter issue was of especially high concern to the women, who were nearly unanimous in their assessment that their medical complaints were never believed or taken seriously.

But perhaps the most frequent complaint was about the denial of parole. When parole was denied, the incarcerated wanted to know why—but they found the parole board's process to be so mysterious and opaque as to leave them completely in the dark about this issue of paramount importance to them. Without meaningful feedback about why you were denied parole this time, how could you better situate yourself for next time?

It took a couple of years, but in 1976 the parole board responded to our recommendations and made the pathway toward a successful bid for parole much clearer and easier for incarcerated people to comprehend. Real progress was also made in terms of providing better, more reliable and humane medical services, especially for incarcerated women.

Building my *personal* credibility as ombudsman became even more important when, shortly after the end of the 1973 legislative session, our loaned executive, Richard Conner, returned to Control Data to take up his newly established position. This meant I no longer would have the service of a full-time staff person to assist with legislative relations. I would now have to more fully assume that responsibility, which I felt I could do, in part because the Bush Foundation grant had allowed the hiring of additional staff so I could

The staff of the Office of the Ombudsman for Corrections, about 1973. I am at center, in a white sweater with a stripe; from me, clockwise, are Randall Halverson, Richard Spratt, Maureen Walljee, Mel Brown, and Mary Jo Reiter.

focus on building and sustaining credibility with leadership in the legislature, the governor's office, and the Department of Corrections. One of the new staff hires was Randall Halverson, a research assistant, who would help ensure we were collecting and analyzing the kind of data that could enable us to discern patterns of grievances and demonstrate the effectiveness of our interventions. Halverson also became staff liaison to the legislature. He was immensely effective in organizing the data we were collecting into an annual report that helped to inform the legislature, the governor, and the public of the work we were doing.

After Halverson was hired, we immediately moved to engage the State Planning Agency to conduct an assessment of the agency's progress during its first two years, hoping to use the assessment to remove the sunset provision from the ombudsman bill. We were confident the outcome would be positive. I had hired the right people—and in sufficient numbers—to fill the staff positions that directly responded to prisoners' complaints; they understood what needed to be done, and they understood the value of credible relationships both with the incarcerated and with facility staff. My job was to help them deal with any challenges that might get in the way of developing those relationships. For example, I encouraged my staff to remind corrections staff of their unlimited access to each facility. My staff knew that if they were challenged, I would directly intervene to help clarify the authority of the ombudsman.

The ombudsman had an additional ally. The year the ombudsman was established, the Office of the State Public Defender also received a federal grant to establish Legal Assistance to Minnesota Prisoners (LAMP); Mel Goldberg, a Northwestern University Law School faculty member, was recruited to be its executive director.

In 1973 we saw a good example of how the partnership could work. US Federal District Court Judge Phillip Neville used a court order to require the Department of Corrections to provide due process for prisoners charged with rules infractions in adult correctional facilities. This court order resulted from legal action initiated by LAMP, with collaboration from the ombudsman, on behalf of the inmates at the Stillwater correctional facility. In response, the commissioner of corrections ordered the creation of the Inmates Disciplinary Due Process System at Stillwater, St. Cloud, and Shakopee. The new process gave hearing officers the ability to conduct disciplinary proceedings, provided representation at hearings for accused inmates, gave inmates the ability to challenge their accusers, and established an appeals process.

To ensure the new process was understood, LAMP, public defenders, private attorneys, and the ombudsman participated in the training of the first hearing officers selected for the program. The inmate due process system, with some modifications, is still in force today at all of the department's adult correctional facilities. A representative from the ombudsman's office periodically monitors disciplinary hearings and informs the Department of Corrections when there is a perceived lack of fidelity to its rules.

Sustaining credibility required continuous effort. Our credibility was challenged whenever there were changes in leadership at the various institutions, including the Department of Corrections central administration, the governor's office, and the legislature. I understood that credibility cannot be conferred—it had to be earned—and to keep earning it, we had to keep looking for opportunities. To be sure, even as a newcomer it was easy to see that the corrections system abounded with opportunities for this.

The next credibility test for the ombudsman's office came soon after a disturbance in Stillwater's Cell Block A, which led to a lockdown and strip search of each prisoner and his cell. The facility's approach to the search was as it had always been: cell by cell, staff would enter and force the incarcerated to strip naked and submit to a complete search, including body cavities. All items of clothing, bedding, and furnishings were chaotically tossed aside, with no effort taken to preserve an inmate's property. Then, adding insult to injury, following the search, cells were often left open and unsecured. This kind of search process invariably led to the loss and destruction of prisoners' personal property, which had not been a concern of the prison administration in the past. Historically, the corrections system had never been held liable under any circumstance to respect or protect prisoners' personal property.

Following the reopening of Cell Block A, the ombudsman's office was overwhelmed with prisoners' complaints. In response, we decided to open a group complaint on behalf of all prisoners in the cellblock. Our entire office participated in this investigative process, during which we interviewed all Cell Block A inmates and staff, as well as the warden and members of his administrative staff. We found that the prison was liable for loss and destruction of prisoners' personal property and that it should entertain claims from prisoners for this. We submitted a written recommendation to that effect to Ken Schoen, the commissioner of corrections, but Warden Bruce McManus resisted participating in any such process because he didn't believe there was any way to validate the claims. I responded that I saw a need for the facility to act more responsibly during searches and to respect that prisoners had property rights. After all, the property destroyed or lost during the search was property prisoners were allowed to possess in their cells *according to the rules of the facility*. Finally, I told the warden and commissioner we were prepared to recommend that prisoners use the services offered by LAMP to sue the Department of Corrections.

I was initially reluctant to take this legal route, because the outcome might not be satisfying to any of us. I preferred to use our institutional alliances to generate enough pressure on the Department of Corrections that they would agree to receive and pay the claims voluntarily. I suggested that the ombudsman, in consultation with LAMP, would establish a process to review all individual claims and recommend amounts to be paid. Then, unless the Department of Corrections could demonstrate a compelling reason to appeal the claim to LAMP, the Department of Corrections should commit to pay the recommended amount.

I knew that, system wide, prisoners didn't trust facility staff, and in a heart-to-heart discussion with the commissioner, I shared that as far as the people incarcerated by the system were concerned, it was just part of the culture of corrections system staff to treat inmates in a heavy-handed, disrespectful manner and that corrections facilities would have to offer some positive and tangible changes in inmates' quality of life in order to help create trust. I could tell the prisoners didn't believe anything would happen, and it seemed obvious to me that unless something came along and disrupted that belief, they would simply wait for the next opportunity to explode. I also believed that if we told prisoners we would do something significant and we managed to pull it off, compliance with facility rules would improve—and we would have taken giant steps toward establishing credibility. I saw in our current moment a perfect time to offer something—a simple opportunity to surprise them by coming through for them.

After our conversation, Commissioner Ken Schoen signed off on our approach, as he was happy to do anything that would restore stability. If the commissioner had not agreed, some of the inmates would surely have sued, and the cost for the Department of Corrections to defend the lawsuit probably would have exceeded the payout for the claims. We would also learn that the belief of some facility staff that the inmates could not be trusted to make honest claims *did not hold true*.

Not all inmates who lost property filed claims. When we asked some who were not filing why they made this decision, they replied that they didn't think the value of the loss was worth the time and effort. Furthermore, they didn't believe the Department of Corrections would honor their claims. In the end, we processed approximately 150 claims and we recommended that the Department of Corrections pay the full amount requested, which amounted to $3,000. The claims were paid in full, and the outcome was reported in the press. This result from our negotiations created another boost in the credibility of the ombudsman's office.

A Disturbing String of Events

The next opportunity to earn or lose credibility came a few months later, following the beginning of a series of eight inmate suicides stretched out over twelve months. Seven of those suicides occurred at the Stillwater facility. The first one at Stillwater was a twenty-one-year-old Black male who was found hanging by bedsheets from his cell bars. The officers who found the inmate immediately cut down his body, and the cell reportedly was cleaned before anyone from the Washington County Medical Examiner's Office was summoned to the facility.

This was the first reported prisoner death at the prison in years, and no one on duty at the time had ever had to deal with a suicide. There were, at that time, *no written policies as to how to handle suspected death by suicide*, so the officers did what they believed was right and proper. They didn't want to leave the prisoner hanging there for all to see.

Once word about the prisoner's death began to spread, there was considerable unrest, particularly among Black prisoners. The prison had no systematic way of informing the prisoners of what had happened, although I'm not sure what a systematic way of informing prisoners of such an event would have looked like.

At that time, the practice among corrections facility administrators was not to inform the incarcerated about much of what happened within facility walls. Prison was then—and is still now—a place where very little trust exists between the incarcerated and facility staff. Indeed, the complicated realities of life within these facilities makes trust difficult.

Many of the inmates were unwilling to accept that this deceased inmate, in particular, had committed suicide. He hadn't been there long, but he had seemed to many like someone more likely to commit homicide within those walls than suicide. This was especially the view of many of the Black prisoners with whom he'd connected most. Beyond that, given the long, complicated history between police departments and Black communities, Black inmates would have grown up on stories about an incarcerated person from their community turning up dead in jail or prison and suicide being blamed for the death, but it seemed deeply suspicious and many people suspected he may have been murdered instead. The deceased had been incarcerated on assault and robbery charges and had been confined to the segregation unit—out of sight and out of mind—where the reported suicide occurred. As a result, the warden was concerned about growing unrest among the Black prisoners and contacted the ombudsman's office for assistance.

I visited the facility and conferred with the warden. I also met with representatives from the Afro Culture group to discuss their concerns. They were highly suspicious of the prison staff, especially the officers who found the prisoner dead in his cell. They were concerned that no one else saw the body hanging from the cell bars. The prisoners had seen only the cut bedsheet, and some wondered why the cell was cleaned up so quickly—was the facility frantically trying to hide something? Some of the Black prisoners were spreading a rumor that the officers who found the deceased had killed him as payback for some prior run-in.

The word "investigation" hadn't been spoken yet, but what this crisis surfaced once again was the fundamental fact that Black inmates, especially, didn't feel safe around facility staff. As ombudsman, I had to figure out a way to lessen the growing tensions and move forward. I had developed a solid relationship with many of the men, especially the Black inmates, so I asked them to trust me, not do anything stupid, and allow me time to investigate. I promised to keep them informed of my office's progress. The ombudsman's office soon reached a consensus with the Department of Corrections and other state agencies that I would be permitted to conduct an investigation and report the outcome.

About forty-eight hours later—before I'd even *begun* to wrap my head around how to investigate the suicide—my office phone rang with a frantic call from Warden Bruce McManus. "T, you've got to help me out," he shouted. When I asked him to explain what was so urgent, he told me one of his officers had pulled a Black inmate from a burning cell and taken him to St. Paul–Ramsey Hospital in St. Paul. The inmate had been admitted to the burn unit there and was not expected to survive.

"Can you go over to the hospital and talk to him before he dies?" McManus asked. He described the chaos developing at the facility among the Black inmates. "Can you imagine how upset they are, just forty-eight hours after one Black inmate is found dead in his cell, when another one is pulled from a blazing cell?" McManus said. I told McManus I would go to the hospital.

Fortunately, my office at the Dahl House was just one block from the hospital. I grabbed my portable tape recorder and ran over there as quickly as I could. The tape recorder had been given to me as a gift when I ended my work with the Urban Coalition. I'd never used it in connection with my work as ombudsman because I felt inmates and facility staff alike would think I was trying to catch them at something. This time, however, I was truly thankful I had it.

When I arrived at the burn unit, the prisoner's parents were standing by the door leading to his room. I didn't want to disrespect them by rushing into the room without acknowledging their presence, so I stopped, introduced myself, and told them why I was there and how important it was for me to speak to their son. They nodded and gave their approval.

I entered the room and introduced myself to their son, who was awake, bandaged, and in traction. I asked if he could speak. In a raspy voice, his vocal cords extremely damaged, he muttered that he could. I told him how important it was for me to ask him about what had happened to him at the facility, because some of his fellow inmates had whipped themselves into a frenzy in the belief that a corrections officer or officers had done this to him. "No," he said resolutely. "I did this to myself."

He told me how he had been despondent because of a "Dear John" letter he had received from his girlfriend. He had taken valium and Thorazine for a couple of days after getting the letter. Once his despondence over the breakup had reached the point where he wanted to kill himself, he drank Drano plumbing fluid, doused himself and his cell with cigarette lighter fluid, and then set fire to himself. Before that final act, he had taken the padlock that prisoners were issued to secure their cells while away and turned the hasp inside the cell, making it much more difficult for the facility staff to cut it open with their bolt cutter.

I'd recorded our entire conversation and, when it ended, I thanked him and headed straight for Warden McManus's office at the prison. Together, we went out into the facility and met with a handful of inmates chosen from among the different ethnic culture groups represented in the population. There were just under a dozen or so inmates in the room. The tension was tight as a wire, so we got straight to the task of rumor control. I told them I had visited and spoken with the prisoner, but instead of trying to tell them what I learned from him, I played the tape. Letting the injured man tell his own truth in his own raspy voice was sobering—and a hundred times more powerful than my attempting to tell it secondhand could ever have been. Some of the prisoners acknowledged an awareness of a letter from his girlfriend and his despondency after reading it.

I'm convinced that if I had not been able to record my interview with the injured prisoner, who died the next morning, the other prisoners would not have believed any report I provided them. Keeping order in the prison would have been deeply challenging.

I began to pull together my team to investigate these two deaths. Our approach would not be like a law enforcement investigation. We were not challenging whether these men died by suicide—we accepted that. Our inquiry would focus on what was happening in the lives of these two men during the days, weeks, and months before their deaths that might provide some insight into why one hanged himself and the other set himself on fire. We wanted to determine how aware the prison staff and administration were of what was going on in the lives of these inmates that could negatively affect their mental health. We wanted to consider how the prison officials could have acted on any such information they had about these prisoners.[1]

The credibility of the ombudsman's office with the warden, the facility staff, and the inmates grew once again following this investigation because, without a doubt, my intervention provided something of value to both sides. The warden was able to avoid what could have been a major disturbance causing harm to people and property. The inmates learned that they had a reliable external source for information on issues and matters affecting their safety and well-being and tangible proof that someone in the system cared not only about their safety and well-being but also about their dignity as human beings.

And as for me, I recognized that the work of developing and sustaining credibility was an ongoing process, important at every level: the wardens, the superintendents, the leadership in the Department of Corrections and the governor's office, key members of the legislature from both political parties—all needed to understand what the Office of the Ombudsman for Corrections was, how it operated, and how it was positively affecting the administration of justice in the corrections system. To help with this effort, all of the ombudsman's special investigation reports were shared with both the governor's office and the legislature. Throughout my more than ten years as Minnesota's ombudsman for corrections, all parties connected or related to the corrections system saw the Office of the Ombudsman for Corrections as an important asset to the administration of justice in the state of Minnesota.

21

ADVOCATING FOR STAFF AND MOVING ON

The ombudsman's office was established to receive and investigate prisoners' complaints, but staff sometimes submitted complaints on behalf of inmates they thought were not being treated justly by the facility's administration. They believed the ombudsman's office was better situated to assist an inmate than any staff person could. We always followed up on staff complaints, and we found many of them to be warranted.

Staff Complaints, Women's Roles

We occasionally received complaints from staff about work conditions and issues. When the complaint was about how an individual staff person was being treated, we approached with caution. We always asked whether the person had asked the union for assistance, and if we decided to open an investigation, we let the staff person know we would initiate our inquiry in partnership with the union. At that point, the staff person would often withdraw the complaint.

The process was quite different, however, in the case of Susan Czech. She was a St. Cloud State University student who was working part-time as a correctional officer at the St. Cloud State Reformatory. Ombudsman staff frequently encountered Sue because she worked in the front area of the facility. She helped check visitors and all others who needed entry through the locked gates separating inmates from the outside, and she also worked in the front office and visitors' room. Susan expressed dissatisfaction with her assignment to the ombudsman's staff every chance she got. What she really wanted was an opportunity to work as a regular corrections officer with the inmates. She shared with Mary Jo Reiter, the member of the ombudsman's staff who visited this facility most frequently, that she wanted to pursue a career working in corrections but did not see a future working at St. Cloud because the women on staff were not allowed to work beyond the front office. When Sue had asked why, the superintendent told her it was not safe for women to work with inmates inside in their living area because a female presence would represent an invasion of the inmates' privacy at this all-male facility. The superintendent, supported by the Department of Corrections, held the position that women officers would always be at high risk of sexual assault in this environment.

But Sue didn't accept their rationale. She asked if the ombudsman's office would accept a complaint challenging the position. Our office wanted to know if she had asked the labor union that represented her for assistance. She said she had, and that they had refused because they agreed with the facility and the Department of Corrections.

We accepted and investigated Sue's complaint, finding in her favor, and recommending to Commissioner Jack Young that the department employ women to work inside adult male correctional facilities. When Young rejected our office's recommendation, we advised Sue that she and other women with like interests could band together to pursue legal action against the Department of Corrections on grounds of sexual discrimination in employment.

With the support of our office, she and several of her female colleagues filed a complaint with the Minnesota Department of Human Rights. I asked the commissioner of human rights to consider using private attorneys if the case required litigation, and he was not opposed but said doing so would require the prior approval of the attorney general. I submitted a formal request to the attorney general describing the ombudsman's role in the complaint and requested that the human rights commissioner be permitted to engage private counsel for this case.

Private counsel was permitted, and the complainants prevailed. The Department of Corrections was ordered to pay the complainants $150,000 and offer them job opportunities at adult male correctional facilities without restrictions. Shortly before I left my position as ombudsman, I received a copy of a letter Commissioner Young had sent to his correctional facilities administrators and office staff. The letter stated that the department could have saved $150,000 if they had accepted the ombudsman's original recommendation.

Our office also demonstrated its value to the state of Minnesota through our public information and education function. During my first five years in office, the high level of interest in Minnesota's ombudsman for corrections continued, with inquiries coming in from all over the United States, Europe, and Africa. We also received visitors from corners of the world as diverse as the United Kingdom and Zaire. A producer from CBS's *60 Minutes* visited to determine if the program was worthy of a spot. We never got our cameo on *60 Minutes*, but we did end up featured in *Visions USA*, a documentary film about life in the United States produced for international distribution by the United States Information Agency (USIA).

The independent filmmaker hired to make the film selected the subjects, and we were pleased that he chose the Minnesota ombudsman for corrections as one example of something positive and progressive that was making a difference in terms of social change somewhere in America. The filmmaker followed me around with a professional camera crew for three days. They filmed in the office, in my car driving to the Stillwater correctional facility, and in a cellblock interviewing inmates. The completed film was seen only in foreign countries because, at the time, USIA documentaries could only be shown abroad. It would take ten years before that documentary could legally be shown in the United States.

When the filmmaker shared his work with some of his colleagues, the documentary generated additional interest in the ombudsman's office, including the interest of a Hollywood producer who wanted to film a made-for-television movie based on the work of our office. The producer and writer visited Minnesota and wrote a script for the film they planned to make, but it was never produced. Each time there was a visit from a filmmaker, producer, or foreign government official, I made sure to introduce them to the governor or someone on the governor's staff, as well as the leadership in the legislature. I also introduced them to the commissioner of corrections and members of his staff, because all of these people could claim some credit for the successes of the program during those years. When all is well, everyone benefits.

We also gained visibility when public officials from Pennsylvania and Kansas invited me to speak with and meet with members of their legislatures, both of which had committees considering ombudsman legislation. Kansas created a corrections ombudsman partially modeled after Minnesota's program, and Pennsylvania considered, but did not adopt, legislation. Neither of those states currently has an ombudsman.

At the time, discussion about creating an ombudsman program in other states also raised a specific question about how the Office of the Ombudsman for Corrections should operate in Minnesota: should the ombudsman report to the governor or to the legislature? There was some agreement on the advantages of reporting to the legislature, which allowed the program to be more effectively shielded from partisan politics. Under this model, the ombudsman is appointed by and reports to a legislative committee. In 2025, Iowa's Citizens Aide Office (ombudsman) reports to the legislature, as do both the Hawaii and the Nebraska ombudsman programs. These are the only three other states with statewide programs.

The reporting relationship for the Minnesota ombudsman was not an issue because it was created by executive order. The governor avoided the appearance of political consideration by creating the Ombudsman Commission and charging it with the responsibility for screening applicants and recommending final candidates to him. The Ombudsman Commission was later eliminated in the legislation because, in the executive order, the governor had given it no role beyond screening candidates. The ombudsman office then reported only to the governor.

I supported eliminating the commission because I wasn't sure about how to work with such a group. I perceived that it would be cumbersome in making its recommendations, and I foresaw the likelihood of recommendations or decisions made by the ombudsman being appealed to the commission by corrections officials who disagreed with the findings.

Changing of the Guard

I was appointed ombudsman for corrections by Governor Wendell Anderson. When he resigned during his second term to engineer his own appointment to the US Senate, I was retained in my position by his successor, Governor Rudy Perpich.

I had developed a personal relationship with Governor Anderson and was equally well known and respected by his chief of staff and other key members of his administration. But I didn't really know Governor Perpich, so I asked for and received a meeting with him early on in his administration. I made sure that he understood how the program worked, and I emphasized that the ombudsman's only authority was to investigate complaints and to recommend solutions. My effectiveness depended entirely on the credibility I had earned. I assured him I would not be coming to his office seeking intervention, but he clearly understood that this was the governor's program and it could make him look good or bad. I offered to take him on a neighborhood tour of North Minneapolis, and he accepted.

The day of our tour, media followed us as we spent a couple of hours visiting Pilot City Regional Health Center (now NorthPoint Health and Wellness Center), First Bank on Plymouth Avenue, and the Red Owl supermarket. It was a good visit, and it resulted in what felt like a promising degree of rapport with the governor's office.

But as the relationship developed, I began to see how much of the credibility of the ombudsman for corrections was tied to my *personal* credibility. I needed to do what I could to ensure that, should the new governor choose to name his own pick as ombudsman, the ombudsman's office had its own *institutional* credibility and would be seen as capable of continuing its good work even if I were no longer at the helm.

Governor Rudy Perpich visited North Minneapolis, October 1977.

Governor Perpich with John Warden at the First Bank on Plymouth, 1977.

However, Governor Perpich decided he was happy with my leadership. In 1977 Governor Perpich was succeeded in office by Governor Al Quie, and the new governor also retained me in the position. I first met Governor Quie when he was still a member of the US Congress. When he became governor, I took the same approach I'd followed with Governor Perpich: I wanted to make sure he fully understood the ombudsman's office and how the program functioned. Governor Quie was very personable and eager to get to know the people working in his administration, so I invited the governor and his wife to my church in North Minneapolis. They accepted.

All three of these governors made me feel like a valued member of their administrations. I was invited to participate in cabinet meetings, and I was also invited to high-profile social events hosted by each of them. The ombudsman's office didn't flourish equally under these governors, however. Of the three under whom I served, Governor Anderson, who'd created our office, clearly had the best understanding of how the program worked and what it could be; Governor Perpich, who was elected to his first full term in 1982, probably understood the program the least.

A Short but Instructive Interlude

With Rudy Perpich's 1982 election, I started giving serious thought to moving on as well. More than ten years on the job was a long time for me, and I didn't want to get to the point where I or others believed I was indispensable. Nor did I want to become synonymous with the job, which I felt was beginning to happen. Years earlier at Phyllis Wheatley, I was feeling increasingly uncomfortable with my identity being so tightly linked to my workplace. It felt limiting and claustrophobic, and I had come to believe it was neither in my best interest nor in the best interest of the organization and the community it served for me to stay.

Now, as the ombudsman, that old, familiar feeling had returned. But it occurred to me that this time, the feeling might be a little harder to shake. I had a greater sense of ownership over the ombudsman's office, having developed and shaped the program from its inception.

Realizing that at some point my leaving was inevitable, I notified incoming Governor Perpich that I was interested in being considered for other opportunities in his administration. I had been contacted by Bob Dronen, deputy director of the Minneapolis Community Development Agency (MCDA), who visited with me in my office about the availability of a director of public housing position with his agency. He said he had spoken with people who recommended me highly. And there were people still in the organization who remembered me from the partnership relationship between Phyllis Wheatley and the Minneapolis Public Housing Authority. I was flattered, but I told him I had no background or experience in housing management, public or private. He didn't see this as an issue, citing my legacy of leadership at the Office of the Ombudsman for Corrections and Phyllis Wheatley. I promised to give his offer some thought, but I was waiting to hear from the governor about my future in his administration. Dronen promised to hold the offer open for one week.

Shortly after that conversation, Governor Perpich announced my reappointment as ombudsman without consulting me. Apparently, he had not given my request for other opportunities in his administration any consideration. I discussed the MCDA offer with Mary Lou, who didn't think it was a great fit for me, but she said if I wanted to take it she would support my decision.

I agreed to meet with Dronen to learn more. He explained that the Minneapolis Housing and Redevelopment Authority had recently been absorbed into the MCDA and no longer operated as an independent agency. Its functions of housing and redevelopment were redistributed and were now divisions of MCDA. I was being recruited as director of the housing division, reporting to the MCDA deputy director.

There were four other divisions—finance, technical services, development, and administration—and technical services was interlocked with housing. There were a lot of red flags going into this job, the biggest being that housing and technical services were separate divisions, each with its own director. I could foresee problems there, because the most tangible product a housing manager has to offer the customer (resident) is reliable service: if something is broken, fix it; if something needs cleaning, clean it; and if something needs moving, move it.

With separate divisions, the capacity for the housing manager to deliver good customer service would be challenging, because the service provider was not accountable to the housing director. Dronen assured me my concern wouldn't be a problem. He promised I would have the authority to address any of the issues I raised. I still had some concerns but told Dronen I was looking favorably upon his offer and would let him know within the time frame he requested.

Meanwhile, I was feeling somewhat disrespected by Governor Perpich—he seemed to be taking me for granted. He apparently was uninterested in considering me for any position other than ombudsman. It was time for me to move on while I had an opportunity, so I asked for a meeting with the governor to let him know I was accepting the offer I had received from MCDA. I thanked him for the opportunity to serve in his administration and discussed how important the ombudsman was to the administration of justice in the corrections system. I encouraged him to consider naming my deputy, Melvyn Brown, as my successor. I reminded the governor that the ombudsman's only authority was to investigate and recommend. Consequently, credibility becomes the most effective tool an ombudsman can have. Brown had been with the program since its inception, and he had been a part of building the excellent credibility the program has enjoyed both within and outside the corrections system.

The governor made no promises about my successor, and it was difficult to tell whether he agreed with me about the legacy of the ombudsman's office. He simply thanked me for my many years of service and wished me well in my new position.

While I was concerned about the impact my leaving would have on the program, I believed it could survive because I had assembled an excellent staff that understood how the program worked and the value of credibility to its success. Unfortunately, Governor Perpich's first appointee did not fully recognize the role he was to play. Within three months, after some missteps, he was replaced by John Poupart, who brought a great deal more work-related experience to the position. John had been the executive director of a halfway house operated by the Minnesota Department of

Corrections that used culturally sensitive approaches in treatment. He had developed credibility with many of the top corrections officials, and he wanted to keep it intact. He rehired Mel Brown and served successfully in the position for eight years.

Twelve years after Poupart left office in 1991, in the middle of an economic downturn that forced many cuts to the state budget—and with leadership that had earned less credibility—the Office of the Ombudsman for Corrections was eliminated. The ombudsman was reestablished by the 2019 Minnesota legislature with little or no fanfare. It is a very low-key operation. I will always believe that those early years of the Minnesota Office of the Ombudsman for Corrections had a lasting and positive impact on the inmates of the Minnesota corrections system and the facilities in which they serve their time.[1]

22

PUBLIC HOUSING

Much of my life story can be seen through the lens of my commitment to institutions: family, church, school, public, nonprofit, and private. My family and friends and my community have all benefited from or been harmed by one or more of these institutions. Throughout much of my adult life, I have sought ways to minimize the harm and maximize the benefits. At the very least, I've endeavored to personally do no harm, and that's not always easy to maintain when serving an institution in a managerial role.

In February 1983 I accepted the position of director of public housing for the Minneapolis Community Development Agency and bade farewell to my loyal and dedicated staff at the Office of the Ombudsman. Over the next two years in my new position, I learned just how challenging it could be to hold onto my values.

I would learn the hard way that taking the MCDA position was not the right move for me at the time. Not only was the job not the best fit, given my experience and skill set, but it was also the one time in my long public career when I felt I was offered a position in large part to serve as window dressing: a Black face where an organization felt it could strategically use one.

Mary Lou, who worked as an aide for Minneapolis Mayor Don Fraser at the time, had foreseen problems and encouraged me not to take the job.

She told me she thought the newly organized Minneapolis Community Development Agency needed to have a Black person as one of its five division directors. "They do not want you for your skills—they want your race and your reputation. They want a Black person in that position for its visual effect, and they are bringing you in because you're well known, with high community credibility. Don't be disappointed when they don't let you do your job."

I saw from the very beginning of my tenure that she was right. It took almost eight months for me to hire an assistant director. One of my conditions for accepting the job had been that I'd be able to make such a hire, but it wasn't until I'd been there a while that I came to understand how difficult making this one hire could be. Part of the challenge was the need to reassign the person who held the position at the time. I didn't have the authority to make the reassignment, and the people who *did* have the authority were reluctant to move forward.

For the next two years, the MCDA's organization confounded my best efforts to achieve the most desirable solution to a problem. I saw the mission as providing safe and secure housing to families and individuals who met the eligibility requirements. My job performance would be evaluated on how well we were able to meet the needs of residents, maintain the facilities, and keep vacancies low, but the only one of those services directly under my control was vacancies.

The lines of authority were blurred and didn't always adhere to agency policy and procedure. My title, director of public housing, implied that I had direct responsibility for the overall management and operations of all Minneapolis low-income public housing units. My division was responsible for leasing all of the units ready for occupancy, but it was the responsibility of technical services to make sure units were ready for leasing. Staff from the housing division had to formally requisition needed maintenance and technical services from the technical services division. There were established lines of communication between housing and technical services to resolve production issues, but the issues often went unresolved. My standards for providing public service simply didn't align with those of MCDA's leadership.

I often reflect on the role of institutions in our lives, especially public and nonprofit institutions. They are there to help improve the quality of life for the people they serve—and also for those providing the services. We are dependent upon the well-being of service providers for the delivery of high-quality goods and services to the community. In spite of the difficulties I encountered as public housing director at MCDA, I can think of four instances when I was able to act on my values and understanding of public service.

The first of these instances involved the hiring and mentoring of a promising intern. I had finally succeeded in hiring an assistant director, Vincent DeLusia, and we had an opportunity to acquire a paid intern from the city through the Comprehensive Employment Training Act (CETA), a federally funded program intended to train workers and provide them with jobs in public service. We interviewed a young Black man from the program with a college degree and hired him for six months. If things worked out well with him, the plan was to look for an opportunity to offer full-time employment. He reported directly to my office, assigned to work with my assistant director. Vincent mentored him, helping him think strategically about finding a way to make his services indispensable.

As it happened, it didn't take too terribly long for him to make himself indispensable. Public housing was spending significant sums on contractors for pest control services, without much success. We assisted our intern in taking the necessary training to become a licensed pest control specialist. Suddenly, he was credible as an in-house resource, and management grew to rely on his counsel when it came to more effectively utilizing the contracted services. Ultimately, this man retired from the Minneapolis Public Housing Authority after thirty years as deputy director of the agency's maintenance services.

The second example also occurred during my first year on the job. The director of administration, human services division, asked to consult with me on a proposal to terminate a recently hired Black employee. This person had been named in a news story as participating in some illegal activity for which he had not been charged. They had yet to speak with the employee, but I was told that this employee was going to be dismissed primarily because of the "optics"—the allegations might take months to go away. I questioned such a decision. I suggested that as far as relations with the Black community were concerned, the negative "optics" that *should* worry them were about how letting this employee go would be perceived as discrimination and an utter lack of caring and empathy for a member of the MCDA family who deserved to be presumed innocent unless and until proven otherwise in a court of law.

I recommended they meet with the employee and reserve any action regarding termination until a final outcome of the legal case had been determined. Termination was stayed, and the legal issue was resolved in the employee's favor. This employee also retired from Minneapolis Public Housing, after thirty years as director of procurement. I'm convinced that if I had not intervened, this employee would have been dismissed, and the agency and public housing community would have been deprived of a good person's services.

These first two experiences were both uplifting and positive, to me and to everyone involved. This was not necessarily so with my next two decisions, which determined my future with the organization and helped ensure that my tenure there would be brief.

One day, I received a telephone call from a member of the Minneapolis City Council. He requested that I authorize the move of his father, who lived on a lower level in one of the senior high-rise apartment buildings in Northeast Minneapolis, to an apartment on a higher level with a view of the downtown Minneapolis skyline. However, the agency's policy required that any unit vacancy be filled with an applicant from the agency's waiting list before an internal move could be approved. I shared the agency's policy with the council member and advised him that I needed the written approval of the MCDA executive director to authorize such a move. When the executive director called and encouraged me to authorize the move, I told him I would do so as soon as I received his written approval. I never received that written approval.

At this point in my tenure, I was beginning to realize that my skills, experience, and values were not the best fit for how the leadership wanted to run this organization. It became more obvious to me when the agency was reorganized, bringing technical services under the management and direction of the housing division, and a new director was named. I was informed after all the changes had been made and was offered the opportunity to fill a newly created position as director of community relations, a role without a position description. I was assured that my salary would be unchanged. They needed to know right away if I would take the position, and right away I said *no*. I didn't want to be in a position in which I was being paid to do nothing. I quickly secured the pro bono services of an attorney I had gotten to know through my work with the Urban Coalition to help me constructively end my employment relationship with MCDA.

I told Mary Lou what I had done and she was very supportive, without saying, "I told you so." She reassured me that we'd get through it. I appreciated her support and encouragement, but for the first time in my professional career, I was unemployed. In the past, jobs had come to me—I hadn't had to search. And while I didn't second-guess my decision to reject the MCDA offer, I was a little anxious about how to move forward.

23

IN SEARCH OF EMPLOYMENT

I remained unemployed from April to September 1985. During that time, I had several short-term consultant opportunities, notably from Geri Carter, executive director of Survival Skills, Inc. I was also offered a position as human services director with Scott County, for which I was well qualified. I declined the offer because we couldn't fully agree on the terms of my employment, especially benefits and compensation.

My Network Comes Through

I still had access to the great network I had developed during my association with the Urban Coalition, which I had never used for my personal benefit. As spring gave way to summer, I decided to tap into it. I found out about and applied for the executive director position at a large nonprofit social service agency for which my qualifications were a good fit. To enhance my chances for an interview, I contacted the board chair of the hiring organization, who was also vice president of one of the Urban Coalition's founding corporations. I was surprised and disappointed by the response I received when I called him. He told me the executive director position was "not an affirmative action hire" and that they would only interview potentially qualified candidates.

I reminded him of my exceptional qualifications, letting him know how angry and disappointed I was with his attitude and response. I was surprised and disappointed because of my prior relationship with him. We'd spent three days together at a seminar that focused on issues of race and poverty. Apparently, he'd only been pretending to understand the gravity of the issues, because now, somehow, he couldn't see me as qualified to lead an organization that historically had been identified with the white community.

This bitter experience taught me that my networks as a Black person may not yield the same results as a white person's networks. I was interviewed by the two Black members on the board of directors, but they acknowledged the interview as perfunctory and had no expectations that I would get any serious consideration for the position. That entire experience, with both the white corporate executive and the two Black board members, exemplified an aspect of the systemic racism that Black professionals have far too often had to battle. The clear message for me, as a Black man, was "stay in your lane." The "lane" for me was to confine my upward mobility to leadership positions within Black institutions. I was not allowed to change lanes, no matter my personal strengths and capabilities.

I continued my search. In about 1980, I had been the community representative on a University of Minnesota search committee for dean of the Humphrey Institute of Public Affairs when Harlan Cleveland was hired. I had had several opportunities to visit with Harlan during my last two years as ombudsman, and he was impressed with my work, stressing that he was particularly a fan of my style of community engagement. He let me know of his interest in someday finding an opportunity for me to collaborate with the Humphrey Institute on projects of mutual interest.

Recalling my conversation with Harlan led me to contact philanthropist Russ Ewald. Shortly after the 1967 street violence, Ewald had told me how much he admired my work at Phyllis Wheatley and the work Larry Harris and I had done with the Urban Coalition. He'd then said that if I needed help with my career in the future, I should let him know and he would make every effort to assist. I secured a meeting with Russ and shared with him my conversation with Harlan. Russ agreed to contact Harlan to discuss an opportunity for me at the Humphrey Institute. Following several consultations between Russ and Harlan, the McKnight Foundation made a $150,000 grant to the Humphrey Institute of Public Affairs to support my work there.

In September 1985, Harlan offered me the untenured position of senior fellow at the Humphrey Institute, with a salary commensurate to that of either an assistant or associate professor. Senior fellow positions at the Humphrey Institute, then and now, were mostly self-sustaining and untenured. A self-sustaining position requires fellows to think entrepreneurially, which is to say they must strategize how to secure the funds that will support their work from sources other than the Humphrey Institute's budget. The other requirements I had to meet were to conduct a project with a public policy focus and to teach a course or offer at least one seminar per calendar year.

The project on which I chose to focus was entitled "Fairness and Social Justice," with an emphasis on educational reform and community development. I may have been informed of the need to continue to generate funds to support my work, but I was not fully aware of the need for my position to be self-sustaining. I was so pleased to be working again full-time, and in an area relevant to my background, interest, and experience, that I was thinking, *Let me get there and I'll figure out how best to stay there.*

I seemed to do alright, and funds were available for nearly six years at the Humphrey Institute. I was the only African American with faculty status as senior fellow. I also assisted the Humphrey Institute in its efforts to recruit and retain students of color. I had the honor and pleasure of mentoring several African American students, providing some of them with paid graduate assistant positions within my projects. I communicate with several of those students to this day. My research and teaching focused on issues of social justice and racial inequality. I conducted a series of forums on educational reform initiatives and how the reformers seldom, if ever, consulted with those most directly impacted by their reform proposals before pursuing them. My aim was to illustrate why so many of the reform initiatives missed the mark, because they were not engaging the people who most needed to be involved in order to achieve meaningful and lasting progress.

My primary focus was on how certain institutions, such as churches and community-based organizations, played critical mediating roles in the lives of community residents. I focused on nonprofit and religious institutions located in communities of color, particularly African American, because I wanted to find examples of how these organizations, working in partnership, were making a difference in people's lives. I wanted to look at the church in particular, because it remains the most trusted institution within the African American community. Historically, it has also been among the most *resourceful* institutions in the African American community.

I learned more about the work of some of these institutions, particularly churches, during my planning for a 1987 forum titled "Venture Capital and Job Development Strategies for the Black Community," cosponsored by the host, Wingspread Conference Center, in Racine, Wisconsin. Forum participants represented business, government, nonprofit, civic, civil rights, religious, and academic institutions across the country. They were convened to explore options for raising venture capital for both job creation and Black business development.

I learned a great deal about the work churches were doing in several communities, and I decided the best way for me to report on the impact of the Wingspread forum was to conduct one or more case studies on their projects. My plan was to conduct case studies at Lawndale Community Christian Church in Chicago; Mount Pleasant Baptist Church in Kansas City, Kansas; and the Black Baptist Ministers Union in Kansas City, Missouri.

I was successful in completing two of the case studies with the assistance of Bakama Bakanume, a geography PhD candidate graduate assistant. Lawndale Community Christian Church (LCC) on Chicago's West Side was established in 1975 by Wayne Gordon, a graduate of Wheaton College in Wheaton, Illinois, and a teacher and coach at Farragut High School. The founding members of the congregation consisted of the Gordon family and approximately fifteen students and parents from Farragut.

In 1987, LCC, working with a neighborhood health clinic, established the Lawndale Christian Community Development Corporation (LCDC).

Our case study was conducted in 1988. The church acquired abandoned housing properties from the city of Chicago and rehabilitated them as lease-to-purchase affordable housing for Lawndale families. Families living in the community in need of better housing were given priority to occupy the units. They would move in, pay rent, and have a portion of the rent placed in escrow until a sufficient amount could be acquired for a down payment on a purchase agreement.

The LCDC also worked with these families to repair and restore their credit scores so they could qualify for loans. By 2024, LCDC's work had resulted in more than $100 million in commercial and residential development, including more than 360 units of affordable housing.[1]

Our second case study, conducted in Kansas City, Missouri, involved a partnership between the Black Baptist Ministers Union (BBMU) and the Kansas City Community Development Corporation (KCDC). This study illustrates the value of protest, community organizing, and institutional credibility. The Linwood neighborhood had seemingly been abandoned by the city and other decision-makers, to the dismay of the residents. Several city blocks lay vacant and undeveloped following the closing and demolition of a public hospital.

Things began to change when the BBMU partnered with the KCDC, under the leadership of Don Maxwell. Through the BBMU's organized protest, the vacant land was secured from the city along with a loan from a local bank to build senior housing, a library, and a neighborhood shopping center. The new shopping center brought a sense of pride to the community, along with some essential goods and services that had been missing for a long time. Unfortunately, the shopping center was negatively impacted by the 2008–09 recession, causing most of the stores to close. The former KCDC executive director, now in private business, is working with the city on a plan to revitalize and reopen this vital neighborhood commercial and social hub.

The Kansas City case study highlights how organizing and protest can be important tools for successful intervention. The BBMU forced the city to sell the land to the developer, and a group of members from BBMU congregations threatened to close their private and church bank accounts if the neighborhood bank did not grant KCDC a loan for the project.

My work at the Humphrey Institute helped me more fully understand and appreciate the value of community institutions in helping improve citizens' quality of life. I learned that when churches work with other institutions to solve community problems, the collaborative effort tends to achieve a higher level of credibility than would otherwise be the case.

In both case studies, it was the credibility of the churches that enabled community development organizations to do the kind of work they were established to do. In Chicago, the church enabled the establishment of the LCDC. In Kansas City, the church organization's BBMU ran interference for KCDC, enabling it to build the shopping center.

My commitment to the Humphrey Institute, and its commitment to me, was nearing an end when I was approached by Steven Mayer to consider joining Rainbow Research, Inc., to work with the team on a project called Religious Institutions as Partners in Community Based Development. They had become aware of my work at the Humphrey Institute, and they believed I would be an excellent addition to their team. They had also received a major grant from the Lilly Endowment to implement the project. So it was that in 1990, I said goodbye to the Humphrey Institute and became a project associate at Rainbow Research.

24

RAINBOW RESEARCH

Rainbow Research is a nonprofit research and evaluation agency established in 1974 to work with diverse communities on providing capacity building, organizational planning, and research and evaluation. The Lilly Endowment is a major national foundation that has funded the work of religious organizations throughout the country. In 1990, Rainbow Research received a significant multiyear grant from the Lilly Endowment to provide research and planning support to twenty-eight religious institutions and community organizations that were engaged in collaborative partnerships throughout the country.

A New Role

During my fifteen-year tenure at Rainbow Research I expanded my knowledge about the role of institutions as mediating forces in the community. The Lilly Endowment initiative project demonstrated how churches could partner effectively with community-based organizations to produce outcomes beneficial to community residents in diverse arenas, including housing, education, and economic development.[1]

In 1998, while still working at Rainbow Research, I used the experience gained from the Lilly Endowment project to assist Redeemer Lutheran in North Minneapolis in establishing an affiliate nonprofit, Redeemer Center for Life (RCFL). The organization partnered with the church to help provide housing and economic development opportunities in the community, a goal entirely in keeping with the church's mission to be a "beacon of hope" to the people in the neighborhood.

Rainbow Research's Ford Foundation initiative further enhanced my knowledge. In 1996, the Ford Foundation awarded Rainbow a significant four-year grant to work with twenty community foundations (CFs) across the country to strengthen their diversity efforts and grant-making capacities in underserved communities. We began by reviewing the relationships that these twenty CFs had with residents in the marginalized communities where they were involved.

Seventeen hundred community foundations exist around the world, with more than seven hundred in the United States; the first, the Cleveland Foundation in Cleveland, Ohio, was established in 1914. A community foundation receives its funds from a diverse group of donors, including individuals and private organizations, whereas private foundations receive funding from a single source, such as a family or corporation. This project in many ways was designed to determine to what extent these organizations were operating with fidelity to their missions.

The Ford Foundation, a private foundation, had a particular interest in examining how the CFs we'd been asked to study were using their resources to address the needs of the most vulnerable people in their communities. At the time of this initiative, the demographics of our country were rapidly becoming much more diverse, while our established institutions, such as CFs, were still largely operating as if the demographics of the communities they served hadn't changed much at all.

Rainbow Research worked with the CFs to help them explore ways to incorporate changing community demographics into their programs making grants to nonprofit community entities that aim to create meaningful social progress. Most of the seven hundred CFs in this country are located outside of the communities identified as most vulnerable. At the time of this study, CFs were still working to build visibility and credibility in their respective communities. Many people who could qualify for grant considerations were unaware of the existence of these valuable community assets.

Seventeen of the twenty CFs in this project agreed to work toward changes that would make them more inclusive and more accessible. This marked an important and necessary shift in the priorities of these CFs, because so many of the people on whom their activities are focused are low-income residents of *every* color, immigrants, and newcomers from other areas of the United States.

I believe this project was important because CFs are among the more significant mediating institutions our communities can lean on. They have resources, flexibility, and community influence, ingredients important in helping build community capacity and stability. We learned through the Community Foundations Project that many of the seventeen CFs that committed to work toward changing their foundations found it difficult to understand the value of cultural and racial diversity and inclusiveness in achieving their mission. It was especially challenging when they were asked to apply that principle throughout every function of the organization. For example, we noticed that it was acceptable to have diversity at the staff level, but less acceptable when it came to governance. The areas of finance and asset development and investment were most resistant to change.

Some of that resistance may be attributed to ignorance or lack of knowledge—the notion that, "If I haven't seen it, it doesn't exist." For example, one CF board member had never heard of Black-owned investment banking firms. Rainbow Research's approach to working with this CF project was to encourage the organization to broaden its networks and look beyond its immediate environments.

Throughout my tenure at Rainbow Research I retained my interest in education issues, taking advantage of several opportunities to work on education-related projects. These included evaluation studies of the first two years of the New Vistas School and a consultation with Hennepin County Human Services on its School Success project. New Vistas was a school for adolescent pregnant or parenting girls located in a space at Honeywell's corporate headquarters. This was a Minneapolis Public Schools program that provided wraparound services for up to twenty-four girls utilizing volunteers and other support from Honeywell. Basic program findings show that New Vistas students' attendance and academic performance was significantly better than students with similar characteristics who were not a part of the New Vistas School.

Project School Success, launched in 2003, was a consultation with Hennepin County Human Services staff, tasked with helping Minneapolis Public Schools staff find ways to help improve student retention and academic performance. Our focus in this project was to help identify factors that supported school success. Our findings included that positive relationships with family, teachers, and community members and institutions were important factors for student success. Barriers to success included lack of parental and other adult support, lack of teacher support, and unstable living arrangements. Most of these factors are beyond the control of students and require action from the school and the community.

Over and over again, in municipalities across the country, activists had been frustrated by the same familiar cycle: a school district will pay significant money for a study to determine what issues might account for the serious disparities in academic achievement that so commonly exist between white students and students of color (or, looked at through another lens, between the children of affluent families and those of economically disadvantaged families). Such studies have generally uncovered very similar lists of the most glaring issues, capped by an equally similar list of recommendations. But in case after case, municipalities have balked when it comes to creating and implementing bold programs to *address and disrupt* these disparities.

Fortunately for the community, even though the Urban Coalition had dissolved by this time, the kind of change the coalition had created in our local corporate culture proved to be having a long and vigorous afterlife. The leadership at Honeywell, one of the companies that had anchored the Urban Coalition, understood that state, county, or federal funding for initiatives like these would likely be very slow to come, if it ever came at all. They stepped up to offer enough support to implement pilot programs like New Vistas and Project School Success that could potentially serve as models for communities to follow and expand upon. In addition to financial support, Honeywell provided a steady stream of volunteers to help these programs run. Honeywell also partnered with the United Way program

Success by Six. And in the tradition of the creative, common-sense, Urban Coalition approach to problem-solving, barriers that often limit parent involvement in programs like these were anticipated and planned for: a nutritious meal was served during a class or workshop; childcare was available at no cost to participants; and vital links were provided to resources that families struggling with multiple issues might have—for instance, connections to help with alcohol and drug dependency, or family violence, or assistance with housing.

By the time I became involved with Project School Success, I had been at Rainbow Research for approximately fifteen years, longer than any other place of employment for me. It was time to contemplate my exit strategy. I knew I wanted to stay engaged with my community in some capacity where I could make a difference. The deep dive into education issues afforded me by involvement with Project School Success motivated me to seek election to the Minneapolis School Board.

I took the leap, my campaign was successful, and my retirement from Rainbow Research in 2006 was simultaneous with my election to a four-year term on the Minneapolis School Board on November 6, 2006.

25

MINNEAPOLIS SCHOOL BOARD

This had been another one of those times in my career when I felt I really needed to shift gears. My career was waning, but I also knew I wasn't done yet. I'd always had a certain sense of mission about leaving this world at least a little better than I found it. I'd taken advantage of every opportunity that came my way to live up to that mission, but I firmly believed there was still more waiting for me to do, even if it required working in a different arena than the ones I was used to.

I've always believed that an excellent education is among the most important assets one can have. And for most, the best source for achieving that education—at least, the foundational kindergarten-through-twelfth-grade (K–12) education to which everyone should have access—is the public schools. All of my elementary and secondary education was attained through the public schools, as was the case for my three children, who completed their K–12 careers in the Minneapolis public school system. That entire time, this system was being challenged to deliver a higher quality education to students of color. The disparity that existed between white and Black student achievement was intolerable. So, I ran for the Minneapolis

While serving on the Minneapolis School Board, I met former Vice President Walter Mondale at a Habitat for Humanity event in 2009 or 2010.

Board of Education, the school board, in 2006 and was elected to a four-year term, beginning in 2007.

Why? Because I understood that the school board set the policies that both guided the practices and provided the resources governing every aspect of how the schools ran. Well, that's how it should operate. The reality is that it is the leadership in the *district* and in the *classrooms* that drives the educational improvements that may lead to enhanced student performance. After learning my limitations as a board member, I decided not to pursue any plans I had prior to my election. I would become a good listener and learn about the challenges involved in governing and managing a large public school district. I would also look for opportunities to influence board decisions that could have the greatest impact on the lives of our most vulnerable students. Ultimately the greatest impact a school board can have on a school system is its choice of its top leadership—the superintendent.

We played it safe during my tenure on the school board in selecting top leadership. We chose not to seek a superintendent who might significantly change the direction of the school district. This meant things got locked in place and educational improvements for marginalized students would be incremental at best. It was difficult for me to see how the decisions I was making at the school board level were affecting the learning outcomes of students in the classrooms. I began to wonder if there would ever be an opportunity for me to connect decisions I was a part of directly to changes within the school buildings.

When I first became a board member I raised a question about the adequacy of the district's central office accommodations. The district was located in a hundred-year-old renovated light bulb factory with poor lighting and poor ventilation that was impossible to adequately heat in the winter or cool in the summer. Part of the building had been permanently sealed off because the space was uninhabitable. In my view, the work environment was negatively affecting the overall work output, and I believed we were being irresponsible as a board of directors not to seek ways to improve it. I supported the board resolution instructing the administration to study the district's central office space needs and report back to the board in a timely manner. My recommendation set in motion the wheels that led to the relocation of the central office from 807 Broadway Northeast to 1250 West Broadway.

I served one four-year term on the Minneapolis school board, but I failed in my efforts for a second term. My activity on the board may have impacted my efforts to be reelected. I can identify three votes I cast. One was the deciding vote to select the new site for the central administration headquarters. This was not a popular decision among a significant group of Northeast Minneapolis residents because it relocated the headquarters outside of Northeast. But renovating a century-old building originally built as a light bulb factory didn't make good economic sense. Minneapolis Public Schools were losing credibility among the people who needed them the most—the poor and people of color. Locating the district's main offices in a community of color was symbolic at least and at best could afford the district an opportunity to more constructively engage with the community.

My second unpopular vote affected the size of the school board. The Minnesota legislature had granted Minneapolis Public Schools permission to increase the number of the school board members from seven to nine and have six members elected from districts drawn by the school board. The change would occur only by affirmative action of the school board. There was no way I would support such a plan. I saw that as a fragmentation of the school district, which would make it more challenging to achieve equity in education. The "haves" would be pitted against the "have-nots," and the balance of power rests with the haves. The board voted to add members, but I did not have an opportunity to serve on a nine-member board and experience how it functioned because I was not elected to serve a second term. My observations since then suggest there has been no discernible improvement in school board behavior or accomplishments.

Finally, I cast the deciding ballot not to close North High School. My vote to keep North High School open and provide it with the resources needed to help it succeed may have been my most impactful vote as a school board member. The support provided by the district and the community enabled the school to downsize, hire a strong principal, and bring in new teachers, which resulted in improved student achievement. The basketball and football athletic programs were also reinvigorated, garnering significant community support within the first two to three years and, eventually, leading to state championships in both football and basketball. To North Minneapolis residents, North High School is more than a school. It has been a mediating institution, particularly through its athletic program. It's a symbol of community pride and achievement, which is important to a community often perceived by outsiders as decadent and immoral. To have a group of young people from the community be the very best at something important is redeeming.

My success in life could not have been accomplished without Mary Lou's unwavering support and guidance. She retired from Augsburg University in 2000 as an associate professor of social work, then spent several years helping with childcare for our grandchildren. My sister Leola had pushed me toward law school or medical school, but it was our older son, Christopher, who fulfilled his aunt's dream. He is a pediatrician practicing in Minneapolis. Jeffrey, our middle child, embraces education and following his passion. He is a middle school teacher in Minneapolis public schools and a filmmaker. He graduated from Colgate University with a bachelor's degree and subsequently attended Howard University, where he earned a master's degree in film, and his productions have won many awards. Our daughter Laurie earned her bachelor's degree, with dual majors of professional communications-speech and creative writing. After also earning a master's in human resources management, she became an employee benefits account specialist.

Mary Lou and me, late 1980s.

I hold grandsons (left to right) Marsell, Beanie, and Hugh, 1998.

Our children have given us grandchildren and great-grandchildren, and each member of our family is unique and thriving in their own right. My life would not have been as enjoyable without my children, grandchildren, and great-grandchildren. They exemplify everything I have learned and strived to communicate over the years.

26

FAST-FORWARD TO 2020

On May 25, 2020, the video of a white Minneapolis police officer kneeling on the neck of a Black man flashed around the world. A seventeen-year-old passerby from the neighborhood used her cell phone to capture the event and post it on the internet, enabling millions to watch in horror while the police officer's knee remained on George Floyd's neck for more than nine minutes, ultimately strangling him to death. The recording's audio is punctuated by repeated exclamations to the officers on the scene from another passerby to please allow Floyd to get up and Floyd's frequent cries of, "I can't breathe . . . I can't breathe"—climaxing, toward the end, with his desperate cries for his mother.

Widespread protest spontaneously burst forth, including property damage with fires and looting throughout the neighborhood and elsewhere in the city. And over the coming days, similar outbursts of anger and grief spread to diverse places across the United States as well as around the world. There was at least one other death related to the incident in Minneapolis and property damage in the hundreds of millions of dollars, including the destruction of the Minneapolis Police Department's Third Precinct Station. The National Guard was eventually called up to control the situation.

In the aftermath of the George Floyd killing, I had flashbacks to 1966–68. What immediately came to mind was the uncertainty in the community about what to expect following the April 5, 1968, assassination of Dr. Martin Luther King Jr. The fear was that there would be massive demonstrations followed by street violence and property destruction. This was exactly the scenario that unfolded in Detroit, Chicago, Washington, DC, and a long list of other cities and towns across the nation. But not in Minneapolis.

Why? Perhaps the most salient answer is that much of the visceral anger and potential violence on Minneapolis streets during those critical nights immediately after the assassination were blunted by the activity of the Soul Patrol—the public safety group of volunteers created through the grassroots, people-power process enabled by the Urban Coalition during the mid-sixties. The Soul Patrol and Red Patrol were groups of mostly young adults organized by leaders from the Black and Native communities to provide the *first* layer of public safety for neighborhoods where community members generally lacked trust in the Minneapolis Police Department.

There has been a long, bitter history in this country of encounters between police officers and people of color that end badly—with police violence, too often fatal, that almost certainly could have been avoided had the officers involved been more tightly embedded and integrated into the life of the neighborhoods they are charged with protecting. Instead, across the country in the mid-sixties, police departments had been making a major shift toward a military style of policing, which people in communities of color were consistently critiquing as a strategy that leaves residents feeling like the police are an occupying military force, rather than a respectful, creative community partner in building and sustaining the tangible sense of *public safety* that communities crave.

Why is it so important to remember the example of the Soul Patrol and the Red Patrol? It was an idea that bubbled up from the grass roots, an idea that was seen, heard, and respected by the newly built institution of the Urban Coalition—an institution that stood ready to fund and support the patrols through an accessible process that was speedy, nimble, and transparent.

Furthermore, the Urban Coalition was flexible enough to allow the Soul Patrol and the Red Patrol to evolve beyond the immediate goal, forged in crisis, of helping to tamp down dangerous rumors and divert angry community residents from the path of violence. The patrols became a force that offered a glimpse of what public safety might look like if a core group of community people could be trained and deputized as protectors and peacemakers. It cost the Urban Coalition $8,000 to support the Soul Patrol for one week. The cost of calling up the National Guard to restore public order following the George Floyd killing was $12.5 million.[1]

What were our community leaders doing in 2020 to respond to the issues being raised by the protesters, and did they have a strategy to prevent a recurrence of the street violence? The possibility of yet another wave of violence during and after the George Floyd murder trial kept city and county officials awake at night. How did we respond as a community in 1968, after the assassination of Dr. Martin Luther King Jr., a crisis that led to widespread violence in urban centers across the country? Due in large part to the presence on the streets of the Soul Patrol and the Red Patrol, Minneapolis remained calm.

But the immediate community response to George Floyd's murder was disappointing on several levels. I will leave it to the experts to speak to what the appropriate law-and-order response should have been. My concern is with the inadequacy of the social justice response.

———

I understand the "why" of the protest, because protest is an appropriate response to deep dissatisfaction. The goal of the protesters was to seek to bring about change in the behavior of police whenever they encounter Black people, especially Black men. Far too often, the encounters have had fatal consequences for Black victims. The demonstrations that followed

Floyd's death were not limited to expressing dissatisfaction with the police and policing. The concerns so urgently raised included big-picture issues like the need to rethink what we really even mean when we talk about public safety, not to mention all the persistent issues our nation still wrestles with in terms of racial injustice and inequality. The protests are ongoing, and the responses to them are still a work in progress. And now, as then, there are many in the community who feel extremely frustrated with the slow pace of change.

To date, it seems as though community responses are being formulated without drawing upon the historical experience of this community in dealing with crises of this magnitude. Not only is Minneapolis formulating its responses without any consideration of the historical perspective, but many of the national correlated responses seem to follow the same pattern. The local respondents are seemingly unaware of what happened in this community in the summers of 1966 and 1967.

For those who may have forgotten, we had what was labeled as "street riots" on Plymouth Avenue. The 1967 outbreak was of a greater magnitude than the incident that occurred in 1966. Community leaders were startled into action. The property and human damage from those two events was nowhere near the scale of damage that resulted from the aftermath of Floyd's death. However, the community response to what happened more than fifty years earlier seems to be of a much greater value.

Let me refresh our collective memory. In 1967, there were 159 disturbances across the country labeled as "riots." Most were sparked by incidents of police misconduct or by violence against a community member by a shopkeeper in predominantly Black neighborhoods; some were triggered by violent police responses to demonstrations against the war in Vietnam. One key part of the national response to urban violence was President Lyndon Johnson's convocation in Washington, DC, in the fall of that year. Hundreds of high-ranking elected officials, academics, grassroots community leaders, and clergy from all four corners of the country came together at the president's request to learn from each other and to strategize ways to prevent further turmoil. He convened these leaders to cajole them to go back to their respective communities and do something about the urban crisis. Minneapolis had a delegation of over forty people at that convocation who listened, came back, and started the Urban Coalition.

Many of the people engaged in developing responses to the current crisis seem to be unaware of the community's experience from that era. I would strongly encourage them to study that experience, read about it, talk to someone old enough to remember, and integrate what they learn into how they respond.

Many of the issues from more than fifty years ago were similar to current issues, as questions were being raised about police misconduct against Black people, particularly Black men. Poor people and people of color also dealt with issues of racial inequality, high unemployment, inadequate housing, unequal education, and inaccessible health care. The community's capacity to respond to some of those issues then was not impacted by the presence of a worldwide pandemic, but the response often was influenced by the presence of an unpopular war in Vietnam. In 2025 the country is still reeling from the bitter taste of yet another messy, haphazard withdrawal from yet another lost foreign war, this time in Afghanistan—as well as from both an economy and a severely strained social safety network struggling to recover from a pandemic in which far too many died, disproportionally the poor and vulnerable. And even though there are no American "boots on the ground" in either Russia's needless war of aggression against Ukraine or Israel's relentless assault against Palestinians in Gaza, war and the specter of war cause constant anxiety. Massive American military aid makes the United States a proxy participant in these conflicts, and many Americans are acutely aware of how much the upkeep on the world's largest military costs.

Dr. Martin Luther King, in his 1967 "Beyond Vietnam" sermon, said, "A nation that continues year after year to spend more money on military defense than on programs of social uplift is approaching spiritual death." Those prophetic words resonated with many of the most socially and economically vulnerable among us back then, and still resonate today.[2]

The community's response to some of the protesters' current demands must be formulated within the context of its response to the COVID-19 pandemic and the outcome of a very divisive national election. What is most disappointing about how the community is responding to the current crisis is its failure to be informed by the history of the crises of the sixties and seventies.

The creation of the Office of Ombudsman for Corrections in 1972 was influenced by the September 9, 1971, Attica Prison riot. Forty-three people were killed during that rebellion, and Minnesota wanted to avoid a similar crisis in its prison system. Governor Anderson used his executive powers to establish the office, and I was named to implement it.

I've offered a historical account of two separate crises and how Minnesotans responded to each. Are there any lessons from those historical experiences that can be beneficial in resolving our current crisis?

There were some important factors I believe contributed to the more constructive responses of that era. President Johnson, though harassed by opponents of the Vietnam War, was committed to his Great Society programs, many of which were designed to address some of the more challenging issues of race and poverty. Central to those programs was the Office of Economic Opportunity (OEO), which provided financial support to many local social, education, and economic programs in low-income and minority communities. Every community interested in securing OEO funding was required to establish a local Community Action Program (CAP) controlled by local citizens. And any program or project for which OEO funding was requested had to show that there was local citizen involvement in developing and managing such projects. The phrase associated with all OEO programs was "maximum feasible citizens' participation." It was precisely this principle that we were able to implement in a very real way, over and over again, during the Urban Coalition years, and it was key to the success of the coalition's primary initiatives.

The Urban Coalition provided a vehicle—an infrastructure—that was used to engage well-meaning corporate leaders, who learned while doing. The Urban Coalition model emphasized corporate community leadership because corporations were lagging behind the public and non-profit sectors in using their assets and resources to focus on the issues—and the hopelessness—that had sparked the street violence. And while our corporate community leaders may not be expected to lead the charge in responding to any current crisis, they must be identifiable in that leadership group.

It would be difficult to replicate the corporate role from the 1967 crisis in 2020. In 1967, most of our top corporate leaders were native Minnesotans, leading primarily national corporations and, in some instances, only local entities. Today many of the corporations led by those fourteen executives are global, and their leadership's knowledge of community life in Minneapolis and Minnesota may be limited. The leadership of those 1967 corporations may have been more vested in place-based outcomes than current corporate leaders.

The changing politics of the 1980s, beginning in the 1970s during the Nixon years and extensively expanding during the administration of President Ronald Reagan, were marked by the systematic dismantling of Johnson's Great Society programs. I label that period "Post Reconstruction, Revisited." Richard Nixon had rapidly reduced the principal elements of Johnson's War on Poverty, and then Reagan came along and eliminated any last vestiges of evidence that the country had ever attempted to fight a war against poverty. In fact, a strong case can be made that through their concerted campaign to dismantle nearly every Great Society institution and initiative, root and branch, Nixon and Reagan provided the one-two punch that assured poverty at least a temporary victory.

Just as we in the Black community knew this wasn't the first time there had been such a dramatic reversal of public policy, we knew it wouldn't be the last. We remember that we're looking at a pattern with deep roots in American history. It's like the swinging of a pendulum. And it always has been. Every single time the Black community experiences a period that represents some kind of significant step forward toward equity and justice, there is a period of reaction, marked by efforts to undo and reverse significant portions of that progress.

The OEO requirements for residents' participation helped engage poor people and people of color—populations that historically had been left out of the decision-making process. This led to the creation of new community institutions whose missions were to help improve the lives of poor people and people of color.

The Urban Coalition evolved into an institution that could respond quickly to community needs on micro *and* macro levels, in ways that tangibly enhanced the lives of community members. I can provide an example of a response to a small, personal crisis. In the summer of 1984, a family who lived in a Northside public housing apartment had their refrigerator fail on them. I called Jim Shannon, from General Mills Foundation, whom I knew through my Urban Coalition connections, and asked if he knew of any emergency resources that might be available to help the family in need. The weather was hot, and they had a refrigerator full of freshly bought food they didn't want to see go to waste. Shannon found money in a small emergency fund appropriate for this use, called a Sears Roebuck store, found a comparable new refrigerator, and had it delivered to the family that same afternoon.

An example of nimble Urban Coalition change-making on the macro level is the creation of the Legal Rights Center in 1970. Attorneys like Doug Hall and Peter Dorsey banded together with activists like Syl Davis, Gwen Jones Davis, and Clyde Bellecourt to present a proposal to the Urban Coalition board for the creation of a center where low-income people could get free or low-cost legal advice, or find an attorney willing to represent them in court, or help them navigate a complex legal issue. They made a compelling case, pointing out that although the public defenders are very good at their jobs, the caseloads they are asked to carry are so high that they are often unable to give their clients the quality of service the system should ensure to *everyone*, regardless of income. The Urban Coalition funded the Legal Rights Center in order to at least make a start at leveling the playing field and democratizing access to legal criminal representation.

—••—

How can we use the knowledge of this history to promote social and economic justice in our own time?

Whereas it may be impossible to replicate the historic roles that a consortium of corporations played during the late sixties, when the Urban Coalition was most active, it is not difficult to discern some of the lessons from that time.

1. Value an inclusive process. Find seats at the table for all who want to be a part of the solution.
2. Look for potential allies where you least expect to find them. Once you've found such an ally or two, look for those places where you can establish common ground with them, and be creative about how you might forge avenues for collective action on tackling issues of common concern.
3. Patience is more than a virtue; it's a necessity.
4. Make maximum use of existing resources, including homegrown institutions.
5. Build (and work hard to maintain) bridges across racial, cultural, and socioeconomic divides.
6. Networking is a critical tool. Value it and use it often.
7. Dissatisfaction drives change, and confrontation can be a useful tool.
8. Change can be a slow and tedious process, especially if it is to be sustained. Know the difference between the capacity to confront and the capacity to implement, and respect it. In any group of potential allies or collaborators, work to identify complementary skill sets, and assign tasks accordingly. The person who is especially gifted at speaking truth to power through confrontation may not be the person who's best suited for the tasks of helping the group identify specific goals and then guiding the group toward implementing them.

9. Be optimistic! Your optimism can have a positive, contagious effect that can actually be the difference sometimes between project success or failure.

———◆———

The image of the Sankofa bird from the Akan culture of Ghana, in West Africa, offers powerful advice: a bird, bending its long neck back over its body, holds an egg in its beak. The word means, literally, "to go back and fetch it," reminding us that before we march off into whatever future we are going to make for ourselves, we need to take a few steps back and make sure we retrieve the elements of our heritage *that we're going to need* for our journey; that wisdom collected by our elders and our ancestors reminds us who we are and why we're *on* this journey in the first place. May we always remember how our elders told us that when the path ahead turns ill-defined and hard to follow, "Sometimes, we have to make the road by walking." May our walk make our ancestors—and our children—proud.

The Sankofa bird, an Akan cultural symbol. *Lucy Treat*

ACKNOWLEDGMENTS

To my wife, Mary Lou, who supported our move out of Chicago to Minneapolis and who has been my partner and my most steadfast supporter in everything I have ever done; to Phyllis Wheatley Community Center, whose board put the future of their historic and iconic organization in the hands of a thirty-one-year-old inexperienced executive; to former Minnesota governor Wendell Anderson, who took a chance in naming me the nation's first ombudsman for corrections; to Charlotte and the late Cyrus Johnson and his family for their encouragement and support throughout this project and our many years of friendship; and finally, to the Minnesota Historical Society Press, especially gifted editor Ann Regan, who never wavered in her belief that this book represents an important part of Minnesota history that needed to be told.

NOTES

Notes to Introduction

1. Reverend Martin Luther King Jr., "The Other America," speech delivered at Grosse Pointe (MI) High School, March 14, 1968, https://www.gphistorical.org/mlk/mlkspeech/mlk-gp-speech.pdf.
2. Michael J. McManus, "A Case Study of Launching the Urban Coalition of Minneapolis," copy at Gale Reference Library, Minnesota Historical Society, St. Paul (hereafter, MNHS).
3. Hawaii established a state ombudsman to investigate complaints against state and county agencies in 1969.
4. Peter L. Berger and Richard John Neuhaus, *To Empower People: From State to Civil Society*, 2nd ed. (Washington, DC: American Enterprise Institute Press, 1996), 51.
5. Jon Collins and Elizabeth Shockman, "Outsiders, Extremists Are Among Those Fomenting Violence in Twin Cities," Minnesota Public Radio, May 30, 2020; Mia Bloom, "Far-Right Infiltrators and Agitators in George Floyd Protests: Indicators of White Supremacists," Just Security, May 30, 2020, just-security.org.

Notes to Chapter 2: A New World

1. Christopher R. Gabel, *The Vicksburg Campaign: November 1862–July 1863* (Washington, DC: US Army, Center of Military History, 2013), 43.
2. Anthony Williams in Ancestry.com, U.S., Colored Troops Military Service Records, 1863–1865 (Lehi, UT: Ancestry.com Operations, Inc., 2007), from Compiled Military Service Records of Volunteer Union Soldiers, National Archives, Washington, DC.

3. USA Track and Field, the sport's national governing body, finally changed all American track and field events to the metric system in 1974.

Note to Chapter 8: Beginning at Phyllis Wheatley

1. On W. Gertrude Brown, see Michiko Hase, "W. Gertrude Brown's Struggle for Racial Justice: Female Leadership and Community in Black Minneapolis, 1920–1940," PhD diss., University of Minnesota, 1994.

Notes to Chapter 9: Establishing the Urban Coalition

1. The coalition's papers are preserved in the Urban Coalition of Minneapolis Organizational Records, 1967–2004, Gale Reference Library, MNHS.
2. Copy in author's possession. The speech is also summarized in McManus, "A Case Study of Launching the Urban Coalition of Minneapolis," 5.
3. Eric Foner, *Reconstruction: America's Unfinished Revolution, 1863–1877* (New York: Harper and Rowe, 1988).
4. Martin Luther King Jr., *Where Do We Go from Here: Chaos or Community?* (1967; Boston: Beacon Press, 1968); Harry Belafonte with Michael Shnayerson, *My Song: A Memoir of Art, Race, and Defiance* (New York: Alfred A. Knopf, 2011), 328.
5. US National Advisory Commission on Civil Disorders, *Report of the National Advisory Commission on Civil Disorders* (Washington, DC: Government Printing Office, 1968), 1. The eleven-member body was chaired by Governor Otto Kerner Jr. of Illinois.
6. Alice George, "The 1968 Kerner Commission Got It Right, But Nobody Listened," *Smithsonian Magazine*, March 1, 2018.
7. Ralph Ellison, *The Invisible Man* (New York: Random House, 1952).
8. Copies of these documents are in the author's possession and in the Urban Coalition of Minneapolis Organizational Records, 1967–2004, Gale Reference Library, MNHS. An account of these meetings and the list of recommendations, presented by Syl Davis, were printed in the *Minneapolis Tribune*, April 7, 1968.
9. Jayne Williamson-Lee, "Has the City of Minneapolis Paid Out 'Almost $80 Million' in Police Conduct Settlements Since 2019?," *MinnPost*, July 3, 2023.

Notes to Chapter 10: Urban Coalition Legacies

1. GMHC, 2017 Report to the Community, December 31, 2017, www
   .gmhchousing.org/annual-reports.
2. MEDA, "Our History," https://meda.net/our-history; "Our Vision," https://
   meda.net/our-vision; "Metropolitan Economic Development Association,"
   ProPublica Nonprofit Explorer, https://projects.propublica.org/nonprofits/
   organizations/410977257; "US. Department of Commerce Names MEDA Top
   Business Center for the Fourth Time," *Insight News*, June 24, 2019.
3. Randy Furst, "Hennepin County to Terminate Diversion Program Contract
   with Operation de Novo," *Minneapolis Star Tribune*, March 30, 2017.
   Other information from Operation de Novo files now in the possession of
   JusticePoint, Inc.

Notes to Chapter 12: Crisis at the University of Minnesota

1. For quotations and other information on the work of the committee, here and
   below, see University of Minnesota Investigating Commission on Morrill Hall
   Sit-In, "Report," 1969, available at the Gale Reference Library, MNHS (hereafter Morrill Hall Investigating Report).
2. Lonnie G. Bunch III, "Why Is America Afraid of Black History?," *The Atlantic*,
   December 2023.
3. Dr. John Wright, who earned a doctorate in African American Studies in 1977
   from the department he helped found at the university, retired as department
   head in 2019.
4. The Inter-University Conference on the Negro is mentioned in the *Racine
   Journal-Times*, February 16, 1964, 6; Eddie R. Cole, *The Campus Color Line:
   College Presidents and the Struggle for Black Freedom* (Princeton, NJ: Princeton
   University Press, 2022), 297.
   "Report of the President's Ad Hoc Committee on the University's Role in
   Social Problems," February 1, 1966, 1, University of Minnesota Archives,
   copy in author's possession; *Minnesota Daily*, May 25, 1966; Morrill Hall
   Investigating Report, 24.
5. Morrill Hall Investigating Report, 29.
6. Morrill Hall Investigating Report, 36.
7. Morrill Hall Investigating Report, 37.

Note to Chapter 13: A Difficult Lesson

1. Katarzyna Bryc et al., "The Genetic Ancestry of African Americans, Latinos, and European Americans across the United States," *American Journal of Human Genetics* 96, no. 1 (2015): 37–53, https://www.ncbi.nlm.nih.gov/pmc/articles/PMC4289685/.

Notes to Chapter 15: Increasing Phyllis Wheatley's Community Visibility and Viability

1. *Minneapolis Tribune*, June 10, 1988.
2. *Minneapolis Star*, May 3, 1968.

Notes to Chapter 17: My Bush Fellowship Experience

1. I would reencounter John Kretzman and John McKnight some twenty years later, after they had written *Building Communities from the Inside Out: A Path Toward Finding and Mobilizing a Community's Assets* (Chicago: Acta Publications, 1993), a book frequently used by community leaders and organizers involved in the work of community development. Much later, I would regularly use Kretzman and McKnight's research and findings in the work I did at Rainbow Research toward the end of my career.
2. The term "benign neglect" was coined by presidential adviser Daniel Patrick Moynihan in a controversial report to President Richard Nixon that suggested the best way toward continued progress for Black America might be to just step back from further government intervention and instead allow the gains made during the height of the civil rights movement to grow and take full effect.

Notes to Chapter 18: Minnesota Gets an Ombudsman for Corrections

1. Anna Stitt, "Minnesota State Prison, Stillwater," MNopedia.
2. In addition, the racial disparities in the prison population were clear. In 1970, 157 whites and 54 Blacks were admitted to state and federal prisons in Minnesota; in 1974, 547 whites and 114 Blacks were admitted: Patrick A. Langan, "Race of Prisoners Admitted to State and Federal Institutions, 1926–86," US Department of Justice Report, May 1991, NCJ-125618, 31, 32. Blacks made up 9 percent of the state's population in 1970 and 1.3 percent in 1980.
3. See Minnesota Legislative Reference Library, Wendell R. Anderson, Executive Order #14, 1972, https://www.leg.mn.gov/archive/execorders/72-14.pdf.

Note to Chapter 19: Establishing the Ombudsman's Office

1. See Minnesota Legislative Reference Library, Wendell R. Anderson, Executive Order #18, 1972, https://www.lrl.mn.gov/archive/execorders/72-18.pdf.

Note to Chapter 20: Building and Sustaining Credibility

1. "Final Investigation Report: Deaths of Love and Durham, December 12, 1973," in Files of Theartrice Williams, 1972–1989, Minnesota Ombudsman for Corrections, Gale Reference Library, MNHS.

Note to Chapter 21: Advocating for Staff and Moving On

1. Minnesota Legislative Reference Library, "Information on Minnesota State Agencies, Boards, Task Forces, and Commissions," https://www.lrl.mn.gov/agencies/detail?AgencyID=2374.

Note to Chapter 23: In Search of Employment

1. See Lawndale Christian Community Church website, https://online.lawndalechurch.org.

Note to Chapter 24: Rainbow Research

1. Rainbow Research, Inc., "Religious Institutions as Partners in Community Based Development: Findings from Year One of the Lilly Endowment Program," 1991, 2–4, 15–22.

Notes to Chapter 26: Fast-Forward to 2020

1. Brian Bakst, "Cost for National Guard Deployment Near $13 Million," Minnesota Public Radio, June 9, 2020.
2. King delivered the speech on April 4, 1967, at Riverside Church in New York City: https://www.americanrhetoric.com/speeches/mlkatimetobreaksilence.htm.

INDEX